# Globalization and Health

# International Studies
# in Sociology
# and Social Anthropology

VOLUME 95

# Globalization and Health

edited by

Richard L. Harris
Melinda Seid

BRILL
LEIDEN · BOSTON
2004

This book is printed on acid-free paper.

**Library of Congress Cataloging-in-Publication Data**

Globalization and health / edited by Richard Harris, Melinda Seid.
    p. cm. — (International studies in sociology and social anthropology, ISSN 0074-8684 ;
    v. 95)
    Includes bibliographical references and index.
    ISBN 90-04-14145-6 (pbk. ; alk. paper)
    1. Globalization—Health aspects. 2. World health.  I. Harris, Richard L. (Richard Legé),
1939-  II. Seid, Melinda.  III. Series.

RA441.G585 2004
362.1'042—dc22

                                                                        2004048880

ISSN  0074-8684
ISBN 90 04 14145 6

PRINTED IN THE NETHERLANDS

# CONTENTS

Editors' Preface........................................... vii

Acknowledgements ....................................... ix

List of Contributors...................................... xi

1   Globalization and Health in the New Millennium........... 1
    RICHARD L. HARRIS AND MELINDA J. SEID

2   Globalization, Health, and the Free Trade Regime: Assessing
    the Links................................................ 47
    RONALD LABONTE

3   The Social Dimension of Globalization and Health ......... 73
    ABOUBAKR A. BADAWI

4   Globalization and Health: The Paradox of the Periphery .... 91
    CHRISTINE MCMURRAY

5   Health Transition and Globalization in the Pacific: Vestiges of
    Colonialism? ............................................ 109
    SITALEKI A. FINAU, IRIS L. WAINIQOLO AND GIUSEPPE
    G. CUBONI

6   Globalization and Health Policy in South Africa............ 131
    DI MCINTYRE, STEPHEN THOMAS AND SUSAN CLEARY

7   Global Challenges to Equity in Safety and Health at Work:
    Struggles for Fair Work in Southern Africa................. 153
    RENE LOEWENSON

8   Reproductive Health in Post-Transition Mongolia: Global
    Discourses and Local Realities............................ 171
    KIMBERLEY RAK AND CRAIG R. JANES

9   Access to Healthcare via Telehealth: Experiences from the
    Pacific................................................. 197
    ROY SMITH

10  Globalization of Risks for Chronic Diseases Demands Global
    Solutions............................................... 213
    DEREK YACH AND ROBERT BEAGLEHOLE

11   The People's Health Movement: A People's Campaign for
     "Health for all – Now!" .................................   235
     RAVI NARAYAN AND CLAUDIO SCHUFTAN

12   The Globalization of Health: Risks, Responses, and Alterna-
     tives ....................................................   245
     RICHARD L. HARRIS AND MELINDA J. SEID

     Index ...................................................   271

# Editors' Preface

This international collection of essays on globalization and health examines the global health issues associated with the economic, technological, political, social, cultural and environmental effects of globalization. These essays analyze the complex linkages between globalization and health, the health effects of globalization at all levels (global, national, and local), and the policy and institutional responses associated with the health consequences of globalization.

This collection combines essays that are global or broadly comparative in scope with those that focus on health issues in a single country or region. The contributors of these essays are international experts, officials, and scholars who are deeply concerned about the global health problems and issues addressed in this collection. They provide important information, insights, and conclusions about the linkages between globalization and health, the health effects of globalization, the major global health issues faced by humanity, and the responses that have been and need to be developed to these issues.

The health risks and challenges faced by humanity today are enormous. The global increase in chronic diseases as well as the spread of new and reemerging communicable diseases is unprecedented. The globalization of contemporary economic, technological, political, social and cultural forces and the health effects of these forces are increasing the risks to population health around the world. This collection of essays was organized to contribute to the global search for effective responses to the global health problems confronting humanity at the outset of the twenty-first century. Hopefully, it will contribute to increasing awareness about these problems and to the ongoing efforts to resolve them.

RICHARD L. HARRIS and MELINDA J. SEID

# Acknowledgements

First, the editors wish to acknowledge the indispensable support they received from their respective universities – California State University, Monterey Bay and California State University, Sacramento – for the sabbatical leaves they were granted by these institutions. This sabbatical support enabled the editors to develop the proposal that was accepted by Brill to publish this collection, to undertake the preliminary research, travel to various countries where they made contact with some of the contributors, to solicit the various contributions, and to complete the initial organizing tasks associated with the publication of this international collection of essays on globalization and health.

The editors also wish to acknowledge their appreciation for the invitation they received from the Institute of Global Conflict and Cooperation at the University of California, San Diego to participate in the Teaching Seminar on Health and Global Politics held on February 18-19, 2000 at the campus of the University of California, San Francisco. The conceptual origins of this collection of essays arose out of the stimulating dialogue engendered at this seminar between the participants and the international team of presenters.

Acknowledgement is also gratefully extended for the support and hospitality provided by the Institute of Latin American Studies at LaTrobe University in Bundoora, Australia, especially by Professors Barry Carr and Steve Niblo, who hosted the editors during their two-month stay in Melbourne during the fall of 2002. Appreciation is also extended to Professors Vivian Lin and David Legge of the School of Public Health at LaTrobe for sponsoring a seminar at which the editors where able to present this project and receive valuable input from the seminar participants.

Moreover, the editors are grateful to Professors Deborah Black and Anthony Zwi of the School of Public Health and Community Medicine at the University of New South Wales in Sydney, Australia who invited them to give a seminar on the issues addressed by this collection of essays. The faculty and students who attended this seminar also provided valuable input that contributed to the development of this project.

Professors Abebe Zegeye of the University of South Africa and Julia Maxted of the University of Pretoria also deserve special mention for their gracious hospitality and collegial support during the editors' research visit to South Africa in 2002.

Last, but certainly not least, the editors wish to express their appreciation for the editorial support and collaborative assistance they have received from Dr. Rubin Patterson, Editor of *Perspectives on Global Development and Technology*; and from the editorial staff of Brill Academic Publishers, especially Joed Elich, Pim Rietbroek and Laura ten Wolde. And, of course, the editors wish to gratefully acknowledge that this unique collection of original essays on globalization and health would not have been possible without the invaluable contributions and professional collaboration of the international team of scholar and experts who produced the essays contained in this collection.

RICHARD L. HARRIS and MELINDA J. SEID

# Contributors

**Dr. Aboubakr A. Badawi**, Senior Specialist on Vocational Training, International Labor Organization, and ILO Representative, Kuwait

**Dr. Robert Beaglehole, M.D.**, Director of Chronic Diseases and Health Promotion, World Health Organization, Geneva, Switzerland

**Susan Cleary**, Researcher, Health Economics Unit, School of Public Health, University of Cape Town, Cape Town, South Africa

**Dr. Giuseppe G. Cuboni**, Senior Lecturer, School of Public Health & Primary Care, Fiji School of Medicine, Suva, Fiji

**Dr. Sitaleki A. Finau**, Professor and Head of School, School of Public Health & Primary Care, Fiji School of Medicine, Suva, Fiji

**Dr. Richard L. Harris**, Professor of Global Studies and World Languages and Cultures, California State University, Monterey Bay, Seaside, California, United States of America

**Dr. Craig R. Janes**, Professor, Departments of Anthropology and Health & Behavioral Sciences, University of Colorado-Denver, Denver, Colorado, United States of America

**Dr. Ronald Labonte**, Director, Saskatchewan Population Health and Evaluation Research Unit, and Professor of Community Health and Epidemiology, University of Saskatchewan, Saskatoon, Saskatchewan, Canada

**Dr. Rene Loewenson**, Director, Training and Research Support Centre, Harare, Zimbabwe; also Coordinator of the Southern African Network on Equity in Health (EQUINET)

**Dr. Di McIntyre**, Associate Professor, Health Economics Unit, School of Public Health, University of Cape Town, Cape Town, South Africa

**Dr. Christine McMurray**, Associate, Australian Centre for Population Research, Australian National University, Canberra, Australia

**Dr. Ravi Narayan, M.D.**, Coordinator, People's Health Movement Secretariat and Community Health Advisor, Community Health Cell, Bangalore, India

**Kimberly Rak**, Researcher, Departments of Anthropology and Health & Behavioral Sciences, University of Colorado-Denver, Denver, Colorado, United States of America

**Dr. Claudio Schuftan, M.D.**, Exchange Moderator, People's Health Movement, Ho Chi Minh City, Vietnam, and a consultant in public health and nutrition in Africa and Asia

**Dr. Melinda J. Seid**, Professor and Program Coordinator of Health Science, California State University, Sacramento, Sacramento, California, United States of America

**Dr. Roy Smith**, Programme Leader in International Relations, Co-Director of the Centre for Asia-Pacific Studies, Nottingham Trent University, Nottingham, United Kingdom

**Dr. Stephen Thomas**, Director of the Health Economics Unit, Department of Public Health and Family Medicine, University of Cape Town, Cape Town, South Africa

**Dr. Iris L. Wainiqolo**, Lecturer, School of Public Health & Primary Care, Fiji School of Medicine, Suva, Fiji

**Dr. Derek Yach**, Professor of Public Health, Yale University, New Haven, Connecticut, United States of America

# Globalization and Health in the New Millennium

## Dr. Richard L. Harris[*] and Dr. Melinda J. Seid[**]

### Abstract

This essay provides an overview of the linkages between globalization and health. It examines many of the global health issues associated with the globalization of economic, political, social, and cultural forces in the world today. The conceptualization and analysis of these linkages between globalization and health and the effects of globalization on population health are discussed from the vantage point of various perspectives. Particular attention is given to the global spread of disease, the diseases of globalization, the health inequities associated with globalization, the effects of globalization on environmental health, and the globalization of health-related technologies.

As a new millennium in human history unfolds, there is increasing evidence that the health of humanity and the sustainability of the entire biosphere of the planet are threatened by the global effects of contemporary forms of human technology, production, consumption, transportation, governance, and warfare. Although the global expansion or "globalization" of these technological, economic, social, cultural, and political forces benefits some members of humanity (and in some cases humanity as a whole), it also harms or threatens to harm a large proportion of humanity, particularly the poor and most disadvantaged sectors (McMichael and Beaglehole 2000). Some of the effects of these forces threaten the long-term health and

---

[*] Global Studies Program, California State University, Monterey Bay, Seaside, California, USA.

[**] Health Science Program, California State University, Sacramento, Sacramento, California, USA.

even the survival of the human race since they are disturbing the delicate balance of the natural ecosystems and the planetary biosphere upon which all life depends. As a result, humanity is confronted at the beginning of the twenty-first century with a series of global health threats that endanger not only its survival but also the survival of many other life forms on the planet. Global warming, depletion of the ozone layer, and the increasing contamination of the earth's limited sources of fresh water are disturbing evidence of the harmful effects of humanity's global footprint on the planet (Karliner 1997).

### Globalization: A Contested Discourse

The concept of "globalization" has generally been used to both describe as well as prescribe the transnational economic, social, and political relations that prevail in the world today (UNDP 1997). As a descriptive concept, it is often used to describe the global proliferation of cross-border flows of trade, finance, and information as well as the emergence of a single, increasingly integrated global economy. When used as a prescription, it usually calls for the liberalization or deregulation of national markets in the belief that the unrestricted or free flow of trade, investments, and profits across national boundaries will facilitate global integration and produce the best economic, social, and political outcomes for humanity. These outcomes or effects of globalization are usually equated with economic growth, increased personal incomes, improved living conditions and liberal democracy. Globalization presented in these terms is often prescribed with an air of inevitability, moral superiority, and overwhelming conviction (UNDP 1997).

Even a brief encounter, however, with the expanding body of literature and the political debates on globalization reveals a lack of consensus on both the use of the concept of globalization as well as the phenomena it is used to describe and/or prescribe. In fact, the existing body of literature on globalization and the debates on this subject involve a highly contested, complex, and multidimensional discourse on the nature of the present world order, its historical antecedents, underlying causative forces, and future evolution. As noted by Lee et al. (2002), most definitions and conceptual applications of globalization, including those concerned with health, tend to be highly value-laden. That is to say, globalization tends to be defined in either explicitly positive or negative terms, and rarely used as a "neutral" concept. Thus, it is "positively equated with openness, cosmopolitanism and integration" by most of its proponents and supporters, and negatively equated with "western imperialism, corporate domination and rampant consumerism" by many of its critics and opponents (Lee et al. 2002).

Globalization and topics closely associated with it have become the subject matter of a burgeoning international and interdisciplinary literature

(Harris 2002; Harris and Seid 2000; Held et al. 1999). In fact, globalization in its various conceptualizations and applications has become "the primary attractor of books, articles, and debate" in much the same way "as postmodernism was the most fashionable and debated topic of the 1980s" (Kellner 2002). It has also become a "buzzword," perhaps "*the* buzzword of the new millennium" (Doyal 2002:1), and is used frequently with a great deal of "hype" in the mass media, government propaganda, and corporate advertising.

More often than not the concept is used both uncritically and critically to focus attention on the increasing flow across national boundaries of capital, labor, technology, products, services, information, values, and cultural practices. Some observers and pundits believe that this transnational or global diffusion of investments, goods, technology, practices, and ideas is integrating humanity within a single global system of interdependent economic, political, social and cultural relations. As a result, the concept of globalization is used frequently to describe the increasing global "interconnectedness" or global interdependence of humanity in nearly all spheres of human endeavor, including health. In this sense, Giddens (1990) uses the concept to describe the intensification of social relations on a worldwide scale; Ianni (1998) defines globalization "as a vast process that is not only politico-economic, but also socio-cultural, and that includes demographic, ecological, gender, religious, linguistic, and other problems." Probably most of those who use the concept in this way would agree with Albrow that globalization encompasses the "diffusion of practices, values and technology that have an influence on people's lives worldwide" (Albrow 1997).

The concept is also used to call attention to the development of a new global consciousness based upon changing conceptions of time and space—what has been referred to as the "shrinking planet phenomenon" (East-wood 2002:224). Lee (2002) suggests that globalization is "changing the nature of how humans interact across three types of boundaries—spatial, temporal and cognitive" (p. 5). Robertson contends that globalization involves both "the compression of the world and the intensification of our consciousness of the world as a whole" (Robertson 1992:8). Castells (1996) stresses the informational aspects of globalization and argues that the so-called information revolution has helped to create a new "network society" and global economy that, for the first time in human history, has "the capacity to work as a [single] unit in real time on a planetary scale" (p. 92).

Most of those concerned with analyzing contemporary globalization acknowledge that this global process of transformation involves costs, risks, challenges, tensions, and conflict as well as many potential benefits. Thus, the World Health Organization (WHO) report on "Macroeconomics and

Health" (WHO 2001) claims that "the benefits of globalization are potentially enormous, as a result of increased sharing of ideas, culture, life-saving technologies, and efficient production processes," but emphasizes that "globalization is under trial, partly because these benefits are not yet reaching hundreds of millions of the world's poor, and partly because globalization introduces new kinds of international challenges" (WHO 2001:1).

*Globalization and Health: Frameworks for Analysis*
It has been argued that "from a public health perspective, globalization appears to be a mixed blessing," since certain aspects of global economic and technological developments have "enhanced health and life expectancy in many populations," while other aspects of globalization "jeopardize population health via the erosion of social and environmental conditions, the global division of labor, the exacerbation of the rich-poor gap between and within countries, and the accelerating spread of consumerism" (McMichael and Beaglehole 2000). These aspects of globalization provide many of the challenges confronted by public health researchers, practitioners, and policymakers today.

McMichael and Beaglehole (2000) provide a relatively comprehensive list of the "primary health risks" posed by globalization. This list includes:

- The perpetuation and exacerbation of income differentials, both within and among countries, thereby creating and maintaining the basic poverty-associated conditions for poor health.
- The fragmentation and weakening of labor markets as internationally mobile capital acquires greater relative power. The resultant job insecurity, substandard wages, and lowest-common denominator approach to occupational environmental conditions and safety can jeopardize the health of workers and their families.
- The consequences of global environmental changes include, change in atmospheric composition, land degradation, depletion of biodiversity, spread of "invasive" species, and dispersal of persistent organic pollutants.
- The spread of smoking-related diseases, as the tobacco industry globalizes its markets.
- The diseases of dietary excesses, as food production and food processing become intensified and as urban consumer preferences are shaped increasingly by globally promoted images.
- The diverse public health consequences of the proliferation of private car ownership, as car manufacturers extend their marketing.
- The continued widespread rise of urban obesity.
- Expansion of the international drug trade, exploiting the inner-urban underclass.

- Infectious diseases that now spread more easily because of increased worldwide travel.
- The apparent increasing prevalence of depression and mental health disorders in aging and socially fragmented urban populations.

These authors call attention to the fact that "globalizing processes" have become a major determinant of national health polices and they contend that the "fundamental social, economic and environmental determinants of population health are becoming increasingly supranational" (McMichael and Beaglehole 2000).

As indicated above, the linkages between health and globalization, particularly the effects of globalization on health, are increasingly the focus of research, debate and policy analysis at both the national and international levels. In many respects, however, this still is a new field of inquiry and empirical analysis. As Drager and Beaglehole (2001) have observed, "public health scientists are still in the early stages of gathering concrete evidence on the effects of globalization on population health" (p. 803). They also note that it is evident already "that policy measures are required to rectify the adverse effects of globalization on health and strengthen the positive ones" (p. 803).

Generally speaking, the health community has not received much help in examining the health effects of globalization from most of the scholars and researchers that have been concerned with conceptualizing, analyzing, and theorizing about globalization *per se*. As Lee (2002) notes in a recent volume she has edited on the health effects of globalization, there has been a "limited analysis of the global dimensions of health within the mainstream globalization literature" (p. 2). Nevertheless, the interest in global health issues is expanding at both the national and international levels. As a result, there has been a "steady growth of global health-related initiatives in major public health institutions" (Lee 2002:3) as well as the appearance of "a growing literature on the importance of globalization for health" (Woodward et al. 2001:875).

However, like the larger body of literature on globalization *per se*, there is a lack of consensus and considerable disagreement in the expanding literature on globalization and health. This is evident in the increasing polarization that characterizes the intellectual and policy debates about the health impacts of globalization between those who contend that the health effects of globalization are mostly positive and those who contend that they are mostly negative (Lee 2002:4).

In the last few years, several attempts have been made to provide a conceptual framework for systematically analyzing and assessing the health effects of globalization. One of the best attempts in this regard is the framework developed by Woodward et al. (2001). These scholars have

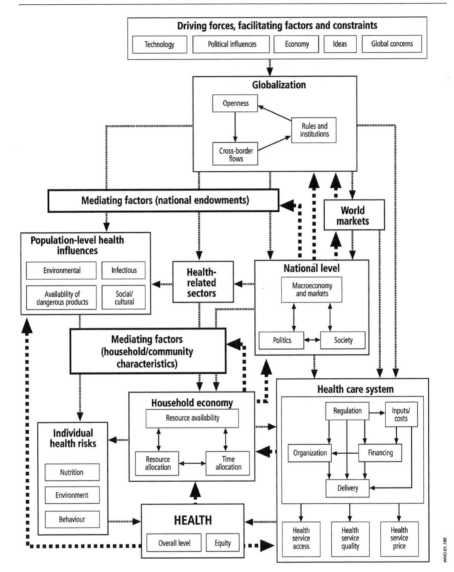

Figure 1. Detailed conceptualization of globalization and health.
Source: Woodward et al. (2001).

formulated an analytical framework for assessing the linkages between globalization and health and for "synthesizing the existing evidence on the relationships between economic, social and health variables" (Woodward et al. 2001:877). Figure 1 provides a detailed illustration of the variables in their analytical framework as well as the types of linkages and feedback effects they posit between these variables. Woodward and his colleagues at the WHO hope that this framework will provide a useful checklist for researching and analyzing the effects of globalization on population health in countries around the world.

This framework emphasizes the economic aspects of globalization. Like most observers and researchers concerned with globalization, Woodward et al. (2001) argue that, "economic globalization has been the driving force behind the overall process of globalization over the last two decades" (p. 876). They conceptualize economic globalization largely in terms of a dramatic growth in the volume of cross border flows of international trade, financial investments, development assistance, human migration, travel and tourism. They contend that this dramatic growth in cross-border flows has occurred largely in response to International Monetary Fund and World Bank programs, and in the case of trade, has been consolidated by the Uruguay Round Agreements of the General Agreement on Tariffs and Trade (GATT), which established the World Trade Organization (WTO).

Included in this conceptual framework are various driving and constraining forces that shape economic globalization, including "technological developments, political influences, economic pressures, changing ideas, and increasing social and environmental concerns" (Woodward et al. 2001: 876). The framework breaks globalization down into three processes that have a circular relationship. That is to say, it posits that increasing cross-border flows of economic activity contribute to the development of global institutions and regulations, and that the development of these global institutions and regulations promote "the opening up of economies," which in turn facilitates greater cross-border flows of trade, investments, tourism, and other activities.

As Figure 1 indicates, Woodward et al. contend there are "multiple direct and indirect linkages between globalization and the proximal determinants of health" (p. 876). Their framework delimits three categories of direct "linkages" between globalization and health at the national level. These direct effects of globalization include "population-level health influences" (environmental health risks, infectious diseases, availability of dangerous products, and social/cultural practices); effects on "health-related sectors;" and effects on the inputs, thru-puts, and outputs of the national "health care system." Woodward and his colleagues give as examples of globalizing influences the rules and regulations of the General Agreement on Trade in Services (GATS) and the agreement on Trade-Related Aspects of Intellectual Property Rights (TRIPS) that are enforced by the WTO; the marketing and sales strategies of the transnational tobacco companies; the international operations of the pharmaceutical corporations; and the transmission of infectious diseases through international travel, migration, and tourism.

The framework presented by the Woodward team also posits the effects of globalization operate indirectly through the national economy on the health sector. These effects work through the "macro-economy and markets, national politics, and the social structure of the society." A good example is "the effects of trade liberalization and financial flows on the availability of the resources for public expenditures on health" (p. 876). In addition, there are "mediating factors" at the national level which these researchers refer to as "national endowments," and mediating factors at the community and household levels which they refer to as the "household/community characteristics" that are particular to each society (see Figure 1).

Woodward and his colleagues suggest in their framework that there are linkages that go both ways between globalization and health. Thus, the heavy dotted lines in Figure 1 indicate that health indirectly affects globalization through the same channels that globalization affects health. However, they believe the effects of health on globalization are limited, whereas the effects of health on both household and national economies are direct and important (p. 876). Their framework is designed, therefore, to facilitate policy-oriented analysis hoping that it will provide "a basis for developing and promoting pro-health policies in national economic policy-making and international negotiations." They also state that they hope it will provide a conceptual tool for identifying and researching the "major gaps in our knowledge concerning the nature of the linkages between globalization and health in different economic and geographic contexts" (p. 877).

The essay by Labonte in this collection draws upon the analytical framework that he, Drager and Torgerson (Drager, Labonte, and Torgerson 2002) developed for "tracing the impacts of globalization on health." Labonte defines globalization as "a process by which nations, businesses and people are becoming more connected and interdependent across the globe through increased economic integration and communication exchange, cultural diffusion (especially of Western culture) and travel." Labonte's framework seeks to identify the multiple pathways through which globalization affects peoples' health as well as the key elements that condition the health effects of globalization. In his framework the economic, political, and social "historical context" of each country and its "pre-existing endowments" are key elements that condition or mediate the impact of globalization on health. These endowments are similar to the mediating factors in the framework proposed by Woodward and his colleagues. The endowments include the "level of economic development, environmental resources, and human capital development" in each country.

Labonte's framework traces the impact of the global context on the national, community, and household contexts of health. The global context consists of globalizing influences such as the macroeconomic policies imposed by the IMF and the World Bank (e.g., structural adjustment programs and privatization), enforceable trade agreements and the associated trade flows, as well as "largely unenforceable multilateral agreements" on human rights and environmental protection, "intermediary public goods," and the various forms of international development assistance. These global influences affect the national or domestic context of health, including domestic policy capacity as well as the specific content of policies concerning access to health care. They also affect labor rights, food security, and restrictions on tobacco, the provision of public goods and services, and environmental protection.

In this framework, the effects of globalization (the global context) on the national or domestic context have an indirect impact on the community context of service and program access, geographic disparities, community participation and urbanization. The conditions at all three levels (global, national, and community) combine to condition the household context of health (i.e., household income, health behaviors, and expenditures on health, education, and social services), which in turn condition health outcomes. Moreover, in Labonte's framework, "each level affects, and is affected by, environmental pathways" such as resource depletion, pollution, and the loss of biodiversity. Labonte contends that the impacts of globalization during the last 20 years of economic globalization "have been largely negative" on the "two fundamental health-determining pathways" of poverty/inequality and environmental sustainability.

A similar framework for analyzing the links between globalization and health in developing countries has been developed by Diaz-Bonilla, Babinard, and Pinstrup-Andersen (2002) (see Figure 2). In their broad definition of globalization, they use the concept to refer to "the multiplication and intensification of economic, political, social and cultural linkages among people, organizations and countries at the world level" (pp. 3-4). As examples of these types of linkages, they cite increased levels of global interaction in the form of trade, financial flows, international communications, international contacts among political groups and non-governmental organizations (NGOs), and increased international tourism.

In their conceptualization, globalization encompasses "the tendency toward universal application of economic, institutional, legal, political and cultural processes" as evidenced by the "codification of trade rules under the WTO [World Trade Organization]" and "the spread of democracy, the increase in the number and coverage of environmental treaties and ... cultural homogenization in entertainment, food, and health habits."

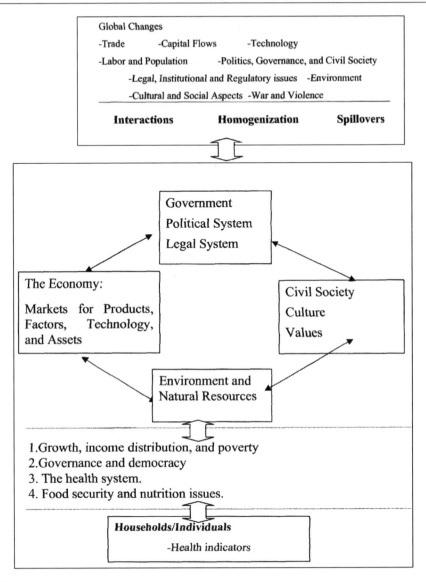

Figure 2.   Framework for health-globalization interactions.
Source: Diaz-Bonilla, Babinard, and Pinstrup-Andersen (2002).

In addition to this tendency toward homogenization, they also view globalization as contributing to "the emergence of significant spillovers to the rest of the world coming from the behavior of individuals and societies." These scholars give the following examples as the "spillover effects" of globalization: global warming, cross-border pollution, financial crises, the spread of HIV/AIDS, and international crime.

Thus, Diaz-Bonilla and his colleagues (2002) delineate three dimensions of globalization, which they label: "interactions, homogenization, and spillovers" (p. 4). They contend that these three dimensions are interrelated. Increased transnational "interactions" tend to contribute to both increased "homogenization" as well as more "spillovers." And the development of global norms and institutions (homogenization) is generally a response to controlling spillovers and regulating interactions. With regard to the impact of globalization on the developing countries, which is their primary concern, they maintain that these three main dimensions of globalization (interactions, homogenization, and spillovers) have an impact on (1) the functioning of the political system, including the government and the legal system; (2) the economy; (3) the environment and natural resources; and (4) the culture and civil society of these countries. They contend the changes induced by globalization in these four interrelated areas influence household and individual health outcomes in these countries. However, in their conceptual framework, they suggest that the effects of globalization on health work through the following five "channels" or pathways: "(1) economic growth, income distribution, and poverty; (2) democracy and governance; (3) health services; (4) nutrition and food security; and (5) other risk or mitigating factors" (p. 6). It is through these channels or pathways that they believe globalization influences health at the household and individual levels.

In a paper commissioned by the WHO, Drager, Labonte, and Torgerson (2002) have assessed the strengths and weaknesses of the various frameworks that have been developed in recent years to conceptualize and/or analyze the relationships between globalization and health. They consider the framework developed by Woodward and his colleagues at the WHO to be the most comprehensive and explicit. Based on their review of the literature, they conclude that "the utility of any framework is that it should identify a number of elements that link globalization to health, through direct, indirect and policy-dependent pathways" (Drager, Labonte, and Torgerson 2002:46). They exclude from their list of framework requirements "any health measures that might be used as endpoint outcomes" in research and policy analyses of the linkages between globalization and health (p. 45). They contend that the use of health measures such as mortality, morbidity, and disability for the assessment of the health effects of globalization is not fruitful because of the difficulty of obtaining reliable data, especially from many of the developing countries, and also because the time-lag and cumulative impact of social and environmental conditions on the health of individuals over their lifespan make it almost impossible to determine the exact cause of health gains or problems at the time of measurement.

Drager et al. argue that "the most useful information, particularly from a policy vantage," will come from comparative case studies in which the linkages between globalization and health are assessed, using a common analytical approach. They note that the impacts of globalization on health are "potentially enormous, for both better and worse," and that "reaching some consensus on how globalization might maximize the former and minimize the latter depends on assembling evidence and undertaking research" that utilizes a "delimited range of frameworks" (Drager, Labonte, and Torgerson 2002:46).

*The Globalization of Disease*
A historical perspective on globalization and health is needed to complement these conceptual frameworks. For example, it can be argued that the "globalization of disease" has its origins in the late fifteenth century when the Europeans "discovered" the Americas and "inflicted one of the earliest examples of genocide on the American peoples through the importation of smallpox, measles and yellow fever" (Walt 2000:1). According to Lee (1999), this view is compatible with Robertson's historical stages of globalization (Robertson 1992) and the findings of many medical historians who view the so-called age of exploration (Robertson's first or "germinal phase" of globalization) and "the arrival of Columbus in the Americas in 1492 … as a significant event in the geographical spread of disease across continents" (Lee 1999:35).

Along with the diseases the European explorers and conquerors brought directly to the Americas from Europe, they also brought diseases such as plague, typhus, and influenza from Asia to Europe and then from Europe to the Americas via the trading routes they established between these continents. Moreover, through the slave trade they established between Africa and the Americas, they "brought hookworm, yaws, filariasis, leprosy and, it is believed, schistosomiasis and malaria to the Americas" (Lee 1999:35), as well as to many of the other areas of the world where they traded.

One of the enduring health impacts associated with the historical development of globalization "has been the uneven spread of communicable disease to disadvantaged individuals and populations" around the world (Lee 1999:36). At each historical stage in the globalization process, the people most vulnerable to the spread of communicable diseases have been the poor and the disadvantaged, while the "wealthier classes have generally experienced a lesser burden of disease since they have greater "mobility, along with access to more and better quality food, sanitary facilities and hygienic conditions" (Lee 1999:36).

During the twentieth century, public health, charitable, social welfare and international collaboration succeeded in controlling many of the worst communicable diseases and significantly lowered morbidity and mortality rates among even the most disadvantaged sectors of the population in most regions of the world (Lee 1999:37). However, there are many who argue that there has since been a reduction in public health expenditures and the deterioration of public health systems in many countries. At the same time, it appears that the spread of infectious diseases has "become increasingly liable—hitting the poor disproportionately" (Walt 2000). Over the last twenty years, new diseases such as HIV/AIDS as well as reemerging infectious diseases such as tuberculosis (TB) have impacted the poor and disadvantaged sectors to a much greater extent than they have affected the more privileged sectors of the population, in both the richer and the poorer countries of the world.

The global impact of high-speed forms of transportation and the increasing movement of people around the world have made it possible for the microbes that accompany them to move faster around the world. This acceleration in the movement of people has had far-reaching health effects. It has given rise to new patterns in the spread of infectious diseases, and facilitated the rapid transmission of these diseases. As the former Director-General of the WHO, Gro Harlem Brundtland (2001) has stated, "with globalization, a single microbial sea washes all of humankind" and as a result "there are no health sanctuaries" (p. 1).

Díaz-Bonilla and his colleagues (2002) also argue that "increases in international travel, tourism and food trade mean ... new insurgent disease-producing organisms can be transported rapidly from one continent to another" (p. 36). They give specific examples of the types of emerging and reemerging infectious diseases that have become major public health problems through contacts resulting from international air travel, which they note has increased over the last 40 years from 2 million to 1.4 billion people per year. They call attention to airborne transmitted diseases such as pneumonic plague, influenza, and TB. They also note that HIV/AIDS has been spread through international sex tourism, and in Africa along the routes taken by international truck drivers. In addition, insects and animal vectors of disease are now being transported around the world in the foods and other goods that are traded globally.

The reaction to the global spread of infectious diseases in the developed countries has generally resulted in two rather inadequate responses: the widespread use of antibiotics and antimicrobials and quarantines (Díaz-Bonilla et al. 2002). These responses are not only inadequate, they may in some cases contribute to the problem. The global health challenge presented by the spread of infectious diseases requires a global response that integrates international with national measures aimed at containing these infectious diseases before they develop sufficient drug resistance to make the task much more difficult. In this regard, Lee (2002) points out that while international travel has facilitated the global spread of microbes, "the ability to communicate faster can also mean enhanced capacity to monitor and report on outbreaks of disease, disseminate guidelines for controlling and treating disease, and coordinate rapid responses when needed" (p. 6). The international response to the rapid spread of Severe Acute Respiratory Syndrome (SARS) offers a recent example of this enhanced capacity to collaborate in the monitoring and control of the spread of a dangerous infectious disease (Mestrel 2003).

The recent outbreak of the virus SARS is a good example of the unprecedented speed by which new infectious diseases can spread globally. This previously unknown but potentially lethal respiratory virus spread around the world within a few months. What the SARS virus reveals is that, as a result of the globalization of air transport, tourism, and trade "the human race has become a vast petri dish for the growth, evolution and spread of microbes" (Mestel 2003:A1). The ease of international movement and an increasingly interconnected world have made it possible for infectious diseases to spread around the world in a matter of hours. For example, health officials in Hong Kong reported the case of a man infected with SARS who "had flown from Hong Kong to Munich, Barcelona, Frankfurt, London, Munich again, Frankfurt again and then back to Hong Kong before entering a hospital" (Bradsher 2003:1). It is believed that this man may have been responsible for spreading SARS to Europe.

Diseases such as HIV/AIDS, SARS, the West Nile Virus, Ebola, Nipah, Hendra, and other new infectious diseases are some of the better known members of a group of some 35 new diseases that have emerged around the world since 1970 (Borenstein 2003). The emergence and global spread of this many new diseases since the 1970s is unprecedented in the history of medicine, according to a recent report released by the Board of Global Health of the Institute of Medicine in the United States. This report attributes the rapid emergence and spread of these diseases to a complex combination of social, economic, political, environmental, ecological, and microbiological factors. Included among this combination of factors are global changes in climate and weather, ecosystem changes, urbanization and the growth of mega-cities, economic development and land use, international travel and commerce, technology and industry, the breakdown or absence of public health measures, poverty and social inequality, and war and famine (Institute of Medicine 2003).

The emergence and global spread of an unprecedented number of new infectious diseases is a result of the confluence of these factors and the fact that they are globally linked. The authors of this report give special attention to the emergence and spread of these diseases in the developing countries, where they contend that "urbanization, deforestation, change in land use and climate, population growth, poverty, malnutrition, political instability, and even terrorism" have combined together to make these diseases serious threats to human health (Institute of Medicine 2003:160). To effectively prevent and control these diseases, the social, economic, political, environmental, and ecological factors in these countries that are contributing to the emergence and recurrence of these infectious diseases "must be recognized and addressed at a global level."

## *The Diseases of Globalization*

McMurray and Smith (2001) contend that globalization fosters deteriorating health through contributing to life style-related noncommunicable diseases and various unhealthy living conditions:

> Although technological progress has brought the means to control infectious diseases, some aspects of globalization have contributed to an increased risk of unhealthy lifestyles. All peoples are at risk, but marginalized groups are more likely to experience inferior living conditions and limited purchasing power. In addition to these economic and environmental constraints there are other aspects of modernization that encourage the adoption of unhealthy lifestyles. These include stress, alienation and the aggressive marketing of fast foods, cigarettes and alcohol. (McMurray and Smith 2001:iv)

These scholars argue that globalization "facilitates uneven growth" and a pattern of socioeconomic development in which some regions "become cores of economic progress" while others are "relegated to the periphery" of the growth and development that take place as a result of globalization (McMurray and Smith:1-2). Within the countries that are experiencing the uneven growth associated with the globalization process, the population tends to experience "a rising incidence of NCDs [non-communicable diseases] related to a shift away from subsistence agriculture to a growing cash economy, urbanization and more sedentary lifestyles." Thus, they refer to NCDs as the "diseases of globalization" (pp. 1-2).

The case studies that McMurray and Smith examine—Mongolia, Uzbekistan, and the Republic of the Marshall Islands—reveal how globalization has affected population health in these peripheral countries. In both Mongolia and Uzbekistan, the transition to a market economy has disrupted the health care systems in these countries, and population health has deteriorated as a result. However, it is in the Marshall Islands, where they find the most evidence of how globalization contributes to lifestyle-related diseases because of "new patterns of aspiration, consumption and lifestyle" (McMurray and Smith 2001:2-3).

Economic development and the introduction of modern medicine have brought about a reduction in the incidence of infectious diseases and a general improvement in health, but "the reduction of mortality from infectious diseases has been paralleled by an increase in NCDs" such as cancer, heart disease and diabetes. This "health transition" has increased life expectancy and shifted the cause of mortality from mostly infectious diseases to mostly NCDs. It has contributed to "a high prevalence of early-onset NCDs," which have "placed an increased burden on health care budgets and generated an increased need for care of the aged" (McMurray and Smith:8).

In most developing countries, this health transition has been slower and more problematic than the health transition experienced by the more developed countries in their transition from agrarian to industrial societies. In many of the developing countries, there is now a high incidence of both infectious diseases and NCDs due to the uneven health effects of the economic and social developments they have experienced. McMurray and Smith argue that this pattern of disease is increasingly common especially among groups marginalized by globalization, they contend that "one of the main causes of this uneven progress in health is the impact of global capitalism and the way it has shaped lifestyles" (pp. 8-9).

The increasing prevalence of NCDs—the "diseases of globalization"—is linked with the increase in certain lifestyle risk factors, such as lack of exercise, excess body weight, smoking, and alcohol consumption as well as "the broader aspects of wealth distribution" and lack of education (McMurray and Smith 2001:9). Globalization promotes these risk factors and the costs of managing the increase in NCDs place a heavy burden on the health care systems of most developing countries. The unhealthy lifestyles associated with globalization include the displacement of the population from their traditional means of subsistence, urbanization without substantial employment generation, substandard housing, low incomes that do not permit the purchase of nutritious food, the marketing and consumption of cheap processed foods (that are high in fat, salt and sugar), and the largely unregulated marketing of tobacco products and alcoholic beverages. Thus, McMurray and Smith conclude that "the Marshallese experience of urbanization without industrialization or substantial employment generation is the underlying factor affecting health and the high prevalence of NCDs" (p. 162).

Health education alone is insufficient to offset the unhealthy lifestyle changes responsible for the increase in NCDs. McMurray and Smith found that the Marshallese are generally well informed about the health risks associated with their adoption of unhealthy lifestyles, but that this has not modified their behavior. Their findings are similar in this respect to those derived from a study on globalization, diet and health education in Tonga carried out by Evans et al. (2001). Their research, like the study by McMurray and Smith, indicates that "one effect of globalization has been to increase reliance on imported foods, rather than traditional foods" and "although educational programs have increased awareness about healthy diets and nutritional foods, people in the Pacific nonetheless choose to consume less-healthy foods because of cost and availability" (p. 856).

These scholars indicate that "one possible answer would be to follow the example of Fiji and ban the importation of fatty foods." As an alternative they could "promote the development of sustainable indigenous fishing and farming industries that could make the preferred and healthier traditional foods readily available at reduced cost" (Evans et al.: 860). However, Evans et al. point out that the trade liberalization provisions of the GATT and the aggressive promotion of these provisions by the World Trade Organization may prohibit these types of solutions.

In their discussion of how certain aspects of globalization may "worsen human nutrition and further aggravate health in developing countries," Diaz-Bonilla et al. (2002) warn that "increasing trade could result in the acceleration of a major shift in the structure of diets, resulting in a growing epidemic of the so-called diseases of affluence" (Diaz-Bonilla et al., p. 31). They note that both under-nutrition and over-nutrition already coexist in many countries and that the patterns of disease in the developing countries "are now shifting away from infectious and nutrient deficiency diseases toward higher rates of coronary heart diseases and some types of cancer."

Diaz-Bonilla et al. refer to the double burden of disease in their discussion of how globalization affects health outcomes in the developing countries (pp. 5-6). The pattern of uneven socioeconomic development associated with globalization contributes to this double burden of disease, especially in the "middle-income" developing countries. Globalization in these countries leads to rising incomes for certain sectors of the population and to lifestyle changes in these sectors that create a new health burden of noncommunicable diseases and injuries. Meanwhile these countries are still faced with "the unfinished agenda of infectious diseases and malnutrition." This old burden of disease is suffered largely by the poorer sectors of the population whose incomes and lifestyles have not changed that much because of the uneven impact of economic development promoted by globalization.

As a result of the double burden of disease, the health services in these countries face the worst of both worlds. They must contend with both the new health burden of noncommunicable diseases among the higher income groups and the old health burden or "the unfinished agenda" of infectious diseases, malnutrition, and the complications of childbirth suffered by the poorer sectors of the population (Diaz-Bonilla et al.: 20-21). At present, their health services are more geared to combating the old burden of

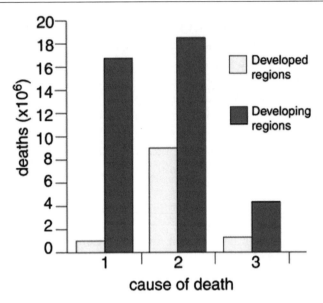

Figure 3. Causes of deaths in developed and developing regions. (1) communicable, perinatal, maternal and nutritional; (2) non-communicable diseases; and (3) injuries.
Source: Murray and Lopez 1997.

communicable diseases and nutritional deficiencies rather than the new burden of NCDs, which require costly interventions.

The Global Burden of Disease project commissioned by the World Bank and the WHO in the early 1990s provides evidence of the "epidemiological transition" and the increasing importance of the so-called diseases of affluence or diseases of globalization in the developing countries. The two researchers who conducted this project, Christopher Murray and Alan Lopez (1997), categorize the causes of death worldwide into three groups: (1) communicable, perinatal, maternal and nutritional; (2) NCDs; and (3) injuries. Among the more important findings of this project was the discovery that heart disease, stroke, and cancer have replaced the major communicable diseases and malnutrition as the prime causes of death worldwide. Moreover, the international health data for 1990 that they use reveal that the total number of deaths from group 2 causes (NCDs) was actually greater in the developing countries than in the more developed countries (see Figure 3).

Out of a total of 50.5 million deaths worldwide in 1990, Murray and Lopez found that 28.1 million deaths were from NCDs and 17.2 million deaths were from communicable diseases, such as malaria, HIV/AIDS, and TB. The vast majority of the deaths from communicable diseases were young children and infants in the developing countries. In fact, 98%

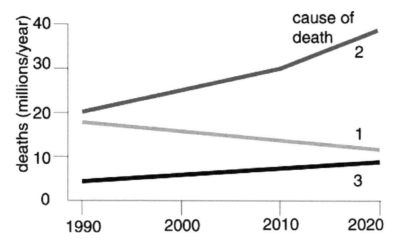

Figure 4.  Trends in causes of death. (1) communicable, perinatal, maternal and nutritional; (2) non-communicable diseases; and (3) injuries.
Source: Murray and Lopez 1997.

of the total number of children's deaths in 1990 occurred in the developing countries. However, the NCDs, normally associated with deaths in the more affluent societies, were also one of the major causes of death even in the most impoverished countries of sub-Saharan Africa, where Murray and Lopez calculated that an adult who lives in this region is now more likely to die from an NCD than an adult in the more developed countries of North America and Europe (Murray and Lopez 1997).

Part of the explanation for these findings is the epidemiological transition that is taking place in these countries (ID21 Insights 2001). This transition in the health of the population is associated with economic development and general improvements in population health that reduce the infant and adult mortality from infectious diseases and increase life expectancy, thereby causing the aging of the population. As a result of this health transformation, "as the number of adults relative to children rises, the commonest health problems become those of adults, producing a surge in NCDs" (ID21 Insights 2001:2). While this transition has taken place in most developing countries, some are still in an early stage of this process of transformation. Thus, infectious diseases are still the main causes of death in sub-Saharan Africa and India (ID21 Insights: 1).

According to the Global Burden of Disease Study, group 2 causes of deaths (NCDs) are expected to rapidly increase while group 1 causes of death (infectious diseases) will decline in the developing regions over the next couple of decades (see Figure 4). In fact, by 2020, deaths from NCDs are expected to double and cause roughly 7 out every 10 deaths in the developing countries (ID21 Insights: 2). As a further indication that globalization is promoting the spread of lifestyle-related diseases, "deaths due to tobacco use are projected to rise from three million worldwide in 1990 to 8.4 million in 2020, surpassing deaths from any single disease, including the HIV epidemic" (ID21 Insights 2001:2).

The WHO's *World Health Report 2002* identifies the health risk factors "responsible for a substantial proportion of the leading causes of death and disability" in the three major groupings of countries used in the report: developing countries with high mortality rates, developing countries with low mortality rates, and developed countries (WHO 2002:82). The top ten risk factors responsible for two thirds of all deaths worldwide are ranked in this report in the following order of importance: underweight (under-nutrition); unsafe sex; high blood pressure; tobacco consumption; alcohol consumption, unsafe water; inadequate sanitation and hygiene; iron deficiency; indoor smoke from solid fuels; high cholesterol, and obesity (WHO 2002:7).

In the developing countries with low mortality rates, the report indicates that NCDs (cardiovascular diseases, cancers, chronic respiratory diseases, neuropsychiatric disorders, and other noncommunicable diseases) are responsible for over half the burden of disease in these countries (WHO 2002:81), while communicable diseases and nutritional deficiencies continue to be responsible for a major portion of the burden. This "double burden" of disease reflects the types of epidemiological transition noted above. However, even in the developing countries with high mortality rates—where communicable diseases, maternal and perinatal conditions and nutritional deficiencies continue to be responsible for more than half the burden of disease, the report reveals that cardiovascular diseases, one of the so-called diseases of affluence, are now responsible for more deaths and disabilities than any other single cause.

The contention that the increase in these cardiovascular diseases in the developing countries is due to the adoption of unhealthy lifestyles is supported by the findings in the WHO report, which indicates that "more than three-quarters of cardiovascular disease—the world's leading cause of death—results from tobacco use, high blood pressure or cholesterol, or their combination" (WHO 2002:8). The report indicates that these risk factors are "now becoming more prevalent in the developing countries" as a result of the globalization of unhealthy lifestyles common to the more developed industrialized countries:

> Until recently, all of these factors—blood pressure, cholesterol, tobacco, alcohol and obesity, and the diseases linked to them—had been thought to be most common in industrialized countries. Unfortunately, as the report demonstrates, they are now becoming more prevalent in developing countries, where they create a double burden in addition to the remaining,

unconquered infectious diseases that have always afflicted poorer countries. (WHO 2002:10)

*The World Health Report 2002* refers to this development as a "risk transition" caused by "changing patterns of living ... changes in food processing and production" as well as "agricultural and trade policies" that have changed "the daily diet of hundreds of millions of people" around the world (WHO 2002:10).

The report also indicates that "tobacco and alcohol are being marketed increasingly in low and middle income countries," where increasing numbers of people "are exposed to such products and patterns, imported or adopted from other countries" (WHO 2002:10). Changes in lifestyle and working conditions are also contributing to less physical activity, which according to the report "causes about 15% of some cancers, diabetes and heart disease." Moreover, the report warns that the increase in "risks such as unsafe sex and tobacco consumption could increase global deaths substantially in the next few decades and could decrease life expectancy in some countries by as much as 20 years" (WHO 2002:10).

Another recent WHO report that focuses on cancer around the world predicts that new cancer cases worldwide will increase by 50% over the next two decades (Ross 2003). One of the main causes for this predicted increase, according to the report, is the widespread adoption of unhealthy life styles by people in the developing countries. It estimates that the number of cancer cases will climb to 15 million per annum by 2020 if current trends in smoking, the consumption of unhealthy diets, and lack of exercise continue. The report expresses particular concern about the increasing adoption of unhealthy patterns of living in the developing regions. According to the director of the WHO's International Agency for Research on Cancer, the report is quite disturbing about the numbers of people in the developing countries who have taken up smoking and are adopting Western lifestyles that are associated with a high risk of cancer (Ross 2003).

In sum, there is considerable evidence that certain patterns of death and disability are caused by the lifestyle changes and the increased consumption of unhealthy products associated with the contemporary aspects of globalization. These lifestyle changes and unhealthy consumption patterns are contributing to an increase in NCDs—the so-called diseases of affluence. In addition, the economic development promoted by globalization is contributing to a problematic epidemiological transition in many of the developing countries. This epidemiological transition is responsible for an increase in NCDs, since it is causing the aging of the population in these societies. At the same time, communicable diseases, especially among the poor and disadvantaged sectors of these societies, continue to be a major

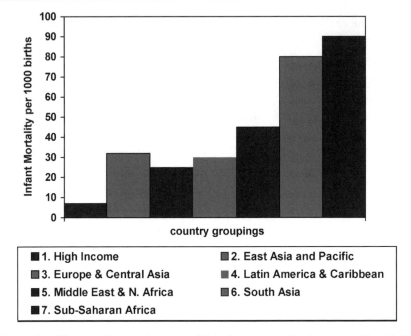

Figure 5. The health gap between high income and other countries. Infant mortality rate = the number of infants who die before reaching the age of one year, per 1,000 live births in a given year.
Source: BBC News Online June 18, 2002—World Bank Data.

cause of death and disability. Thus, these societies suffer the double burden of disease associated with what appear to be the contemporary health effects of globalization.

*Globalization and Health Inequities*
At the outset of the new millennium, "the greatest burden of health risks is borne by the poor countries, and by the disadvantaged in all societies" who suffer the health effects of poverty as well as other unhealthy living conditions (WHO 2002:13). In fact, there is growing evidence that the increasing integration of the developing countries and the former socialist countries into the contemporary global capitalist economy is not, as expected, propelling the populations of these societies into a new era of affluence, rising living standards, and post-modernity. To the contrary, the contemporary forces of globalization appear to be creating more "losers" than "winners" in most of these countries. The "health gap" (see Figure 5) between the developed and the developing countries appears to be one of the consequences of this process.

Many of the critics of globalization see it as a euphemism for the global expansion of what has been called "turbo-capitalism," and they argue that one of the prime characteristics of this global expansion of contemporary capitalism is that it is creating "a small elite of winners, a mass of losers of varying affluence or poverty, and rebellious law-breaking rebels" (Luttwak 1999:236). Even those who view globalization favorably acknowledge that it creates a lot of "road kill" as it runs over the "turtles" in its way. In his book on globalization, *The Lexus and the Olive Tree*, these are the terms that *The New York Times* columnist Thomas Friedman (1999) uses to describe the effects of globalization (Friedman 1999:271). As Friedman's analysis of globalization reveals, even the admirers and proponents of globalization acknowledge that it creates many losers ("turtles" and "road kill").

In fact, most contemporary observers of the current global order are struck by the increasing inequality that has accompanied the growth and global integration of the contemporary capitalist economic system. For example, Korten (1999) has observed that "the great majority of the benefits of global economic growth have gone not to the poor but to those who already have more than they need—often far more" (p. 79). In fact, it is difficult to ignore the economic, political, and social inequality that characterizes the contemporary global order at the outset of the third millennium. Thus, the United Nations Development Program (UNDP) devoted its *Human Development Report 1999* to the unequal effects of globalization on the world's population (UNDP 1999). This report warns that the majority of the world's population is being left behind by the rapid growth of the world economy, which has not been able to meet the basic needs of the world's poor, including their health needs.

The UNDP report provides statistical data that indicate economic globalization as being responsible for a growing disparity in wealth between the rich and the poor, not only in the developing countries but also in the developed countries. The report indicates that the income gap between the top 20% and the bottom 20% of humanity had increased from 30 to 1 in 1960 to 74 to 1 by the end of the twentieth century (UNDP 1999:36). The report reveals that as the current new century in human history began, the richest 20% of the world's population enjoyed 86% of the world's gross domestic product (GDP); whereas the middle 60% shared just 13 percent of the world's GDP; and the poorest 20% had only 1%. These statistics challenge the claims made by some of the proponents of economic globalization who contend that the increasing global flow of trade, investments and information promotes economic growth that improves the incomes and standard of living of people everywhere.

Cornia (2001) provides the results of recent studies that demonstrate convincingly that income inequalities have risen over the last two decades in most countries. The data presented by Cornia reveal that the neoliberal economic reforms and the patterns of economic development associated with globalization have either contributed to income inequalities or have had no impact one way or the other on these inequalities, but that there is no convincing evidence that they have reduced income inequalities. Cornia provides data demonstrating that the so-called structural reforms and patterns of development associated with globalization have not contributed to poverty reduction or to improvements in the health of the poor, as claimed by many of the advocates of neoliberalism and globalization, such as Dollar and Kraay (2002) at the World Bank. In fact, Dollar (2001) has conceded that "globalization can have adverse effects on health," and that these adverse effects "originate most clearly as side-effects of travel and migration, though trade in food and other products can spread disease as well" (p. 830).

Dollar and Kraay (2002) claim that global inequality has declined since 1975, due primarily to the rapid economic growth that has taken place in China and India and to the growth of per capita income that has taken place in the "globalizing economies," but not in the "nonglobalizers" (Dollar and Kraay 2002). Their use of India, China, and Vietnam as globalizing success stories has been criticized (Galbraith 2002), because these countries have not followed the prescribed neoliberal development strategy for the integration of their economies into the global market. To the contrary, they have followed unorthodox development strategies based, not on neoliberal structural reforms, but on capital controls, long-term official development assistance, industrial development financed by internal savings, and/or various types of protectionist trade policies. Moreover, the heavily indebted and bankrupt economies of Argentina and Russia are missing from Dollar and Kraay's globalizing success stories even though these countries were previously touted as the poster children for globalizing economies, and the same goes for the newly industrialized "Asian tigers" who liberalized their economies in the early 1990s, only to suffer a devastating economic crisis in the late 1990s that they are still struggling to overcome (Galbraith 2002).

There is considerable evidence that "world growth rates were systematically higher under the structured international finance regimes of Bretton Woods from 1945 to 1971 than in the era of deregulation after 1980" (Galbraith 2002). Based on his review of the international data on economic growth, Cornia (2001) contends that "there is no evidence that globalization has improved overall growth, indeed the contrary is true" (p. 838). He provides data that reveal "the rate of gross national product (GNP) growth per capita in the world economy slowed from an average 2.6% during the period 1960-79 to an average of 1.0% between 1980 and 1998" (p. 838). Moreover, he finds that during the 1990s, the rate of growth of the world economy decelerated in relation to that of the 1980s. Cornia also finds that "with slow growth and frequent rises in inequality, health improvements during the era of deregulation and globalization decelerated perceptibly, especially during the 1990s" (Cornia 2001:839). He cites UNICEF data that show in 15 of the East European economies in transition "the infant mortality rate was higher in 1994 than in 1990" and "in sub-Saharan Africa as a whole the 1999 mortality rate for children aged under 5 was higher than in 1990." He also cites the deterioration in population health and the drop in life expectancy that took place in Belarus, the Russian Federation, and the Ukraine between 1990 and 2000. These three countries provide the most dramatic examples of the adverse health effects associated with the integration of the former socialist economies into the global capitalist economy.

As McMichael and Beaglehole (2000) note in their analysis of the global context of public health, the "principal promoters" (transnational corporations, IMF, World Bank, and WTO) of the contemporary "globalized market-based economic system" have promoted development strategies and structural adjustments that "have often impaired population health" in the countries affected by these strategies and reforms. They attribute this effect to the "tension" that exists between the "free market" ideology of neoliberalism shared by these promoters of globalization and the "philosophy of social justice" that generally is shared by those who practice and advocate for public health.

Weisbrot and his colleagues (2001), who have produced the "Scorecard on Globalization," find that there is no evidence that the policies associated with globalization in the last two decades or so have improved outcomes for the developing countries. They compare the economic and social performance of all countries over the recent 20-year period of neoliberal globalization (1980-2000) with their performance during the previous 20-year period (1960-1980). This comparison is based on economic and social indicators such as the growth of income per person; life expectancy; mortality among infants, children, and adults; literacy, and education. The comparison of the two periods reveals that slower growth is a clear pattern for countries across the income spectrum in the second period (the period of accelerated globalization) compared to the earlier period of growth between 1960 and 1980 (see Figure 6). Since this pattern of slower growth prevails for countries at all income levels, the authors of the study argue that this rules out the possibility that the slowdown is due to countries exhausting their development strategies during the first period and suggests that the cause of the sharp decline in growth was triggered by structural and policy changes that have affected mostly all countries during the 20 year period of globalization.

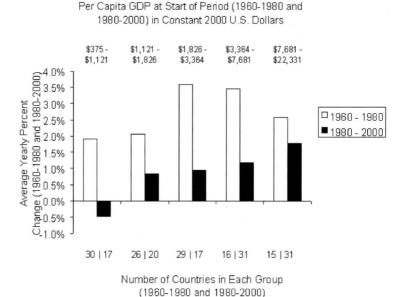

Figure 6.    Scorecard on globalization—real per capita GDP 1960-2000.
Sources: Weisbrot et al. 2001; Penn World Table, International Monetary Fund.

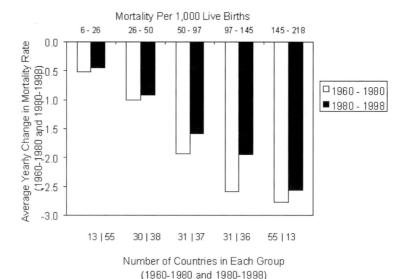

Figure 7.    Scorecard on globalization—infant mortality 1960-2000. Infant mortality rate = the number of infants who die before reaching the age of one year, per 1,000 live births in a given year.
Sources: Weisbrot et al. 2001; World Bank, World Development Indicators 2000.

Most of the indicators of social progress, including the health indicators, generally follow the slower pattern of the per capita income growth during the period of globalization (1980-2000). Thus, the rate of progress in infant mortality, child and adult mortality, and life expectancy is generally greater for countries during the first period (1960-1980) than during the period of globalization (Weisbrot et al. 2001). Among the health indicators, the rates of decline in infant mortality, child and adult mortality, and the rate of increase in life expectancy are significantly less in the period of globalization (1980-2000) than in the earlier period (1960-1980). For example, the data indicate that the rate of decline in infant mortality slowed down for all groupings during the period of neoliberal development and globalization in comparison to the earlier period of national capitalist and state-planned development (see Figure 7).

The data on health outcomes in "The Scorecard on Globalization" reveal less improvement in these outcomes in the poorer performing countries than in the best performing countries during the period of globalization; they reveal that "women appeared to be more adversely impacted by this deterioration than men" (Weisbrot et al. 2001). Although the authors of "The Scorecard" acknowledge that this evidence does not prove that the policies associated with globalization actually initiated the deterioration in performance between the two periods, they point out that it does present a very strong *prima facie* case that some structural and policy changes implemented over the last two decades explain these declines. Moreover, it is certainly the case that there is "no persuasive evidence that the policies formulated in response to globalization have improved outcomes for the developing countries" (Weisbrot et al. 2001).

The possibility that the HIV/AIDS pandemic is responsible for the deterioration in health outcomes revealed by the data on these outcomes during the recent two decades of globalization can be discounted, since "the decline in the progress in health outcomes is reported for the majority of the low and middle-income countries and not just in those countries most affected by AIDS" (Weisbrot et al. 2001). Moreover, the authors of The Scorecard point out that "we do not know how many countries would have been able to contain the spread of HIV and of what rate of infection, if their income growth, education levels, health care spending, and infrastructure had continued to grow at the rates seen from 1960-1980" (Weisbrot et al. 2001).

In fact, it is important to note "that the spread of AIDS pandemic is itself partly a result of the increased trade and travel" associated with globalization (Weisbrot et al. 2001). At the very least, globalization has made the spread of infectious diseases such as HIV/AIDS more rapid. Moreover, the increase in the income gap between most of the developing countries and the developed countries in the current period of globalization is also paralleled by the growing gap between these countries in the global spread of HIV/AIDS. Indeed, most of the people who are infected with this disease live in the developing countries, and it is not a coincidence that the populations most severely affected by this pandemic are the poorest sectors of the population in sub-Saharan Africa.

Recent UNAIDS data also indicate that the percent of the adult population in Botswana infected with HIV has increased rapidly in recent years, from 36 to 39 between 2000 and 2002, while in the United States the number of persons (60,000) infected with this deadly virus has remained approximately the same for the last 10 years (BNS 2002:A1). A similar situation exists in Zimbabwe, where the number of adults infected with HIV increased from one quarter of the population in 1997 to one third in 2002. Moreover, the recent research indicates that, in several sub-Saharan countries, nearly half of all new mothers may die from AIDS in the coming years. This deadly disease is also spreading rapidly in Eastern Europe. In 2001, the highest increase in new cases of HIV occurred in the transitional economies of Eastern Europe, and the number of new cases in Russia is now doubling every year (BNS 2002:A1 and A16). Moreover, UNAIDS experts predict that the number of HIV-positive cases in "globalizing" China will increase from an estimated 1.5 million in 2002 to as many as 10 million in 2010.

The essay in this collection on health policy in post-apartheid South Africa by Di McIntyre and her associates reveals the extent to which the struggle to overcome the "legacy of massive inequalities in income, health status and access to health and other social services" resulting from South Africa's racist and authoritarian past has been hindered by the forces of globalization. Moreover, they reveal that it is not just the obvious forms of global intervention such as IMF loan conditions, externally enforced compliance with the Trade Related Aspects of International Property Rights (TRIPS) Agreement on patented HIV/AIDS medicines, and the World Bank's privatization of health care programs that exacerbate the existing inequities in South Africa, it is also the more subtle and indirect influences of globalization that have led the post-apartheid government to adopt "self-imposed" structural adjustments. These self-imposed policies and practices tend to reinforce the health inequities created by centuries of colonialism and European domination on the African continent.

Furthermore, the health inequities associated with globalization are closely tied to gender inequities. As Doyal (2002) argues "until recently gender has rarely been taken seriously in the broader analysis of globalization" and "the discourse itself has had a predominantly male focus" (Doyal 2002). However, increasingly, attention is now being given to the links between globalization and gender inequities and to the effects of globalization on women's health. Doyal criticizes the structural adjustment programs carried out by governments around the world that have conformed to the global restructuring strategies of international institutions such as the IMF, the World Bank, and the WTO. These programs have responded to the demands of these globalizing agents by reducing public expenditures on health and other social services "to facilitate the repayment of international debt and to realign the spending patterns of individual countries with the perceived needs of a globalizing world economy" (Doyal 2002). They have "hollowed out" the public services capacity of individual states and reduced the provision of health care and other services, particularly to women trapped in poverty.

More women than men are in poverty and poor women make up a larger share than men of the total population that lives in poverty in most countries (Doyle 2002). Thus, the impact of the globally imposed structural adjustment programs on the poor affects women more severely than men. They must suffer the physical and psychological exhaustion that goes with struggling to make sure they and their families survive. Since women have special needs connected to their reproductive capacity, they are vulnerable to a wide range of health problems associated with controlling their fertility, pregnancy, and childbirth. Their struggle to survive under the conditions imposed by structural adjustments increases their vulnerability to the wide range of health problems that are particular to women. Especially if food is in short supply, they are susceptible to iron deficiency, pregnancy-related disorders, and various infectious diseases, including HIV/AIDS.

In fact, as Doyle (2002) notes, the "gendered links between health, poverty and global restructuring" can be seen "with particular clarity through the HIV/AIDS epidemic." This disease started off primarily "affecting gay men in the developed countries but has become a major killer of poor women" in the developing countries. It is possible to attribute the spread of this disease among women (now 47% of those who are HIV positive) to both global restructuring and the poverty associated with it:

> In a situation where they have few options for supporting themselves, many women may feel compelled to stay with a male partner even when this is putting their life at risk. A refusal to participate in unsafe sex may mean the withdrawal of material support leaving a woman and her children with no alternative means of survival. For some, paid sex work may be the only source of income and adolescent girls are particularly at risk in such circumstances. This reflects their greater biological vulnerability but also their lack of alternative means of subsistence where the rapidity of global restructuring has cut away the support networks that previously existed even in impoverished communities. (Doyle 2002)

There are a number of studies that indicate how violence against women is often exacerbated by poverty and social conflict that accompany economic restructuring. A recent World Bank study has found that the increases in gender violence in Eastern Europe and Central Asia are linked to the economic decline and the breakdown of state institutions in these countries that have accompanied their integration into the global capitalist economy (Doyle 2002).

Other gendered links between health, poverty and global restructuring include the following: (1) increased health threats resulting from the entry of women and girls into the workforce of globalized production facilities in countries with weak health, safety, and labor laws; (2) the health effects that result from women's work increasingly combined with childbearing in the informal sector of employment; (3) the health effects of sexual harassment in the workplace; (4) and the health effects on women and on their unborn children as a result of exposure to pesticides through their work in commercial agriculture or chemicals stored inside or near their homes; (5) poor women usually being the most at risk with regard to the consumption of low quality and untested drugs and contraceptive devices that are sold or tested in the developing countries; (6) women being particularly susceptible in certain countries to the marketing efforts of the international tobacco industry at a time when the uncertainties and pressures in their lives make them especially vulnerable to smoking related diseases. Also, the introduction of user fees for health services has had a disproportionate effect on poor women, especially in the area of reproductive health (Doyle 2002).

The essay in this collection by Rak and Janes on reproductive health in post-transition Mongolia reveals how global reproductive health policies, promoted by international NGOs and the governments of developed countries such as the United States, impose family planning methods on women that often run counter to their beliefs, experiences and needs. These paternalistic and ethnocentric family planning methods have ignored local cultures and devalued the alternatives that may already exist at the local level. Rak and Janes reveal the contradictions in this approach within the context of Mongolia's rapidly deteriorating health services caused by the adoption of market-based reforms, the reduction of the public budget for health care and the privatization of the health sector in what was a Soviet-style, state-planned economy for 70 years. The effects have been severe for women in Mongolia: maternal mortality has increased significantly, particularly among women who are socially and economically marginalized. The problem for many women in Mongolia, according to Rak and Janes, is not fertility control but "the often desperate economic conditions that many [women] now find themselves in."

*The Health Effects of Neoliberalism, SAPs, and Privatization*
Over the last two decades, the international financial institutions such as
the World Bank and the IMF, the WTO, the governments of the Group
of 7 countries (led by the United States), the transnational corporations,
and the local political and business elites in the developing countries
have promoted major structural changes called "structural adjustment
programs" (SAPs) in the economies of most of the developing countries
to facilitate the increased integration of these countries into the global
capitalist system. These SAPs and the mutual interests of this coalition
of both the global and local agents of globalization are cloaked with the
contemporary ideology of "neoliberalism," which has its origins in the
Reagan-Bush administrations in the United States and the Thatcher-Major
governments in the United Kingdom (Harris and Seid 2000:11).

The key concepts in this ideology are "the free market" and "free
trade," and the advocates of this ideology generally use these concepts
like a mantra. They believe the triumph of capitalism over communism
and the end to the Cold War are due to the victory of the market
over the state (Korten 1999:37). They also believe that "the more you
let market forces rule and the more you open your economy to free trade
and competition, the more efficient and flourishing your economy will
be" (Friedman 1999:8). In this ideology, globalization is equated with the
"spread of free market capitalism to virtually every corner of the world."

The proponents of this ideology believe they have discovered the universal formula for economic prosperity. As Luttwak (1999) puts it, they believe
this formula is "good for every country, rich or poor," and the formula
is: "PRIVATIZATION + DEREGULATION + GLOBALIZATION =
TURBO-CAPITALISM = PROSPERITY" (p. 25). In applying this ideology, the IMF, the World Bank, the regional development banks, and
the international development agencies of the major donor countries (led
by the United States) have insisted that the governments receiving their
loans, credits, and development assistance adopt a series of so-called structural adjustments and economic reforms. These adjustments and reforms
make the private sector the primary engine of these countries' development efforts, give priority to servicing their foreign debts, deregulate their
commercial and financial markets, reduce the size of their government
budgets and bureaucracies, eliminate all barriers to foreign investments
and imports, sell off their state enterprises and public utilities to private
corporations, privatize as many of their public services as possible, and
terminate all government subsidies and most welfare programs (Balasubramaniam 2000).

The critics of these SAPs and neoliberal reforms contend that they have
had disastrous consequences in most of the countries where they have been

implemented. For example, in his recent book on globalization, Joseph Stiglitz (2002), winner of the 2001 Nobel Prize in Economics and former Chief Economist and Senior Vice President of the World Bank, provides a harsh indictment on the disastrous effects on the structural adjustment programs and neoliberal development strategies of the IMF, the World Bank, and the WTO. Stiglitz claims that what he learned while he was at the World Bank "radically changed [his] views of both globalization and development," because he "saw firsthand the devastating effect that globalization can have on developing countries and especially the poor within these countries" (p. ix).

Stiglitz, who was also the Chairman of the U.S. Council of Economic Advisors and a cabinet member in the Clinton presidential administration, provides a scathing critique of what he calls the "free market fundamentalism" that underlies the structural adjustment and monetary policies that the IMF, the World Bank, and the U.S. Treasury have imposed on the countries they provide loans, credits, financial aid, and/or advice. The neoliberal policies that the IMF and the other international financial and trade agencies have imposed on these countries have been "an almost certain recipe for job destruction and unemployment creation at the expense of the poor," and they have contributed to the instability of their economies (p. 84).

It also appears that many of the policies these institutions have imposed on countries around the world have been a recipe for weakening their public health systems and reducing their efforts to improve the health of their populations (Balasubramaniam 2000). The countries that have implemented SAPs and neoliberal structural reforms under the aegis of the World Bank and the IMF have generally increased the commercial presence in their health systems with what are often disastrous results (Hilary 2001). For example, Hilary gives particular focus to the impact on children's health of neoliberal cost-recovery programs, about which he says the following:

> The introduction of cost recovery programs in the health sector is now widely accepted to have been disastrous, forcing many families and their children into a "medical poverty trap" characterized by untreated illness and long term impoverishment. Even the World Bank, while it continues to support user fees for health in national Poverty Reduction Strategy Papers, has acknowledged that they are responsible for denying poor families access to health care. (Hilary 2001)

As Hilary notes, many countries that have followed the World Bank's private sector development strategy have experienced negative consequences: (1) commercialization has led to increased inequality in access to health care; (2) private investment tends to be concentrated in the more affluent areas and in profit-maximizing activities; (3) health maintenance organizations and health insurance companies favor the healthy and wealthy; (4) the private sector draws health personnel away from the public health system (causing a "brain drain") and worsens the shortage of trained personnel in public health; (5) many conflicts of interest between the pursuit of commercial interests and public health goals have arisen; (6) profit-motivated health care gives excessive focus to curative rather than preventive health measures; (7) limited funds are often diverted toward nonpriority areas; (8) privatization schemes have restricted the access of poor families to not only health but to water and sanitation; and (9) rising prices in the health care system are often accompanied by a decline in the quality of service.

With increasing globalization and the promotion of neoliberal policies by the World Bank and the IMF, there has been a marked shift in global health strategies away from national government responsibility for providing health care for all members of the population to new strategies that are based on so-called public-private partnerships, the privatization of health care, and the provision of selective primary health care (Balasubramaniam 2000; Khor 1995; Shrestha, Shrestha, and Maskey 2002). Many of the critics of the present global strategies regard them as a betrayal of the commitment of certain national governments to provide primary health care for all. This commitment was made by the national governments that endorsed the Alma Ata Declaration formulated at the 1978 International Health Assembly that WHO and UNICEF held in Alma-Ata in what was then the Soviet Union (Mokhiber and Weissman 2000). This declaration to achieve "Health for All by the Year 2000" called upon health ministries and health workers around the world to provide comprehensive primary health care for their populations, ensure that the basic needs of all people are met, and hold themselves accountable to the people and communities they serve.

Since the 1980s, the shift in global health strategy that has accompanied the promotion of neoliberal policies by the IMF and the World Bank has replaced the goal of providing comprehensive primary health care with that of providing selective primary health care, reducing government budgets for health and other social services, downsizing the public health sector, privatizing hospitals and clinics, charging fees for health and other public services, eliminating or greatly reducing food subsidies, and freeing the prices of drugs and health services so that they are no longer within the reach of large sectors of the population (Devraj 2000; Hilary 2001; Walt 2000). Many critical observers and activists (Devraj 2000; Khor 1995; Shrestha, Shrestha, and Maskey 2002; Walt 2000) have criticized the World Bank for this shift in strategy and for the adverse health effects of the neoliberal policies this shift in global health strategy has caused.

They argue that the Bank's promotion of neoliberal policies has placed the burden of health care costs on the shoulders of the poor, drastically reduced public health services, turned over to private doctors and businesses most of the health services that used to be provided free or on a subsidized basis, and priced many medical interventions beyond the capability to pay of those who have the greatest need for these interventions.

The World Bank's market-oriented health policies have come under severe criticism from health activists in the new People's Health Movement (PHM), who accuse the Bank of having contributed to the deterioration of health conditions around the world. They also charge that the World Bank has "hijacked health" from the WHO (Devraj 2000), since the Bank now provides more funds for health-related programs than the WHO. The PHM is an international movement that has affiliates in five continents. It represents a primary example of what has been called "globalization from below," that is, the kind of global solidarity and collaboration that occurs when groups of people at the grassroots level around the world link up to protect their interests against the forces of globalization from above (Brecher, Costello, and Smith 2000).

The PHM emerged out of the People's Health Assembly (PHA) that brought health activists from some 92 countries together in Savar, Bangladesh, in December 2000 (Mokhiber and Weissman 2000). This international assembly produced a People's Charter for Health (PHA 2000), which has since been translated into 35 languages. The Charter is aimed at combating the negative effects of globalization and at making health a fundamental human right that is respected by all national governments and intergovernmental organizations.

The PHM advocates comprehensive primary health care for all (as envisioned in the Alma Ata Declaration); calls for the radical transformation of the World Bank, the IMF, WTO, and the WHO to make them more responsive to poverty alleviation and promoting health for all; demands that the foreign debts of the developing countries be cancelled; calls on national governments to protect the health rights of their citizens; demands that transnational corporations (particularly those involved in health) be effectively regulated so that they do not exploit or harm people's health; opposes the privatization and commodification of health care; and calls for the establishment of people's organizations and movements to work at the global, national, and community levels for a healthy, ecologically sustainable and more democratic world order (PHA 2000). Representatives of the PHM met with the WHO Director-General at the May 2001 World Health Assembly in Geneva, and the PHM sent the largest civil society delegation to the May 2002 World Health Assembly (Chetley and Narayan 2002). It is engaged in organizing regional and country "circles" to build awareness about and mobilize support for the movement around the world. The PHA Charter concludes that although governments are responsible for promoting health equality, people's organizations are required to force them to meet this responsibility (PHA 2000).

*The Effects of Globalization on Environmental Health*
There is mounting evidence that the globalization of the patterns of production and consumption developed in the Western industrial societies is responsible for global environmental effects that are harmful to human health. These environmental effects of globalization include: global climate change, the depletion of the planet's stratospheric ozone layer, the destabilization and destruction of natural ecosystems, desertification, and a wide variety of chemical pollution. McMichael and Beaglehole (2000) emphasize in their work the health consequences of global climate change and stratospheric ozone depletion. These global threats to health are the result of the globalization of modern production and consumption patterns based on the use of fossil fuels and man-made gases such as chlorofluorocarbons. The United Nation's Intergovernmental Panel on Climate Change and other scientific agencies have assessed the potential health risks associated with global warming, in particular the potential health effects of increased exposure to extreme temperatures, the disruption of complex ecosystems that increase the range of vector-borne and water-borne infections, the salination and contamination of fresh water supplies as a result of rising sea levels, the reduction of agricultural yields, more frequent and severe droughts and floods, and the increased production of photochemical air pollutants.

Among the various health effects of global climate change are a projected 500% rise in skin-cancer among the population of Europe and the United States during the middle decades of this century (McMichael and Beaglehole 2000). There are also the health risks posed by the proliferation of invasive plant and animal species that is taking place as a result of global climate change and the breakdown of natural ecosystems under the pressure of human contamination. Many of these invasive species are providing a breeding ground for water-borne diseases and diarrhea organisms. There is also evidence of an estimated worldwide reduction of 24% in cereal grain yields as a result of global climate change, particularly in areas where there is already a high risk of hunger (McMichael and Beaglehole 2000). These grains represent two-thirds of the world's food energy, and the expected decreases in crop yields in already food-insecure regions of the developing world could have grave health effects on their populations. Finally, there are many other types of global environmental health risks linked to the increasing water demands of commercial agriculture and industry that are depleting and/or polluting the world's finite fresh water supplies. Current projections indicate that these trends will result in serious public health crises in the coming decades (McMichael and Beaglehole 2000).

The increased burning of fossil fuels and the emissions of other greenhouse gases that are entailed in the socioeconomic development processes associated with globalization are causing climate changes that threaten to reduce crop yields in Africa, South Asia, and South America by as much as 30% by 2050 (Hong 2000:68-69). Hong claims that these climate changes are not only threatening the food security and nutritional health of large numbers of people but that they are also increasing the global range of vector-borne infections such as malaria, dengue fever, yellow fever, certain types of encephalitis and leishmaniasis. In addition, Hong blames the climate changes resulting from globalization for the health risks associated with the increased frequency and intensity of droughts, heat waves and floods.

Most of sub-Saharan Africa, South and Southeast Asia, and the Pacific islands are the most vulnerable areas to global climate changes that pose health risks because of rising temperatures, increasing intensity in tropical storms, rising sea levels, and/or salt-water intrusion into fresh water supplies (Diaz-Bonilla et al. 2002:39). As a result of expected climate changes in these regions, the number of people at risk of hunger is projected to rise between 38 to 300 million by 2060. Diaz-Bonilla and his colleagues consider these environmental health threats to be examples of what they regard as the "spillovers" from globalization, and they claim that "poor environmental quality has been calculated to be directly responsible for around 25 percent of all preventable ill-health in the world today" (38).

The United Nations Intergovernmental Panel on Climate Change has identified the Pacific Island Countries (PICs) and other small island states as the countries that are most vulnerable to the effects of climate change (Parker and Corvalan 2000:132). These small societies are limited in their ability to adapt to climate change because they are relatively isolated, quite susceptible to weather disasters, and have restricted resources. The South Pacific Regional Environment Program reports that in the PICs, "changes consistent with global climate change have already been observed in the region such as increased coastal erosion, more saline soils, shifting fishing grounds, more droughts and water shortages, and increased reports of malaria and dengue" (p. 132). These effects of climate change exacerbate other conditions associated with economic globalization that contribute to the vulnerability of the PICs, such as the overexploitation of their limited resources, pollution, and changes in the social structure of these societies (WHO 2000).

Epstein (2002) contends that "diseases relayed by mosquitoes—such as malaria, dengue fever, yellow fever and several kinds of encephalitis—are among those eliciting the greatest concern" as the world warms up as a result of global warming (p. 2). He indicates that some studies project that global warming will extend the scope of malaria transmission from the present area containing some "45 percent of the world's population to an area containing about 60 percent." There is evidence already that malaria is extending its range since it has recently appeared as far north as the Korean peninsula and the former Soviet Union and as far south as the South African coast of the Indian Ocean, and is moving into the previously malaria free higher elevations in northern India, central Mexico, Central and South America, and East and Central Africa (Epstein 2000).

The increased climate variability that results from global warming will probably fuel the spread of vector-borne diseases such as St. Louis encephalitis and other infections such as the West Nile virus that have recently found their way to the United States (Epstein 2000). The hantavirus in the United States and Latin America in the 1990s is an example of other disease-conveying vectors, such as rodents and other "pests" that appear to be facilitated by the disrupting effects of climate variability on the natural balance of animal and plant ecosystems. In addition to contributing to these vector-borne illnesses, Epstein (2000) predicts that "global warming will probably also elevate the incidence of water-borne diseases, including cholera" and pathogens such as Cryptosporidium through causing a heightened incidence of floods and droughts that "wipe out supplies of safe drinking water and concentrate contaminants that might otherwise remain diluted" (p. 4). As examples of what can be expected from global warming, Epstein cites the epidemics of cholera, malaria and dengue fever that have taken place in the Horn of Africa, Central America, Mozambique, and Madagascar since the late 1990s as a result of the unprecedented torrential rains and storms that have occurred in these areas.

However, it is not only through climate change that the environmental effects of globalization are increasingly threatening human health. Globalization is accompanied by a developmental model of production and consumption that is responsible for many devastating effects on the physical environment that have adverse effects on human health (Hong 2000:68). Hong provides a long list of how the environmental impacts of this developmental model threaten human health and the life support systems of the planet. This list includes the following (see Hong, pp. 68-72):

- As a result of losing access to their main source of protein, the health of some one billion people in 40 Third World countries is threatened by the over-fishing and the depletion of fish stocks that is taking place in response to the increasing export demand for fish-based animal feeds and oils.

- A sixth of the world's land area has already been degraded by human-induced soil erosion, salination, water logging and chemicalization; and by 2050 more than two billion people will suffer the health risks associated with living in regions facing land scarcity and/or increasing desertification as a result of these processes of environmental degradation.

- Human populations are exposed to a growing number of endocrine disrupting synthetic chemicals that are being introduced into the environment and that cause male and female reproductive disorders, neurological toxicity, low birth rates, and slowed fetal development.

- Ozone depleting gases resulting from industrial processes and the consumption of manufactured goods have already reduced by some ten percent the ozone layer in the temperate regions of the planet resulting in ultra violet light induced cataracts that claim the sight of millions of people every year.

- Increasing lead emissions (most of them in the Third World) are impairing the development of children's brains and reducing their IQ levels.

- Infrastructure development, urbanization, poverty and pollution have combined to create new environmental niches for a wide range of disease causing agents.

- Chemical-based and commercialized farming and food preservation have resulted in salmonella and listeria epidemics, the transference of antibiotic resistance to humans from livestock and poultry; and new diseases (such as mad cow disease) which can be transferred to humans from animals as a result of large-scale methods of breeding and feeding livestock.

- The environmental effects of globalization are responsible for the loss of biodiversity, which in turn means the loss of food, medicines, energy, and fibers that translate into destroyed livelihoods and the deprivation of human needs for two thirds of humanity.

According to Hong, these and other "global environmental and ecological crises ... are threatening the biosphere and its capacity to sustain healthy human life" (p. 69).

Hong contends that "global economic forces have given rise to a situation where exposure to pathogenic microorganisms has increased and human resistance has been weakened," and she cites research by the Harvard Working Group on New and Resurgent Diseases to support her claim that the "major economic strategies of privatization, export agriculture, deregulation and free trade, and economic growth have altered the epidemiology of our species through multiple pathways" that are now contributing to new emerging diseases and the comeback of old diseases (p. 71). Hong, who is associated with the Third World Network (based in Penang, Malaysia), provides a Third World view on the health impacts of globalization, which holds the dominant neoliberal model of globalization responsible for promoting patterns of production and consumption that are unsustainable and that benefit only a minority of the world's population. In Hong's view, the health effects of globalization "have been devastating for societies everywhere" (p. 75), but especially for the majority of the population in most of the Third World societies of Africa, Asia, the Middle East, Latin America, and the Pacific Islands.

*Globalization and Health-Related Technologies*
There are those who argue rather convincingly that the development of health-related technologies has largely benefited the developed rather than the developing countries. Elmendorf (2002) argues that "the present global market for health research and development is not responding adequately to the interests of developing countries in the development of new technologies appropriate to their health conditions." The United Nations Development Program (UNDP 2001) has offered the following observations on this situation:

- The technology divide does not have to follow the income divide; throughout history, technology has been a powerful tool for human development and poverty reduction.
- Markets are powerful engines of technological progress, but they are not powerful enough to create and diffuse the technologies needed to eradicate poverty.
- Developing countries may gain especially high rewards from new technologies, but they also face especially severe challenges in managing the risks.
- National policies—important though they be—will not be sufficient to compensate for global market failures. New international initiatives and the fair use of global rules are needed to channel new technologies towards the most urgent needs of the world's poor people.

The challenge is for the international community to act on these propositions, and to organize and finance more effectively than in the past the development and distribution of the new health-related technologies that are needed by the populations of the developing world "in the face of the growing pressures of globalization" (Elmendorf 2002).

Moreover, those who are responsible for promoting globalization in the developed countries will have to adopt this course of action in their overall policy programs, if globalization is to benefit both the poor and powerless as well as the rich and powerful. In this regard, Elmendorf notes that there have been a large number of global initiatives in the areas of health technology and research, such as the Global Forum for Health Research, the Global Alliance for Vaccines and Immunizations, the joint WHO/World Bank/UNDP Program of Research on Tropical Diseases, and the UNDP/UNFP/WHO/World Bank Program of Research, Development and Research Training in Human Reproduction. However, although health care technology is becoming a critical public policy issue in the developing countries, so far health technology assessment and choice have received little attention (Elmendorf 2002). Elmendorf predicts that globalization and the changing epidemiological patterns in the developing countries will make these issues increasingly more important.

In this regard, it is interesting to note that an international panel of scientists have recently identified what they consider to be the top ten biotechnologies for improving health in the developing countries (Daar et al. 2002). They argue that, while most research into genomics and other biotechnologies is primarily concerned with the priorities of the developed countries, a limited number of projects have demonstrated that many of these technologies could improve health in the developing countries. This panel of 28 well-known experts from around the world identified the following as the top ten biotechnologies for improving health in the developing countries:

1. Modified molecular technologies for affordable, simple diagnosis of infectious diseases.
2. Recombinant technologies to develop vaccines against infectious diseases.
3. Technologies for more efficient drug and vaccine delivery systems.
4. Technologies for environmental improvement (sanitation, clean water, bioremediation).
5. Sequencing pathogen genomes to understand their biology and to identify antimicrobials.
6. Female-centered protection against sexually transmitted diseases, both with and without contraceptive effect.
7. Bioinformatics to identify drug targets and to examine pathogen-host interactions.
8. Genetically modified crops with increased nutrients to counter specific deficiencies.
9. Recombinant technology to make therapeutic products (e.g., insulin, interferons) more affordable.
10. Combinatorial chemistry for drug discovery.

This panel of experts argue that biotechnology can be made affordable for the developing countries. However, they note that 90% of all health research funds are spent on the health problems of only 10% of the world's population (p. 229). These experts also state that they do not wish to diminish the importance of proven health strategies in the developing countries, such as health education and improvements in sanitation. To the contrary, they argue that the appropriate balance between these conventional strategies and new health-related technologies needs to be achieved and pursued in the developing countries. They urge individual countries to assess the appropriateness of these technologies to their needs and their national contexts. They also encourage regional associations of developing countries to determine how they can collaboratively improve health in their regions by promoting some of these technologies, and they lastly encourage the WHO to conduct formal technology assessments of these technologies to determine their cost effectiveness.

Roy Smith in his contribution to this collection of essays examines how new information and communication technologies (ICT) have been applied to healthcare in some of the more remote areas of the world, especially in the Pacific islands. In particular, he analyzes the use of telehealth and telemedicine in certain Pacific island communities for remote consultancy, diagnosis and prescription of health care as well as the use of ICT for distance learning for health professionals. He calls attention to how the ownership and usage of this technology can enhance the provision of healthcare to people in remote and marginalized areas as well as potentially reinforce unequal power relationships in the global economy. Smith calls attention to how the life style changes associated with modernization and globalization in the Pacific island communities have brought about a shift in the incidence of communicable to non-communicable diseases. He argues that telehealth strategies in the region need to take into account this health transition since the telehealth technology has the potential to provide "a remarkable expansion of the medical expertise available to act in a curative manner," and to advance a program of preventative healthcare.

*Conclusions about the Linkages between Globalization and Health*
Although the final essay in this collection will examine in some detail the conclusions derived from all the essays in the collection, it is important to note here that the definition, conceptualization, and analysis of the health effects of globalization are part of a highly significant, but contested discourse. The ideological debate, the political implications, and the complexity of globalization make it difficult to conceptualize, theorize, and analyze the linkages between globalization and health. The frameworks for analysis that have been analyzed in this essay attempt to identify in a relatively neutral manner the different pathways, both direct and indirect,

through which the various aspects of globalization affect health and health-related conditions at the national, community, and household levels.

Conceptualizations such as the globalization of disease and the diseases of globalization provide convenient perspectives for analyzing the history and linkages between globalization and health at the macro and mid-range levels of analysis and for fairly high-level and broadly comparative theorizing. However, a wide range of interdisciplinary concepts and units of analysis are needed to comprehend the ideological, political, economic, and environmental forces that are shaping the dynamic relationships between the transnational, international, national, and local agents that are responsible for the globalization of the health care systems and the health of people around the world. The analysis and comprehension of these dynamic relationships and their effects require the use of an interdisciplinary ensemble of concepts and foci of analysis that includes neoliberalism, structural adjustment programs (SAPs), privatization, income distribution, poverty alleviation, globalization from below, ozone depletion, global warming, and sustainable development.

The theoretical, clinical and policy implications of analyses carried out at the mid-range level (national and subnational) as well as at the more macro-level (global and regional) are potentially quite significant at the relatively nascent stage at which the inquiry into the linkages between globalization and health now exists. Micro-level analyses, such as those included in this collection, are of course needed to provide empirical evidence and closer scrutiny of the various effects of globalization on health and the pathways through which globalization impacts local community, household, and individual health. Although there is a rapidly growing literature on globalization and health, the field is still wide open and much work needs to be done to develop the existing body of knowledge on this complex and highly important subject.

# References

ALBROW, MARTIN
2000          *The Golden Age: State and Society Beyond Modernity.* Stanford, CA: Stanford
              University Press.
BALASUBRAMANIAM, K.
2000          "Globalization and Liberalization of Healthcare Services: WTO and the
              General Agreement on Trade in Services." Paper prepared for The People's
              Health Assembly, December 4-8, Savar, Bangladesh (11 pages). Retrieved
              December 9, 2002 (http://phmovement.org/pubs/issuepapers/bala2.html).
BEE NEWS SERVICE (BNS)
2002          "Huge Jump in AIDS Toll Feared." *The Sacramento Bee*, July 3, 2002. p. A1
              and A16.
BORENSTEIN, SETH
2003          "SARS is Latest in Explosion of New Infectious Diseases." *Knight Rid-*

der *Newspapers*, May 1, Washington Bureau. Retrieved on May 10, 2003 (http://www.realcities.com/mld/krwashington/5764247.htm).

BRADSHER, KEITH
2003        "Carrier of SARS Made 7 Flights Before Treatment." *The New York Times*, April 11, p. 1.

BRECHER, JEREMY, TIM COSTELLO AND BRENDAN SMITH
2000        *Globalization from Below*. Boston: South End Press.

BRUNDTLAND, GRO HARLEM
2002        "Globalization as a Force for Better Health." Transcript of lecture at London School of Economics, March 16, 2001. Retrieved March 16, 2003 (http://www.lse.ac.uk/collections/globalDimensions/lectures/ globalizationAsAForceForBetterH.../transcript.html).

CASTELLS, MANUEL
1996        *The Network Society*. Oxford: Blackwell.

CHETLEY, ANDREW AND RAVI NARAYAN
2002        "The People's Health Movement." *Contact* 176 (January-March 2002):1-2.

COLLIN, JEFF AND KELLEY LEE
2002        "Globalization and Public Health: A Review and Assessment of Public Health Measures in the UK Concerned with Transborder Health Risks." Report prepared for The Nuffield Trust, February 2002 (102 pages). Retrieved March 13, 2003 (http://www.lshtm.ac.uk/cgch/globalisation&publichealth.pdf).

CORNIA, GIOVANNI
2001        "Globalization and Health: Results and Options." *Bulletin of the World Health Organization* 79:834-841.

DAAR, ABDALLAH, HALLA THORSTEINSDOTTTIR, DOUGLAS K. MARTIN, ALYNA C. SMITH, SHAUNS NAST AND PETER A. SINGER
2002        "Top Ten Biotechnologies for Improving Health in Developing Countries." *Nature Genetics* 32:229-232.

DEVRAJ, RANJIT
2000        "World Bank's Health Policies Hurting Nations, Say Critics." Third World Network. Retrieved March 15, 2003 (http://www.twnside.org.sg/title/ hurting.htm).

DIAZ-BONILLA, EUGENIO, JULIE BABINARD, AND PER PINSTRUP-ANDERSEN
2002        "Opportunities and Risks for the Poor in Developing Countries" (Working Paper 83). Indian Council for Research on International Economic Relations, New Delhi, India. Retrieved December 9, 2002 (http://www.icrier.res.in/pdf/risk.pdf).

DOLLAR, DAVID
2001        "Is Globalization Good for Your Health?" *Bulletin of the World Health Organization* 79:832-833.

DOLLAR, DAVID AND AART KRAAY
2002        "Spreading Wealth." *Foreign Affairs*, January/February. Retrieved March 22, 2003 (http://www.foreignaffairs.org/20020101faessay6561/david-dollar- aart.../spreading-the-wealth.html).

DOYAL, LESLEY
2002        "Putting Gender into Health and Globalization Debates: New Perspectives and Old Challenges." *Third World Quarterly* 23. Retrieved August 8, 2002 (http://www.womankind.org.uk/main/globheal.htm).

DRAGER, NICK AND ROBERT BEAGLEHOLE
2001        "Editorial: Globalization: Changing the Public Health Landscape." *Bulletin of the World Health Organization* 79:803.

DRAGER, NICK, RONALD LABONTE AND RENEE TORGERSON
2002        "Frameworks for Analyzing the Links Between Globalization and Health" (Draft Document). Retrieved March 30, 2002 (http://dev.www.uregina.ca/ spheru/PDF%20Files/Labonte-Frameworks-Links.PDF).

ELMENDORF, EDWARD
2002        "Globalization and the Choice of Health Technology in the Developing World." Paper presented at the Seventh International Conference on The Impact of Globalization on Development and Health Care Services in Islamic

Countries, March 23-27, Kuwait. Retrieved December 8, 2002 (http://www.islamet.com/ioms/globe/Full_papers/ed_elmend.html).

EPSTEIN, PAUL
2000        "Is Global Warming Harmful to Health?" *Scientific American.Com* August 20, 2000. Retrieved March 16, 2003 (http://sciam.com/print_version.cfm?articleID=0008C7*2-E060-1C73-9B81809EC588EF21).

EASTWOOD, HEATHER
2002        "Globalization, Complementary Medicine, and Australian Health Policy: The Role of Consumerism." Pp. 222-245 in *Health Policy in Australia*, edited by Heather Gardner and Simon Barraclough. Melbourne, Australia: Oxford University Press.

EVANS, MIKE, ROBERT SINCLAIR, CAROLINE FUSIMALOHI AND VILIAMI LIAVA'A
2001        "Globalization, Diet, and Health: An Example from Tonga." *Bulletin of the World Health Organization* 79:856-860.

FRIEDMAN, THOMAS
1999        *The Lexus and the Olive Tree: Understanding Globalization.* New York: Farrar-Straus-Giroux.

GALBRAITH, JAMES
2002        "By the Numbers." *Foreign Affairs* July/August. Retrieved March 22, 2003 (http://www.foreignaffairs.org/2002070faresponse8531/james-k-galbraith/by-the-numbers.html).

GIDDENS, ANTHONY
1990        *The Consequences of Modernity.* Cambridge, MA: Polity Press.

HARRIS, RICHARD
2002        "Globalization and Globalism in Latin America: Contending Perspectives." *Latin American Perspectives* 127:5-23.

HARRIS, RICHARD AND MELINDA SEID
2000        *Critical Perspectives on Globalization and Neoliberalism in the Developing Countries.* Leiden: Brill Academic Publishers.

HELD, DAVID, ANTHONY MCGREW, DAVID GOLDBLATT AND JONATHAN PERRA-TON
1999        *Global Transformations: Politics, Economics, and Culture.* Stanford, CA: Stanford University Press.

HILARY, JOHN
2001        "The World Bank's Private Sector Review: Does the Private Sector Development Strategy Threaten Children's Right to Health?" Save the Children Position Paper. Retrieved on March 15, 2003 (http://www.challengeglobalization.org/html/tools/WB_private_sector.pdf).

HONG, EVELYN
2000        "Globalization and the Impact on Health: A Third World View." Document prepared for The People's Health Assembly, December 4-8, Savar, Bangladesh.

IANNI, OCTAVIO
1998        "Las ciencias sociales en la época de la globalización." *Revista de Ciencias Sociales* 7/8 (Universidad Nacional de Quilmes, Argentina). Retrieved June 7, 2002 (http://www.argiropolis.com.ar/documentos/investigacion/publicaciones/cs/7-8/1a.htm).

INSTITUTE OF MEDICINE
2003        "Microbial Threats to Health: Emergence, Detection, and Response." Washington, DC: National Academic Press. Retrieved May 6, 2003 (http://books.nap.edu/books/030908864X/html/index.html).

ID21 INSIGHTS
2001        "Diseases of Affluence? Global Trends and Predictions." *Insights Health* Issue #1. Retrieved March 16, 2003 (http://www.id21.org/insights/insights-h01/insights-issh01-art01.html).

KELLNER, DOUGLAS
2002        "Theorizing Globalization." Pp. 73-108 in Globalisierung: Ein wissenschaftlicher Diskurs? Mainz: Passagen Verlag. Retrieved June 7, 2002 (http://www.gseis.ucla.edu/faculty/kellner/papers/theoryglob.htm).

KHOR, MARTIN
1995        "Experts Attack Shift in Global Health Strategy." Third World Network.
            Retrieved March 15, 2003 (http://www.twnside.org.sg/title/exp-ch.htm).
KARLINER, JOSHUA
1997        *The Corporate Planet: Ecology and Politics in the Age of Globalization.* San Francisco,
            CA: Sierra Club Books.
KORTEN, DAVID
1995        *When Corporations Rule the World.* San Francisco, CA: Berrett-Koehler Publishers.
1999        *The Post-Corporate World: Life After Capitalism.* San Francisco, CA: Berrett-Koehler
            Publishers.
LEE, KELLY
1999        "Globalization, Communicable Disease and Equity: A Look Back and Forth."
            *Development* 42:35-39.
2002        *Health Impacts of Globalization: Towards Global Governance.* London, UK: Palgrave
            Macmillan.
LEE, KELLY, TONY MCMICHAEL, COLIN BUTLER, MIKE AHERN AND DAVID
            BRADLEY
2002        "Global Change and Health—The Good, the Bad and the Evidence." *Global
            Change and Human Health* 3:16-19.
LUTTWAK, EDWARD
1999        *Turbo-Capitalism: Winners and Losers in the Global Economy.* New York: Harper-
            Collins.
MCMICHAEL, A.J. AND ROBERT BEAGLEHOLE
2000        "The Changing Global Context of Public Health." *The Lancet 2000* 356:49599.
            Retrieved June 6, 2002 (http://thelancet.com/era/LLAN.ERA.1060).
MCMURRAY, CHRISTINE AND ROY SMITH
2001        *Diseases of Globalization: Socioeconomic Transitions and Health.* London, UK: Earth-
            scan Publications.
MESTREL, ROSIE
2003        "SARS May Be Just the Start." *Los Angeles Times*, May 3, p. A1, A15.
MOKHIBER, RUSSELL AND ROBERT WEISSMAN
2000        "The People's Health." Retrieved March 16, 2003 (http://lists.essential.org/
            pipermail/corp-focus/2000/000052.html).
MURRAY, CHRISTOPHER AND ALAN LOPEZ
1997        "Mortality by Cause for Eight Regions of the World, Global Burden of Disease
            Study." *The Lancet* 349:1269-76.
PARKER, CINDY LOU AND CARLOS F. CORVALAN
2000        "Summary of the Regional Workshop on Climate Variability and Change and
            their Health Effects in Pacific Island Countries." *Global Change and Human Health*
            1:133-133.
PEOPLE'S HEALTH ASSEMBLY
2000        *People's Charter for Health.* Bangalore, India: PHM Secretariat.
ROBERTSON, ROLAND
1992        *Globalization: Social Theory and Global Culture.* London, UK: Sage.
ROSS, EMMA
2003        "World Health Body Predicts 50% Rise in Cancer Cases." *San Francisco
            Chronicle*, April 4, p. A15.
SHRESTHA, MATHURA, INDIRA SHRESTHA AND MANESH MASKEY
2000        "New Paradigm of Globalization: Replacing the Existing One of Unequal Re-
            lations Among Peoples and Nations with a Humane Form." Paper prepared for
            The People's Health Assembly, December 4-8, Savar, Bangladesh. Retrieved
            December 9, 2002
            (http://phmovement.org/pubs/issuepapers/shrestha1.html).
STIGLITZ, JOSEPH
2002        *Globalization and its Discontents.* New York: W.W. Norton.
UNITED NATIONS DEVELOPMENT PROGRAM (UNDP)
1997        "Globalization—Poor Nations, Poor People." Pp. 82-93 in *Human Development
            Report 1997.* New York: Oxford University Press.

1999        *Human Development Report 1999: Globalization with a Human Face.* New York: Oxford University Press. Retrieved March 9, 2003 (http://hdr.undp.org/reports/global/1999/en/default.cfm).

WALT, GILL
2000        "Globalization and Health." Paper presented at the Medact Meeting, May 13, 2000. Retrieved December 9, 2002 (http://phmovement.org/pubs/issuepapers/walt.html).

WEISBROT, MARK, DEAN BAKER, EGOR KRAEV AND JUDY CHEN
2001        "The Scorecard on Globalization 1980-2000: Twenty Years of Diminished Progress." Center for Economic and Policy Research. Retrieved April 18, 2002 (http://www.cepr.net/globalization/scorecard_on_globalization.htm).

WOODWARD, DAVID, NICK DRAGER, ROBERT BEAGLEHOLE AND DEBRA LIPSON
2001        "Globalization and Health: A Framework for Analysis and Action." *Bulletin of the World Health Organization* 79:875-880.

WORLD HEALTH ORGANIZATION (WHO)
2000        "Workshop Report: Climate Variability and Change and their Health Effects in Pacific Island Countries." July 25-28, Apia, Samoa.
2001        "Macroeconomics and Health: Investing in Health for Economic Development. Report of the Commission on Macroeconomics and Health." Geneva, Switzerland: WHO.
2002        *The World Health Report 2002.* Retrieved March 9, 2003 (http://www.who.int.whr/2002/).

# Globalization, Health, and the Free Trade Regime: Assessing the Links

## RONALD LABONTE[*]

### ABSTRACT

Globalization can be defined as the increased interconnectedness of peoples and nations through technology, trade, and finance, reinforced by an increasing number of multilateral institutions and rules. Globalization can bring health benefits, but is also associated with health risks. Its direct and indirect links to health present a complex puzzle. This essay provides a framework to help in unpacking the links, including a review of some of the evidence of health impacts along the pathways. Particular attention is given to trade agreements and their potential effects on national regulatory abilities to create healthy living, working, and environmental conditions.

## Introduction[**]

Globalization describes a process by which nations, businesses and people are becoming more connected and interdependent across the globe through increased economic integration and communication exchange, cultural

[*] Saskatchewan Population Health and Evaluation Research Unit, Community Health and Epidemiology, University of Saskatchewan, Saskatoon, Saskatchewan, Canada.

[**] *Acknowledgements:* Some of the arguments presented in this article were first made in briefing papers prepared for the International Union for Health Promotion and Education (Labonte 2000) "Brief to the World Trade Organization: World Trade and Population Health," *International Journal of Health Promotion and Education* VI(4):24-32; and Labonte (2002) "International Governance and World Trade Organization Reform," *Critical Public Health* 12(1):65-86; and for the World Health Organization meeting, "Making Health Central to Sustainable Development," Oslo, Norway, November, 2001 (Labonte 2001) "Health, Globalization and Sustainable Development" (www.spheru.ca).

diffusion (especially of Western culture) and travel. It is not a new phenomenon. One might actually call it a basic human drive. Jared Diamond (2000), in his book, *Guns, Germs and Steel*, recounts how the history of humankind has been one of pushing against borders, exploring, expanding, conquering and assimilating. In ancient Western times, "global" meant the Middle East, once a Garden of Eden that, despoiled by overuse, became an eroding desert that drove people further east to what is now China and west to the Mediterranean and continental Europe. In Western medieval times, "global" meant exploration, colonization and exploitation of the "new world." Eduardo Galeano (1973) thirty years ago, in his polemic, *Open Veins of Latin America*, showed how only the wealth of the exploited colonies — their resources, their peoples — allowed Western capitalism to depose feudalism.

Contemporary globalization, abetted by innovations in communications technologies, is characterized by increasing liberalization in the cross-border flow of finance capital and trade in goods and services. It differs from previous eras in several ways:

1. The scale and speed of such movement, particularly of finance capital. Over US $1.5 trillion (some estimate $2 trillion) in currency transactions occurs daily, more than double the total foreign exchange reserves of all governments. Such transactions reduce the ability of governments to intervene in foreign exchange markets to stabilize their currencies, manage their economies and maintain fiscal autonomy (UNDP 1999).

2. The establishment of binding rules, primarily through the World Trade Organization. Trade agreements are increasingly establishing enforceable supra-national obligations on nation-states. Countries have also entered into scores of other multilateral conventions and agreements on human rights and environmental protection, but few of these carry any penalties. This asymmetry between enforceable economic (market-based) rules and unenforceable social and environmental reciprocal obligations may be the biggest governance challenge of the new millennium (Kickbusch 2000; Labonte 1998; UNDP 1999).

3. The size of trans-national companies involved, several of which are economically larger than many nations or whole regions. Much of the global trade in goods is intra-firm, meaning that a company's subsidiary in one country sells parts or products to a subsidiary in another country (Reinicke 1998). This allows companies to locate labor-intensive parts of the production chain in low-wage countries (often in exclusive export production zones) and to declare most of their profits in low-tax countries (leading to global tax competition

and lower corporate tax revenues in all countries). The Oxford Committee for Famine Relief (OXFAM) estimates that over US $100 billion in potential tax revenue leaves developing countries for offshore tax havens each year, almost double the total amount of aid they receive (Action Aid et al. 2001).

4. The apparent commitment of most countries to continue the project of global economic integration through increased market liberalization. This commitment is built upon two decades' dominance of neo-liberal economic assumptions, reflected in the macroeconomic policies of most governments, the World Bank and International Monetary Fund, and most trade agreements (see Table 1). It is somewhat tempered by the reluctance of many of the world's wealthiest nations to abide by these assumptions if they are not to their benefit, witnessed by the continued presence and even increase of trade-distorting domestic agricultural subsidies in the European Union, Japan, and the United States.

5. Social, economic, environmental, and health issues are becoming "inherently global," rather than purely national or domestic (Labonte and Spiegel 2002). Environmental impacts of human activities are planetary in scale and scope; disease pandemics and economic stagnation partly underpin state collapse and regional conflict (Price-Smith 2002); almost 1/6th of humanity is "on the move" to escape environmental or economic degradation and conflict, straining against the borders of other nations (Worldwatch Institute 2001). The risk of a return to unilateralism by the more powerful nations is always present; the evidence of the need for multilateral (global) solutions is irrefutable.

From a health vantage, there are several compelling pro-globalization arguments. The diffusion of new knowledge and technology through trade and investment, for example, can aid in disease surveillance, treatment and prevention. There is also broad consensus on the positive effects of a globalization of gender rights and empowerment, though with the *caveat* that these rights are not simply an invention of the West but existed (often more strongly in pre-Western colonization times) in many presumably less emancipated countries today (Sen 1999). In economic terms, the pro-globalization argument posits that increased trade and foreign investment through liberalization can improve economic growth. Such growth can be used to sustain investment in necessary public goods, such as health care, education, women's empowerment programs and so on (Dollar 2001; Dollar and Kray 2000). Such growth, particularly in poorer countries, also reduces poverty, which leads, in turn, to better health. Improved population health, particularly amongst the world's

## Table 1

Basic neoliberal economic assumptions drive contemporary globalization

| Objectives | Recommendations and Benefits |
|---|---|
| Liberalization | Open markets work best for everyone |
| Privatization | States should not own or operate productive or profitable sectors of the economy |
| Private sector enhancement | States should not only sell off their assets, but also open their programs or services to private sector competition |
| Deregulation | The fewer the rules on the private sector, the better |
| State minimalism | States should reduce their public spending and taxation rates and introduces cost-recovery program to help pay their debts, balance their budgets, and promote the private sector |

Adapted from Milward (2000).

poorest countries, is increasingly associated with improved economic growth (Savedoff and Schultz 2000; World Health Organization 2001) and so the circle virtuously closes upon itself.

Globalization's skeptics quickly point out that the virtuous circle can have a vicious undertow. This includes the more rapid spread of infectious diseases, some of which are becoming resistant to treatment; and the increased adoption of unhealthy 'Western' lifestyles by larger numbers of people (Lee 2001). The more significant challenge is that liberalization does not always or inevitably lead to increased trade, foreign investment or economic growth and that, when it does, it does not inevitably reduce poverty (Cornia 2001; Weisbrot et al. 2001). Much depends upon pre-existing social, economic and environmental conditions within countries; and upon specific national programs and policies that enhance the capacities of citizens, such as health, education and social welfare programs (UNDP 1999). China, Korea, Thailand, Malaysia, Indonesia, and Vietnam did increase dramatically their role as global traders, but this was primarily in terms of their exports. They maintained public ownership of large segments of banking, retained tariff and non-tariff barriers that shielded important sectors of their economy from competitive imports, and placed restrictions on foreign capital flows—which is precisely how wealthier European and North American economies developed historically (Rodriguez and Rodrik 2000; Rodrik 1999). World Trade Organization rules now largely prohibit poorer countries from doing the same, with only modest provisions for "special and differential treatment" (trade agreement exemptions) that are being actively opposed by many of the world's richest economies. Weaker economies with fewer domestic protections, largely removed through earlier World Bank and International Monetary

Fund (IMF) "structural adjustment" loan conditionalities, have fared poorly under liberalization, particularly those in Africa and Latin America. The net effect for these countries has been suppressed domestic economic activity, depressed wages and tax revenues, and worsened balance of payments (Sustainable Developments 2001). Mexico, Uruguay, Zimbabwe, Kenya, India, and the Philippines all witnessed serious declines in income and corresponding increases in poverty and poor health among its rural farming population following liberalization (Hilary 2001).

## Understanding the Impact of Globalization on Health

Globalization may improve the health of populations in some circumstances but damage it in others, especially when liberalization has been rapid and without government support to liberalization-affected sectors and populations (Ben-David, Nordstrom, and Winter 1999; Cornia 2001; UNDP 1999). Liberalized trade in agricultural products, for example, may provide short-term economic benefit to less developed countries. This can improve citizens' health, depending on how equitably those benefits are allocated among all citizens. But food exports in poorer countries can also increase fossil-fuel based transportation, creating short- and long-term health- and environment-damaging effects; and commodity-led export produces lower long-term economic growth than manufactured ("value-added") export (Kim et al. 2000). Protectionist policies, including subsidies, in turn, may preserve rural life and livelihoods, which is an argument frequently advanced by the European Union and Japan (Labonte 2000). These policies benefit the health and quality of life of rural people. But such policies can also support ecologically unsustainable forms of production and increase oligopolistic corporate control over global food production. Another example of liberalization's mixed effects is that trade openness might increase women's share of paid employment, which is an important element of gender empowerment (Ozler 1999 in UNDP 1999). Yet much of women's employment remains low-paid, unhealthy and insecure in "free-trade" export zones that often prohibit any form of labor organization and employ only single women. Public-caring supports for young children have been declining in many trade-opened countries, portending future health inequalities. There is also evidence of a global "hierarchy of care." Women from developing nations employed as domestic workers in wealthy countries send much valued currency back home to their families, some of which is used to employ poorer rural women in their home countries to look after the children they have left behind. These rural women, in turn, leave their eldest daughter (often still quite young and ill-educated) to care for the family they have left behind in the village (Hochschild 2000).

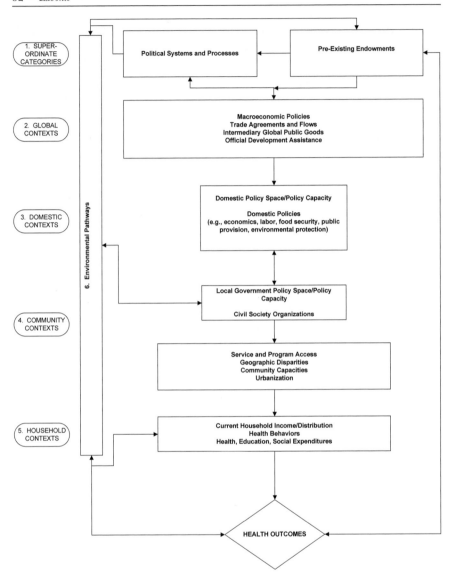

Figure 1. Globalization and health: selected pathways and elements.

What is the gain? What is the loss? Or, more poignantly expressed, who gains and who loses? Tracing the impacts of globalization on health to answer such questions can be a daunting task. Figure 1, based upon a more extensive study (Labonte and Torgerson 2002), provides a simplified framework for understanding how contemporary globalization can affect health.[1] The key points conveyed by this Figure in descending order of scale are:

1. How contemporary globalization affects health depends, first, on the historical context of particular countries, specifically their political, social, and economic traditions (e.g., democratic, oligarchic, patriarchal, theocratic, dictatorial); and their stock of pre-existing endowments (e.g., level of economic development, environmental resources, human capital development).

2. Globally, the major vehicles through which contemporary globalization operates are imposed macroeconomic policies (notably Structural Adjustment Programs, which are the precursors of today's free trade agenda); enforceable trade agreements (notably the World Trade Organization) and associated trans-border flows in goods, capital, and services; official development assistance as a form of wealth transfer for public infrastructure development in poorer nations; and "intermediary global public goods," the numerous yet largely unenforceable multilateral agreements we have on human rights, environmental protection, women's rights, children's rights, and so on (Kaul, Grunberg, and Stern 1999; Kaul and Faust 2001; Sandler and Arce 2000).

3. These vehicles, in turn, have both positive and negative health effects on domestic policy space, by increasing or decreasing public sector capacity or resources and regulatory authority. Key domestic policies that condition health outcomes include universal access to education and health care, legislated human and labor rights, restrictions on health-damaging products such as tobacco, or exposure to hazardous waste and environmental protection. Liberalization, whether through trade agreements or through Structural Adjustment Programs, lowers tariffs on imported goods.[2] This affects the ability of policies to provide the public health, education, and water/sanitation services

---

[1] It is difficult to link directly health outcomes to globalization processes. Other phenomena may affect health status dramatically in the short-term, for example, infectious diseases such as HIV/AIDS, or large-scale immunization programs. These are largely independent of globalization processes, although mass communication, travel, and global economic pressures will change risks of exposure, and the Agreement on Trade-Related Intellectual Property Rights (TRIPS) is affecting access to treatment. Changes in physical environmental conditions, such as increasing the size of a nation's or population group's "ecological footprint," may improve health outcomes in the short-term but not over the long-term. Changes in international trade and investment flows are recent and present-day health gains, at least for older populations, may reflect social and environmental conditions of an earlier period characterized by greater trade protectionism and stronger state welfare programs.

[2] Liberalization therefore has been particularly hard on developing countries, which derive much of their national tax revenue from tariffs and which lack the capacity to

essential both to health and to economic development. Global and regional trade agreements, in turn, are increasingly circumscribing the social and environmental regulatory options of national governments. It is the impact of globalization at this level of national policy capacity and regulatory authority that causes health activists the greatest concern, since it can preclude governments from enacting those policies that lead to health, equity, and empowerment at the local levels.

4. National policies and resource transfers affect the abilities of regional or local governments to regulate their immediate environments, provide equitable access to health-promoting services, enhance generic community capacities (community empowerment), or cope with increased and usually rapidly increasingly urbanization.

5. At the household level, all of the above determine in large measure family income and distribution (under conditions of poverty, for example, when women control household income, children's health tends to be better), health behaviors, and household expenditures (both in time and in money) for health, education, and social programs.

6. Each level affects, and is affected by, environmental pathways, chief among these being resource depletion (water, land, forests), biodiversity loss, and pollution.

While much remains to be understood about how globalization phenomena can be harnessed to improve global health outcomes, we have now lived through 20 years of increased market integration and 10 years of enforceable trade rules. With respect to trends in two fundamental health-determining pathways (poverty/inequality, and environmental sustainability), the effects have been largely negative.

## Poverty and Income Inequality

Globally, the past decade has seen a reduction in poverty rates at the $1/day level, but a worsening in such rates at the $2/day level (Ben-David, Nordstrom, and Winters 1999). This allows us to infer, somewhat cynically, that our recent era of globalization has successfully transferred income from the extremely poor to the absolutely destitute, a conclusion bolstered by more recent evidence that poverty rates at the $1/day level are once again increasing in the least developed countries (UNCTAD 2002). Some counter that this situation exists because poor countries have insufficiently liberalized. If they liberalized more, they would benefit more. A 1999

---

institute alternative revenue-generating sources (Hilary 2001; Rao 1999; Rodas-Martini 1999; World Bank 2000).

UNDP study of 40 developing and least developed nations challenges this assumption. It found that trade openness (liberalization) increased poverty and inequality. Those countries liberalizing most rapidly fared worst (Rao 1999).

While there is still some controversy over whether trade liberalization will or will not succeed in poverty reduction — recalling poverty as one of health's greatest threats — there is much less dispute that trade liberalization is increasing inequality. Whether income inequality is the root of disease inequality remains a disputed topic among population health researchers (Deaton 2001). Poverty, which is higher in high income-inequality countries, may be the bigger problem. But the greater the income inequality, the harder it becomes for the economic growth *presumed* to follow trade liberalization to actually lift people out of poverty. Moreover, inequalities *are* associated with a decline in social cohesion, social solidarity and support for strong states with strong redistributive income, health, and education policies that have been shown to buffer liberalization's unequalizing effects (Deaton 2001; Global Social Policy Forum, 2001; Gough 2001).

The evidence that trade and investment liberalization is leading to growing income inequality is compelling. A review of 313 Structural Adjustment Programs (SAPs) from 1968 to 1994, which increased liberalization and privatization of public services, found that inequality measures worsened dramatically in the first three years following such programs (Lee and Rhea 1998 in Rodas-Martini 1999). While there was some improvement in these measures by the fifth year, they never recovered to their pre-SAP period. A recent review of the health consequences of structural adjustment (Breman and Shelton 2001) found a preponderance of negative effects among 76 studies identified; the impact of structural adjustments was almost singularly negative in Africa. David Dollar (2001) of the World Bank, however, argues that there is no consistent pattern between liberalization and income inequalities and that, on average, incomes in the bottom percentiles rise at the same rate as those in the highest percentiles as economic growth proceeds. Yet the same 10% rise on $1,000 and $100,000 nonetheless creates a larger absolute difference in wealth, health-enhancing capacities, and privileges. Moreover, the very countries cited as evidence of the liberalization, growth, and poverty-reduction relationship (such as China, Vietnam, and India) are the outliers among the average in terms of income distribution. Those market liberalizing developing countries experiencing the greatest growth are also the ones experiencing the sharpest increases in income inequalities.

## The Environment and Sustainable Development

The two primary pathways linking globalization to the environment are the liberalization-induced effects of growth on resource depletion and pollution, and increased transportation-based fossil-fuel emissions. Ecological limits to growth and consumption are rarely considered in economic models, yet if all countries "developed" to the same consumption patterns found in the US, our species would require four more planets to exploit (*Footprint of the Planet Report* n.d.). Worldwide, current consumption outstrips capacity by 35%. There are also numerous case examples where trade and investment liberalization have increased the pace of environmental degradation, for example:

1. The combined effects of deregulation, privatization, and weak governmental controls on the Indonesian logging industry, implemented to increase economic growth through increased trade, have led to the loss of more than 1 million hectares of forest per year through logging in Indonesia. Health effects range from short-term and widespread respiratory disorders associated with extensive burning to long-term ecosystem disturbances and potential climatic change (Walt 2000).

2. In Uganda, trade liberalization in the form of industrial privatization and tariff reduction on fishing technology contributed to over-fishing of the Nile perch in Lake Victoria, and a degradation of the lake's ecosystem and water quality (UNEP March 2001).

3. Mauritania, a poor sub-Saharan African country, has sold fishing rights to factory-ships from Europe, Japan, and China to earn the foreign currency it needs to pay back liberalization-induced foreign loans. Meanwhile, fish, the staple protein for the country's poor, has largely disappeared from local markets (Brown 2002).

4. In Argentina, trade liberalization and promotion of fisheries exports led to a fivefold growth in fish catches in the decade 1985-95. Fishing companies gained an estimated US $1.6 billion from this growth, but depletion of fish stocks and environmental degradation have produced a net cost of US $500 million (UNEP March 2001).

There are also potential indirect climate change effects due to deregulation of foreign investment. A recent example of this was the Brazilian currency crisis of 1998, precipitated by the greatest inflow and outflow of speculative capital ever experienced by a developing country (de Paula and Alves Jr. 2000; UNDP 1999). The government lacked sufficient foreign reserves to stabilize its currency and was forced to borrow from the International Monetary Fund. The rescue package included the requirement for drastic public spending cuts, including a two-thirds reduction in Brazil's environmental protection spending. This led to the collapse of a multination funded project that would have begun satellite mapping of the Amazonian rainforest as a first step in stemming its destruction. This destruction, in turn, may have a profound effect on climate change, with long-term and potentially severe health implications for much of the world's populations (Labonte 1999). The 2002 World Summit on Sustainable Development commitment of the Brazilian government to set aside large tracts of the remaining Amazonian rainforest partly obviates this earlier bleak assessment (Mitchell 2002).

Most empirically based projections on the environmental impacts of trade liberalization show severe ecological damage (Labonte and Torgerson 2002). The only exception is trade agreement requirements to reduce trade-distorting agricultural and fisheries production subsidies. These subsidies go primarily to wealthier producers within wealthy countries, wreck havoc on local production in poorer countries by flooding the market with below-cost commodities, and severely damage the environment. World Trade Organization member nations in November 2001 committed themselves to "reductions, with a view to phasing out, all forms of [agricultural] export subsidies; and substantial reductions in trade-distorting domestic support" (WTO Doha Ministerial Declaration 2001). The EU and Japan, which heavily subsidize their domestic farmers, have been slow to comply; and the US Bush Administration in 2002, despite the Doha agreement, signed into law the largest increase in domestic farm subsidies in American history. [3]

## World Trade Organization Agreements and Health-Determining Pathways

This discussion now shifts to a narrower focus on trade agreements, specifically those of the World Trade Organization (WTO) and their impacts on globalization's health-determining pathways. The WTO was formed in 1995 out of the Uruguay Round of talks on the General Agreement on Tariffs and Trade (GATT). The WTO is the only multilateral organization with enforcement powers in the form of fines or monetized trade concessions. It administers 29 different trade, investment, and "trade-related" agreements. Key principles underpinning all agreements are "national treatment" (in which foreign goods, investment or services are regulated the same as domestic ones); "most favored nation" (whatever special preferences might be given to one trading partner must be given to all

---

[3] The US Trade Representative, Robert Zoellick, subsequently proposed global reductions in such subsidies, including those in the US (*BRIDGES Weekly Trade News Digest* 6 [38] 7 November 2002). This is a common ploy by wealthier countries in the WTO. Before agreeing to reduce trade-distorting tariffs or subsidies in sectors important to their own economies, they first dramatically raise them.

member nations); and "least trade restrictive" (whatever environmental or social regulations a country adopts domestically that might fall within the ambit of WTO agreements must be those that least impede global trade). Several WTO agreements have specific bearing on these broad economic, social, and environmental pathways linking globalization and health.

There is growing consensus that various forms of social investment and worker protections are needed in the transition from a closed to open economy. But these very protections may be eroded through the new trade/investment regime. The Trade Related Investment Measures (TRIMS) agreement prevents countries from placing "performance requirements" on foreign investment. Such requirements have been used to benefit corrupt political leaders, government officials and their families. But such requirements have also proven useful in the development of viable national economies. Their removal benefits investors from developed countries much more than it does people living within developing countries. Many developing countries are requesting exemptions to this TRIMS requirement in order to retain some control over the direction of their local economic development. Such exemptions may prove difficult, since a WTO dispute panel several years ago ruled against the use of import protections by developing nations for purposes of improving poor living standards. "Development [or pro-poor] policy," the ruling concluded, is not the same as "macro-economic policy." Where there is a WTO dispute, the latter shall prevail (Raghaven 1999). Moreover, the exemptions to TRIMS for developing countries are opposed by the so-called "Quad" of rich countries — the US, the European Union, Japan, and Canada (*BRIDGES Weekly Trade News Digest* 6 [20], 28 May, 2002).

The Technical Barriers to Trade (TBT) agreement views any "technical" barriers to trade as restrictions that must be reduced to "international standards." A technical barrier is a domestic regulation that has nothing to do with tariffs (the taxes governments impose on imports) or export subsidies (the assistance they give to exports). The TBT agreement encourages use of international standards and allows domestic regulations to be higher only if they can be justified. Article XX(b) of GATT permits exception to the general GATT rules, including the TBT, that are "necessary to protect human, animal or plant life or health." On the surface, this exception seems to allow for a reasonable level of health protection. But in only one instance has this exception been successful in a trade dispute. In April 2001, the WTO rejected Canada's appeal against the French decree banning the importation of asbestos. Canada argued that its asbestos products were "like" the glass fiber products that France did permit; therefore the asbestos ban was a technical barrier to trade. The WTO dispute panel agreed with Canada, but also considered the large body of research establishing asbestos as a proven human carcinogen. The French ban therefore qualified under the Article XX(b) exception (WTO 2000). Such scientific certainty, however, rarely applies to most human health risks, especially those mediated through the environment. Moreover, countries wishing to derogate from trade rules under this exception are responsible for proving that the measure is not really protectionism in disguise. Many health non-governmental organizations (NGOs) argue that a reverse onus should apply, that is, the complaining country should prove that the exception was *not* invoked to protect human, animal, or plant life or health.

Scientific uncertainty is the premise behind the "precautionary principle," that is, when evidence is suggestive but not conclusive, the benefit of doubt should go to protecting human and environmental health. This principle has been weakened by the Agreement on the Application of Sanitary and Phytosanitary Measures (SPS), which mandates a scientific risk assessment on all regulatory standards. Risk assessments, while an important tool in providing an understanding of human threats to the environment and, in turn, environmental threats to humans, cannot deal with the multiple, cumulative impacts which now typify risk management issues. The SPS risk assessment requirement invariably favors producers and exporting countries over citizens and importing countries, since there is no cost to them if, eventually, their product proves harmful. The higher order of scientific certainty under the SPS than that governing GATT Article XX(b) is one reason why the European Union (EU) lost to the US and Canada on its attempt to ban imports of hormone-treated beef. The WTO dispute panel, which did not include any scientists as its members, rejected as inadequate the EU arguments—including evidence of possible, though not definitive, human carcinogenicity—provided by the independent International Agency for Research on Cancer (Charnovitz 2001; Sullivan and Shainblum 2001). Both the TBT and the SPS constitute what some call "trade-creep," where trade rules limit how national governments can regulate their domestic health and environment affairs even if they treat products from other countries no differently than their own (Drache et al. 2002).

The Agreement on Government Procurement (AGP) requires governments to take into account only "commercial considerations" when making purchasing decisions, specifically banning preferences based on environment, human, or labor rights. Currently a plurilateral (voluntary) agreement to which few developing countries have signed on, there are plans for it to become a multilateral (mandatory) agreement (WTO Doha Ministerial Declaration 2001). Such an agreement might aid in preventing large-scale cronyism or abuse of public monies by corrupt officials. Like the TRIMS agreement, however, it could also signal gradual erosion in the ability of national governments to give preference to domestic suppliers and so direct public revenues to groups or regions in greatest need of economic support and development. Many developing countries are asking for exemptions to the AGP, arguing that government procurement is one of the few means they have to develop socioeconomically disadvantaged areas, groups, or sectors (*BRIDGES Weekly Trade News Digest* 6 [21], 4 June, 2002). Again, most developed countries are opposing this.

Ironically, the Agreement on Trade-Related Intellectual Property Rights (TRIPS) does not "free" trade but is a trade "protectionist" by entrenching intellectual property rights, almost all of which are held by companies or individuals in developed countries. TRIPS requires WTO member nations to legislate patent protection for 20 years, although least developed countries have an exception extended until 2016. Debate over TRIPS, particularly regarding access to antiretroviral drugs, has been extensive and highly public. Few developing countries had any patent protection legislation prior to joining the WTO. One effect of the agreement has been sharply increased drug costs in most countries. This higher cost for drugs decreases the amount of public funding available for primary health care or other public programs, including environmental protection, in first world countries, where 75% of prescription drug costs are publicly or privately insured. But it is particularly hard on persons living in poor countries where the health portion spent on drugs is already much higher and often a direct personal cost.

Current TRIPS clauses allow countries to issue compulsory licenses to generic drug manufacturers in cases of public health emergencies. These provisions were affirmed by the so-called Doha "Declaration on TRIPS Agreement and Public Health" (WTO 2001). [4] While lauded as a major public health breakthrough and a victory by developing countries (particularly the group of African countries) at the WTO, the Doha Declaration failed to deal with how countries lacking generic production capacity would obtain their drugs at lower cost. The TRIPS Council of the WTO was given a year to solve this problem, but was initially blocked by the US, Canada, Japan, and Switzerland, which argued that only time-limited concessions should be made and only for the "big three" diseases of HIV/AIDS, malaria, and tuberculosis (*BRIDGES Weekly Trade News Digest* 6 [19], 22 May, 2002).

The contribution of services to economic growth and wealth has increased rapidly in comparison to the production of goods. Its actual

---

[4] Doha was the secluded location of the 4th Ministerial meeting of the World Trade Organization, November, 2001.

and potential contribution to trade has also grown (Sinclair 2000). The General Agreement on Trade in Services (GATS) was conceived, and continues to be defended, primarily as a vehicle for the expansion of business opportunities for transnational service corporations (Hilary 2001). The key concern is that GATS will ineluctably lead to increased privatization of such essential public services as health care, education, and water/sanitation. Globally, roughly 30% of all economic activity lies in government (publicly) provided services. Most of these services are essential, meaning there is a guaranteed market for them, at least among those able to pay privately. When there is a crisis of overproduction (too many goods for too few purchasers), or a volatile stock market collapsing after almost two decades of excessive speculation, one might expect corporations with capital to look to formerly provided public services as a safe private investment. There is some evidence this may be occurring: services account for 60% of all foreign direct investment (FDI), "much of which is connected with privatization of state entities" (Corner House Briefing Paper 23, 2001:3).

The pro-GATS argument claims that service liberalization can lead to new private resources to support the public system; can introduce new techniques to health professionals in developing countries; can provide such professionals with advanced training and credentials; and can introduce new and more efficient management techniques (Zarrilli 2002). Several developing countries are liberalizing and privatizing health services, becoming centers of "health tourism" for surrounding countries, and exporting health professionals. But these private resources, whether in the form of health tourism, foreign investment or remittances from professionals working abroad, benefit the wealthy and increase the regressive privatization of domestic health systems. There is a global crisis in the "brain drain" of trained health professionals from developing to developed countries, from poorer to richer developed countries, and from poorer to richer regions of developed countries. Developing countries are estimated to lose over US $500 million in training costs as a result of doctors and nurses who migrate each year to wealthier nations (Frommel 2002). The problem is most acute for African countries, but is also a problem for many Caribbean countries (IDRC 2002), and could be worsened by GATS. Furthermore, the new management techniques that are adopted are primarily those that have been developed by private providers, the majority of which are in the US, a country that has the most inefficient and inequitable health care system of all economically advanced nations.[5]

---

[5] There is one country where liberalized trade in health services does work: Cuba. Years ago, Cuba set out to become a "world medical power." It is one of the few nations in

To date, 54 WTO members have made commitments to liberalize some health services under GATS (Adlung and Carzaniga 2002). Many of these are developing countries. The number of health-liberalized countries grows to 78 if one includes private health insurance. GATS has a built-in requirement for "progressive liberalization," meaning that countries can only liberalize more, not less. Once a service sector has been liberalized under GATS, there is no cost-free way of reversing it (CCPA 2002). Imagine a poorer country, where most of its former public services are now privately provided, partly a result of earlier structural adjustment programs. Imagine that trade liberalization does eventually promote long-term economic growth, and the country is able to tax such growth so that it has sufficient revenue to increase its provision of public health, education, or sanitary services. If it committed any of these services under GATS, it would have to pay some compensatory damages (in trade concessions, perhaps as fines) should its public programs force private foreign providers out of the domestic market.[6]

## Summary and Healthy Public Policy Options

Globalization is not new, but it is taking on new forms. Specifically, liberalized trade in goods, services, and capital is now governed by enforceable trade rules. The dominant discourse on globalization is that of a "tide raising all boats." This "tide" has not been empirically demonstrated except in a few countries, where trade liberalization has lifted all boats but has also made the large ones much larger and the small ones much smaller. Environmentally, the seas supporting the boats, the air filling their sails, and the land on which they dock are all experiencing more severe stress. How globalization more precisely determines peoples' health is affected by a complex set of preexisting political conditions and natural endowments, national policy capacities and resources, and

---

the world producing more health professionals than it needs. It has also developed surplus health care facility capacity. Cuban health professionals work abroad, both as acts of international solidarity and as a means of obtaining foreign exchange through remittances. Cuba's high quality health care facilities are "value-adding" to its tourism industry. But Cuba is also unique in having surplus capacity, a fully universal public health care system for all of its citizens and a commercialized health industry that is fully within the public sector.

[6] GATS does offer an exception for "a [government] service which is supplied neither on a commercial basis, nor in competition with one or more service suppliers" (Article 1:3b). This exception is often cited as evidence that concern over privatization is misplaced. This clause, however, may collapse under an eventual challenge, since most countries allow some commercial or competitive provision of virtually all public services (Pollock and Price 2000; CCPA 2002).

publicly provided programs, such as health, education, labor rights and environmental protection. The ability of national governments to self-determine these regulatory policies continues to be constrained by the neoliberal economic prescriptions of the World Bank and the International Monetary Fund, and are increasingly being compromised by World Trade Organization agreements with their "trade creep" effects.

There are, however, several trade policy options that health activists can promote and that might help contemporary globalization's virtuous circle to be realized. These options would:

1. Extend trade agreements' "special and differential" treatment exemptions for developing countries. The European Union, following the lead of many developing countries and development NGOs, is urging that these exemptions be based on the level of economic development within a country rather than on some arbitrary calendar date (*BRIDGES Weekly Trade News Digest*, 6 [39], 14 November, 2002). This small victory was also earned by developing countries at the Doha Ministerial Round of the WTO in 2001, which declared that the WTO should review "all Special and Differential provisions ... with a view to *strengthening them...*" [emphasis added] (WTO Doha Ministerial Declaration 2001). Many developed countries, however, have been reluctant to proceed to do this (*BRIDGES Weekly Trade News Digest*, 6 [34], 8 October, 2002).

2. Ban patenting of life forms, exempt patent protection legislation for poor countries indefinitely, decrease the patent protection period, and permit parallel importing under the TRIPS agreement. These are all positions variously argued by developing and least developed countries, as well as by health, environmental and development NGOs, and many United Nations agencies.

3. Reverse the burden of proof in health and environmental protection cases argued under the exemptions in GATT XX(b), and under the SPS Agreement. Countries claiming that another nation's domestic standards are unnecessarily trade restrictive need to prove that they were *not* imposed for health reasons, and that changing the standard would *not* create a health risk.

4. Institute fines tied to Gross Domestic Product rather than trade sanctions as penalties, since trade sanctions invariably hurt poor countries more than wealthy ones. The WTO has the option to levy fines instead of trade sanctions, but rarely does. Part of the fines could be allocated to global funds for health, education, and social development, allowing the dozens of countries now lagging behind in reaching the Millennium Development Goal targets for infant and

child health, maternal health, gender empowerment, and universal education to start catching up.

5. Impose a "Tobin Tax" on currency exchange transactions (named after the Nobel economist who first proposed the idea). This will dampen excessive currency speculation and, based on 1995 data, would raise about US $150 billion annually. Discussions have already noted that such a tax could be split three ways, with a third going to each of the two national governments whose currencies were being traded, and the remainder to an international development fund. [7]

6. Negotiate an overarching and enforceable rule in all trade agreements that requires, when there is any conflict, multilateral environmental agreements and human rights agreements (including the right to health) shall trump trade agreements. Some 109 countries recognize a right to health in some form in their constitution, and all but a few countries, including the US, have ratified human rights conventions that include the right to health (Blouin, Foster, and Labonte 2002). Several health NGOs have been urging national governments with an interest in health to create a "like-minded group" to pursue negotiation of such an overarching rule within the WTO's ambit. A related reform is inclusion of a special UN rights "clause" in trade enforcement mechanisms, enabling countries to invoke obligations to UN Declarations, Covenants, or Conventions as a shield to any trade-related challenge to a domestic measure that is intended to meet human rights, human development or environmental obligations.

7. Exclude health, education, and other essential services (such as water and sanitation) as commercial services. They are basic essentials to human life and health. Public systems for their provision arose in most countries because private systems proved inadequate and inequitable. Trade treaties, which are intended to promote private economic interests, are no place to negotiate international rules for health, and other essential public services. These require other forms of multilateral agreements freed from commercial economic goals. Canada, France, and other countries are now proposing to create a global cultural diversity treaty that would protect national culture and

---

[7] Other global taxation schemes include a carbon tax, which would penalize high fossil-fuel using countries such as the US and Canada and provide incentives for reduced consumption. Global taxes, under an appropriately transparent and democratic allocation system perhaps governed by the UN or a new multilateral agency, could permit substantial global wealth redistribution without the many problems currently associated with World Bank and IMF grants or loans, foreign direct investment, official development assistance, or debt forgiveness schemes.

minority language rights, and which would remove cultural products from the WTO ambit (*Globe and Mail*, November 29, 2002; p. B5). The WTO itself also needs some overhauling. The WTO dispute settlement process is one of its least transparent and least democratic practices. WTO dispute settlement panels should be opened to greater participation from civil society groups, whether in the form of *amicus curiae* ("friends of the court") briefs or actual representation. All proceedings of each panel should be public in the form of web-postings, except for information that may be legally sensitive or confidential. Such panels should also become "joint panels" involving other specialized multilateral or UN organizations (such as UNEP, WHO, ILO) when the trade dispute has obvious crosscutting effects on human health, human rights, and the environment. Panel members should always include representatives from developing countries (this is optional rather than mandatory at the moment), and should be drawn from experts in disciplines other than simply trade law.

In fairness, the WTO has gone some distance in becoming more open about its trade negotiating agendas, initiating more meetings with civil society groups and convening discussions with UN agencies such as the World Health Organization, the International Labour Organization, and the United Nations Environment Program. These UN agencies, however, are still excluded from any of the negotiating sessions of the WTO, and lack any official observer status. For example, the WTO has a Committee on Trade and Environment. The Doha Declaration mandated this Committee to reconcile conflicts between WTO agreements and multilateral environmental agreements, such as the Convention on Biodiversity and the Convention on International Trade in Endangered Species, both of which require trade restrictions against offending countries. But even observer status at the WTO Committee on Trade and Environment by the secretariats responsible for these environmental agreements is still not allowed.

Developing countries are much better organized and more vocal in WTO negotiations than they were in earlier years. Their ability to influence the WTO agenda and decision-making process, however, remains constrained. Nearly half of the least developed country members of the WTO have no representation in Geneva, compared to the presence of over 250 full-time negotiators from the US alone. Many developing countries have only one representative, who lacks the time and expertise to attend all of the different weekly meetings scheduled by the WTO. The push for expanding existing agreements and introducing new issues for negotiation will only further creation of a WTO biased towards the economic interests of developed nations. As several NGOs have argued, "WTO processes should be designed to suit the capacity of the least powerful members [and] this aim should override concerns about the speed of decision-making" (ActionAid et al. 2001). Among others, this requirement means direct financial assistance from developed to developing countries for WTO participation, reductions in the number of trade-related issues for negotiation at the WTO, fewer meetings, and discontinuing the use of executive body or other subdividing of decision-making away from the General Council.

Finally, existing agreements must continue to be analyzed for their impacts on internationally-agreed basic rights, human development, health and environmental sustainability goals, and changes should be made in WTO agreements when they conflict in any way with the accomplishment of these and other important norms and goals. The WTO, as an institution, should be judged for how it contributes to the accomplishment of these goals and norms, rather than simply on the degree to which it succeeds in promoting trade and investment liberalization.

## Conclusion

We live in perhaps the most important historical moment of our species. There is excessive affluence and poverty. Once far-away conflicts and diseases are now imperiling global health and security. We are struggling forward to some system of global governance for our common good. In Western countries, a similar struggle at the national level took place in the nineteenth century. The first laws and the regulatory system in such countries largely served the interests of the capitalist class, at the expense of the workers, women, the poor, the environment. But such laws became the platform around which progressive social struggles created reciprocal responsibilities from both state and market, creating the twentieth century welfare state.

A similar struggle is taking place globally today. Trade agreements are the first truly enforceable international laws we have created. They benefit the capitalist class. They have also become the focus for progressive social movements that are globally demanding that governments abide by their agreements to protect the environment, promote human rights, achieve health for all, and redistribute wealth through universal education and social support systems. The WTO, originally a vehicle primarily wielded for the benefit of the rich countries, is increasingly under siege by developing countries, UN agencies, and NGOs. Some democratic globalizers urge the WTO's abolition. This would be a mistake, for there is no other vehicle where the unequal balance of economic power globally might be subject to enforceable change. The struggles of civil society and developing countries to wrest reforms in the WTO are giving rise to a new system of global governance for the common good. We cannot say whether these struggles will succeed. But these are global policy options that will work to promote health. We know where these options must be advocated—in our national governments, among our fellow citizens, and in our global institutions.

## Annex 1
## Open Borders May Improve Economic Efficiency, but at What Price?

Following the introduction of NAFTA (North American Free Trade Agreement), the Mexican government ended its subsidies to corn growers, most of whom were small scale and industrially inefficient. The market was flooded by cheaper US imports, where production remained heavily subsidized, and Mexican corn production fell by half (Wallach and Sforza 1999). Mexican poverty rates rose to over 70%, the minimum wage lost over 75% of its purchasing power, infant mortality rates for the poor increased, and wage inequalities became the most severe of those in Latin America, a region already with the greatest income disparity on the planet (*The Economist* 2000; Barlow 2001). Mexico has since reintroduced production subsidies to farmers, and is in the process of increasing them (*BRIDGES Weekly Trade News Digest* 6 [40], 20 November, 2002). Even with subsidies, Mexican farmers are still much less efficient than US farmers, owing partly to the small size of their farms. But should economic efficiency be the only criterion for determining economic "success"?

Zambia, in return for World Bank and IMF loans, opened its borders in the early 1990s to cheap, often second-hand textile imports. Its domestic manufacturing, inefficient by wealthier industrialized nation standards, could not compete. Within 8 years, 30,000 jobs disappeared and 132 of 140 textile mills closed operations, which the World Bank acknowledges as "unintended and regrettable consequences" of the adjustment process (Jeter 2002). Overall, 40% of manufacturing jobs disappeared in the past decade, and huge numbers of previously employed workers rely on precarious street vending. In the early 1990s, user charges for schools, imposed partly because of the loss of public revenues following collapse of the textile sector, led to increased dropout and illiteracy rates. The current government is now seeking to undo many of these policies, including elimination of user fees for education, lower costs for public health care, a reintroduction of agricultural subsidies and support for domestic industries with a potential for growth. But the task is harder than it might have been before the "open borders" had been imposed.

Many of the low wealth/high health countries (such as China, Costa Rica, Sri Lanka and the "exemplar" Indian state of Kerala) have, or had, relatively equitable income distribution, as well as policies supporting social transfers to meet basic needs, universal education, equitable access to public health and primary health care, and adequate caloric intake (Werner and Sanders 1997). These pro-poor policies are being eroded by trade liberalization. In Kerala, a media-developed Western consumerist culture, alongside tariff reductions, is rejecting locally produced goods for imported luxuries, weakening the local entrepreneurial base. Over time, this will erode the State's ability to tax domestic wealth for purposes of income redistribution, gender empowerment, maternal/child health and other low wealth/high health outcomes. Economic growth, measured by GDP, may improve, but masks the more important questions: Who gains? Who loses?

## Postscript

Since writing this article, two significant developments have transpired. In August 2003, the impasse over TRIPS was temporarily resolved when WTO member nations agreed to waive countries' obligations under TRIPS Article 31(f), which requires production under compulsory licensing to be predominantly for the domestic market. The waiver will last until this article is amended. It also includes several conditions to prevent compulsory licensed drugs from re-entering wealthy country markets. Development groups are concerned that these conditions place undue burdens on poor countries, but there is consensus the August agreement is a positive step. Shortly afterwards, WTO talks in Cancún, Mexico, collapsed when the so-called G-21 of developing countries, led by Brazil, China and India, refused the wording of the Ministerial text that failed to adequately address the trade-distorting agricultural subsidies practiced by the US, Japan and EU member nations. The collapse of these talks can be read as a simultaneous success and failure. The success is the increased strength of organized developing countries attempting to shape trade rules more to their benefit, after a decade of such rules working almost singularly to the advantage of wealthy nations. The failure lies in the apparent commitment of wealthier countries, including the US and the EU, to focus now on bilateral and regional trade agreements where their economic might can more easily overwhelm a diluted developing world opposition.

## References

ACTIONAID, CAFOD, CHRISTIAN AID, CONSUMERS INTERNATIONAL, FIELD, OXFAM, RSPB, WDM
2001    "Recommendations for ways forward on institutional reform of the World Trade Organisation" (mimeo).
ADLUNG, RUDOLF AND ANTONIA CARZANIGA
2002    "Health Services under the General Agreement on Trade Services." Pp. 13-22 in *Trade in Health Services: Global, Regional and Country Perspectives*, edited by C. Vieira and Nick Drager. Washington, DC: PAHO.
BARLOW, MAUDE
2001    "The Free Trade Area of the Americas and the Threat to Social Programs, Environmental Sustainability and Social Justice in Canada and the Americas." Council of Canadians. Retrieved November 12, 2001 (www.canadians.org/campaigns/campaigns~tradepub~ftaa2.html).
BEN-DAVID, DAN, HAKAN NORDSTROM AND L. ALAN WINTERS
1999    *Trade, Income, Disparity and Poverty*. World Trade Organization: Special Studies 5.
BLOUIN, CHANTAL, JOHN FOSTER AND RONALD LABONTE
2002    "Canada's Foreign Policy on Health: Towards Coherence." Commissioned Research Paper to the Commission on the Future of Health Care in Canada. Retrieved January 24, 2003 (www.spheru.ca).
BREMAN, ANNA AND CAROLYN SHELTON
2001    "Structural Adjustment and Health: A Literature Review of the Debate, its

Role-Players and Presented Empirical Evidence." (Paper No. WG6:6). Cambridge, MA: Commission on Macroeconomics and Health, June. Retrieved October 15, 2001 (http://www.cmhealth.org/cmh_papers&reports.htm).

*BRIDGES Weekly Trade News Digest*
6 [40], 20 November, 2002.
6 [39], 14 November, 2002.
6 [38], 7 November, 2002.
6 [34], 18 October, 2002.
6 [21], 4 June, 2002.
6 [20], 28 May, 2002.
6 [19], 22 May, 2002.

BROWN, PETER
2002       "Europe's Catch-All Clause." *The Guardian Weekly*, March 29-April 3, p. 26.

CANADIAN CENTRE FOR POLICY ALTERNATIVES
2002       *Putting Health First: Canadian Health Care Reform, Trade Treaties and Foreign Policy.* Retrieved December 14, 2002 (www.healthcarecommission.ca).

CHARNOVITZ, STEVE
2001       *The Supervision of Health and Biosafety Regulation by World Trade Rules.* Retrieved March 26, 2001 (www.gets.org/gets/library/admin/...n_of_Health_and_Biosafety_Regulat_3.htm).

CORNER HOUSE
2001       *Trading Health Care Away? GATS, Public Services and Privatisation.* Sturminster Newton: Author.

CORNIA, GIOVANNI ANDREA
2001       "Globalization and Health: Results and Options." *Bulletin of the World Health Organization* 79: 834-41.

DEATON, ANGUS
2001       *Health, Inequality and Economic Development,* CMH Working Paper Series WG1: 3, World Health Organization: Commission on Macroeconomics and Health.

DE PAULA, LUIZ FERNANDO RODRIGUES AND ANTONIO JOSE ALVES JR.
2000       *External Financial Stability and the 1998-99 Brazilian Currency Crisis.* Retrieved December 8, 2000 (www.adenauer.com.br/HTML/Textos~e/atuais-e-1-html).

DOLLAR, DAVID
2001       "Is Globalization Good for your Health?" *Bulletin of the World Health Organization* 79: 827-33.

DOLLAR, DAVID AND AART KRAAY
2000       *Growth is Good for the Poor.* Washington, DC: World Bank. Retrieved December 8, 2000 (www.worldbank.org/research).

DRACHE, DANIEL, MARC FROESE, MARK FULLER AND NIRMALA SINGH
2002       *One World, One System? The Diversity Deficits in Standard-Setting, Development and Sovereignty at the WTO.* Toronto, Canada: Robarts Centre for Canadian Studies, York University.

*Footprints of the Planet Report*
(n.d.)       Retrieved September 15, 2001 (www.iclei.org/iclei/ecofoot.htm).

FROMMEL, DIANNE
2002       "Global Market in Medical Workers." *Le Monde Diplomatique.* May.

GLOBAL SOCIAL POLICY FORUM
2001       "A North-South Dialogue on the Prospects for a Socially Progressive Globalization." *Global Social Policy* 1: 147-62.

GOUGH, IAN
2001       "Globalization and Regional Welfare Regimes: The East Asian Case." *Global Social Policy* 1: 163-90.

HILARY, JOHN
2001       *The Wrong Model: GATS, Trade Liberalisation and Children's Right to Health.* London, England: Save the Children.

HOCHSCHILD, ARLIE RUSSELL
2000       "Global Care Chains and Emotional Surplus Value." Pp. 130-146 in *Global Capitalism*, edited by Will Hutton and Anthony Giddens. New York, NY: The New Press.

HUMAN RIGHTS WATCH
2002        *The FTAA, Access to HIV/AIDS Treatment and Human Rights* (Briefing Paper),
            October 29.
INTERNATIONAL DEVELOPMENT RESEARCH CENTRE
2002        *Trade in Health Services: Research Priorities to Address Emerging Policy Challenges in Latin
            America and the Caribbean*, Ottawa, Canada: IDRC.
JETER, JAN
2002        "Zambia Reduced to a Flea-Market Economy." *The Washington Post* in *The
            Guardian Weekly*, May 9-15, p. 30.
KAUL, INGE, ISABELLE GRUNBERG AND MARC STERN
1999        "Introduction." Pp. xix-xxxviii in *Global Public Goods: International Cooperation in
            the 21$^{st}$ Century*, edited by I. Grunberg Kaul and M. Stern. New York, NY:
            UNDP/Oxford University Press.
KAUL, INGE AND MICHAEL FAUST
2001        "Global Public Goods for Health: A Framework for Analysis and Action."
            *Bulletin of the World Health Organization* 79: 869-74.
KICKBUSCH, ILONA
2000        "The Development of International Health Policies-Accountability Intact?"
            *Social Science and Medicine* 51: 979-89.
KIM, JIM-YONG, JOYCE MILLEN, ALEC IRWIN AND GERSHMAN JOHN, EDS.
2000        *Dying for Growth: Global Inequality and the Health of the Poor*. Monroe: Common
            Courage Press.
LABONTE, RONALD
2001        *Global Governance and the World Trade Organization Reform*. Brief on behalf of the
            International Union for Health Promotion and Education to the Genoa Non-
            Governmental Organization Consultation, Florence, Italy. Retrieved October
            10, 2002 (www.iuhpe.nyu.edu/whatsnew/amendedBrief.htm).
2000        "Brief to the World Trade Organization: World Trade and Population
            Health." *International Journal of Health Promotion and Education* VI: 24-32.
1999        "Globalism and Health: Threats and Opportunities." *Health Promotion Journal of
            Australia* 9: 126-32.
1998        "Healthy Public Policy and the World Trade Organization: A Proposal for
            an International Health Presence in Future World Trade/Investment Talks."
            *Health Promotion International* 13: 245-56.
LABONTE, RONALD AND JERRY SPIEGEL
2002        "Setting Global Health Priorities for Funding Canadian Researchers." A
            Discussion Paper Prepared for the Institute on Population and Public Health.
            Retrieved December 14, 2002 (www.spheru.ca).
LABONTE, RONALD AND RENEE TORGERSON
2002        *Frameworks for Analyzing the Links Between Globalization and Health*. SPHERU —
            University of Saskatchewan (mimeo, draft report to World Health Organiza-
            tion, Geneva). Retrieved December 14, 2002 (www.spheru.ca).
LEE, KELLEY
2001        "Globalization: A New Agenda for Health?" Pp. 13-30 in *International Co-
            operation in Health*, edited by Martin McKee, Paul Garner and Robin Scott.
            Oxford, United Kingdom: Oxford University Press.
MILWARD, BOB
2000        "What Is Structural Adjustment." Pp. 24-38 in *Structural Adjustment: Theory,
            Practice and Impacts*, edited by Giles Mohan, Ed Brown, Bob Milward, and
            Alfred B. Zack-Williams. London, England and New York, NY: Routledge.
MITCHELL, A.
2002        "Brazil to Conserve Tract of Rain Forest." *The Globe and Mail*, Sept. 7, p. A14.
POLLOCK, ALLYSON AND DAVID PRICE
2000        "Re-Writing the Regulations: How the World Trade Organisation Could
            Accelerate Privatisation in Health-Care Systems." *The Lancet* 356: 1995-2000.
PRICE-SMITH, A.
2002        *The Health of Nations: Infectious Disease, Environmental Change, and Their Effects on
            National Security and Development*. Cambridge, MA: The MIT Press.
RAGHAVEN, C.
1999        "WTO Members Awaiting New Draft Text for Seattle." Third World

Network 10/17/99. Retrieved December 3, 1999 (www:twnside.org.sg/souths/twn/title/new draft).

RAO, J. MOHAN
1999    *Openness, Poverty and Inequality* in Background Papers Human Development Report 1999, Volume 1. New York: UNDP.

REINICKE, WOLFGANG
1998    *Global Public Policy: Governing Without Government?* Washington, DC: Brookings Institute.

RODAS-MARTINI, PABLO
1999    *Income Inequality Between and Within Countries: Main Issues in the Literature* in Background Papers Human Development Report 1999, Volume 1. New York: UNDP.

RODRIGUEZ, FRANCISCO AND DANI RODRIK
2000    *Trade Policy and Economic Growth: A Skeptic's Guide to the Cross-National Evidence.* University of Maryland and Harvard University.

RODRIK, DANI
1999    *The New Global Economy and Developing Countries: Making Openness Work.* Cambridge, MA: Harvard University.

SANDLER, TODD AND DAVID ARCE
2000    *A Conceptual Framework for Understanding Global and Transnational Goods for Health.* World Health Organization Commission on Macroeconomics and Health, Working Group 2, Background Paper 1. Draft Paper, Retrieved October 15, 2001 (www.cmhealth.org/cmh_papers&reports.htm).

SAVEDOFF, WILLIAM AND T. PAUL SCHULTZ, EDS.
2000    *Wealth from Health: Linking Social Investments to Earnings in Latin America.* Washington, DC: Inter-American Development Bank.

SEN, AMARTYA
1999    *Development as Freedom.* New York, NY: Knopf.

SINCLAIR, SCOTT
2000    *GATS: How the World Trade Organization's New "services" Negotiations Threaten Democracy.* Ottawa, Canada: Canadian Centre for Policy Alternatives.

SULLIVAN, TERRENCE AND ESTHER SHAINBLUM
2001    "Trading in Health: The World Trade Organization (WTO) and the International Regulation of Health and Safety." *Health Law in Canada*, November.
2001    "Summary of the WTO Symposium on Issues Confronting the World Trading System." *Sustainable Developments* 55.

UNITED NATIONS CONFERENCE ON TRADE AND DEVELOPMENT (UNCTAD)
2002    *Escaping the Poverty Trap: The Least Developed Countries Report 2002.* New York, NY: United Nations.

UNITED NATIONS DEVELOPMENT PROGRAM (UNDP)
1999    *Human Development Report 1999.* New York, NY: Oxford University Press.

UNDP, UNEP, WORLD BANK, WORLD RESOURCES INSTITUTE
2000    *World Resources 2000-2001* Washington, DC: World Resources Institute.

UNITED NATIONS ENVIRONMENT PROGRAM (UNEP) INFORMATION NOTE 01/18
2001    "Trade Agreements Must Consider Environmental Issues." March.

WALLACH, LORI AND M. SFORZA
1999    *Whose Trade Organization?* Washington, DC: Public Citizen.

WALT, GILL
2000    "Globalisation of International Health." *The Lancet* 351: 434-44.

WEISBROT, MARK, DEAN BAKER, EGOR KRAEV AND JUDY CHEN
2001    *The Scorecard on Globalization 1980-2000: Twenty Years of Diminished Progress.* Centre for Economic and Policy Research (http://www.cepr.net/globalization/scorecard_on_globalization.htm).

WERNER, DAVID AND DAVID SANDERS
1997    *Questioning the Solution: The Politics of Primary Health Care and Child Survival.* Palo Alto, CA: HealthWrights.

WORLD BANK
2000    *World Development Indicators 2000.* Washington, DC: World Bank.

WORLD HEALTH ORGANIZATION
2001        Commission on Macroeconomics and Health (CMH). *Macroeconomics and Health: Investing in Health for Economic Development.* Geneva, Switzerland: WHO.
WORLDWATCH INSTITUTE
2001        *Vital Signs 2001.* New York, NY: W.W. Norton and Co.
WTO
2002        *Implementation of Paragraph 6 of the Doha Declaration on the TRIPS Agreement and Public Health.* Note from the Chairman, Council for TRIPS, WTO; JOB (02) 217, December 16, 2002.
2001        *Declaration on the TRIPs Agreement and Public Health.* WT/MIN(01)/DEC/2. Geneva, Switzerland: WTO, November 20. Retrieved September 18, 2002 (www.wto.org/english/thewto_e/minist_e/min01_e/mindecl_trips_e.htm).
2000        *European communities—Measures Affecting Asbestos and Asbestos Containing Products: Report of the Panel,* WT/DS/135/R (http://www.wto.org).
ZARRILLI, SIMONETTA
2002        "Identifying a Trade-Negotiating Agenda." Pp. 71-86 in *Trade in Health Services: Global, Regional and Country Perspectives,* edited by C. Vieira, C. and Nick Drager. Washington, DC: PAHO.

# The Social Dimension of Globalization and Health

## ABOUBAKR A. BADAWI[*]

### ABSTRACT

Contrary to the hopes created by globalization, most observers report a substantial degradation of living standards, social protection, and basic social services, such as education, employment and health. This paper discusses the social dimensions of globalization with special focus on its impact on health services. Six main issues are addressed, namely, commercial exploitation of health plants, monopoly of health commodities, new food hazards, unfair implementation of intellectual property rights, marketing of tobacco and similar health threatening items, and the brain drain from developing countries. Specific recommended actions are presented, aiming for globalization that is more favorable to the poor.

### The Social Dimension of Globalization and Health

For more than a decade, the world has been witness to unprecedented and rapid economic and political changes. The pace of change is so fast that many are unable to follow it or to assess its impact on their lives. Different names are given to this era, reflecting one aspect or the other of its main features. Globalization is one of these features, but it spreads out in a way that makes it difficult to limit its impact to one particular area or domain. Meanwhile, many specialists debate whether we are still living in a globalized world, or have proceeded to the post-globalization era, where complexity, irreducibility of disorder, indelible contradictions, and uncertainty prevail. Regardless of the outcomes of this debate, many developing countries find it imperative to study the impact of globalization

[*]International Labor Organization (ILO), Safat, Kuwait.

on the standard of living of their citizens. This paper focuses on the social effects of globalization, and does not intend to address the perspectives on complexity, its science or praxis.

## Introduction

It goes without saying that a complex and all-embracing phenomenon such as globalization is difficult to assess. Substantial theoretical, methodological, and empirical problems are involved in such an analysis. Globalization, like many other terms and concepts, stems from an economic context and is focused on the opening of markets to trade. The concept has spread to other fields. The literature is full of writings on the links between globalization and development. Yet, there needs to be fresh thinking about development that goes beyond macroeconomic analysis to a much more multidisciplinary approach. By taking a multidisciplinary approach it is possible to develop strategies that pay due respect both to essential social needs and to progress that is favorable to the poor. The overall objective of development is to ensure better standards of living for all citizens, including affordable social protection and social services (i.e., health, pension, unemployment and other forms of social insurance and welfare services). Through the focus on the social dimension of globalization, assessments can be made of its impact on affordable social protection schemes and health services. Appendix A presents an operational definition of globalization, the social dimension of globalization, and health services. A cause-effect relationship between globalization and the various aspects of its social dimension is almost impossible to prove. This essay attempts to use a more hypothetical approach to examine the social dimension of globalization with a special focus on its relation to health services.

A recent ILO (2001c) report on trade liberalization and employment has found that many developing countries are not benefiting from the increased international trade brought about by globalization. The report goes beyond the issue of whether developing countries should benefit from increased international trade, to how they should benefit. The report notes that democratic, transparent, and competent governance of a well-functioning market-based economic system should be the foundation of sound policies that enhance benefits for all members of the population. This foundation provides a counterweight to unjust economic power. The report highlights the need for better education and skills-training of workers, the upgrading of public transportation networks and other public services, as well as improved social protection. The report also indicates that globalization has a tendency to minimize the importance of natural resources and maximize the role of technology. In doing so, it weakens the national endowments of the developing countries and downgrades their assets, while optimizing the impact of technology, education, research, and training.

When we talk about the social dimension of globalization, we touch on many social aspects or areas; however, the main focus in this essay centers on five major areas: education, employment, social security, equity for special groups, and last but not least, health (ILO 2001b). Globalization's social dimension has created new policy issues for most countries. These policy issues are concerned with questions of equity/equality and attempts to create a level playing field both among and within countries, with the question of fairness being the primary focus. Moreover, most of the studies on globalization link it to the deterioration of basic social services, which used to be the responsibility of governments.

Deterioration of the quality of education and training and overcoming the barriers to accessing these basic tools for development are matters of major concern to the International Labor Organization (ILO 2001c). Loss of labor market and job security, neglect of labor standards, the deterioration of the work environment, erosion of workers rights and benefits are among the major issues of concern in this age of globalization. Substantial declines in earnings and income inequalities have had a far-reaching impact on the standard of living of many individuals. Limited coverage of social insurance and other social safety nets has forced people to accept inhumane work and living conditions. Above all, unavailability or deterioration of health services appears to threaten the social fabric of societies.

In the mid-nineties, with the completion of the last round of international trade negotiations, which gave rise to the creation of the World Trade Organization (WTO), there was hope that a fresh wave of trade liberalization would translate into a substantial improvement of living standards in all countries (ILO 2001c). On the contrary, most observers report a substantial degradation of the standard of living in developing countries, including the new emerging economies. Public concern has increased, and the general tone of the debate has sharpened (see UNDP 1997 and 2001).

This essay attempts to identify some of the negative impacts of globalization on health-related issues and provide specific proposals to address them. It offers some guidance with regard to the specific actions that can be taken by the developing countries, the developed countries, and concerned organizations at the international, regional, and other levels to address the social effects of globalization. The proposed actions are addressed separately for the developing and developed countries, as well as for international, regional, and other organizations that are concerned with human development. It should be noted that consistency of policies and actions in dealing with the different aspects of globalization is crucial to these proposals. Partial or sectorial policies and programs will be far less effective than integrated approaches.

## The Problem

One of the most dangerous aspects of globalization is that it forces developing countries to adopt certain structural and economic changes, which prematurely decrease expenditures on social services, including health care. The anticipated reduction in these expenditures is not counterbalanced with appropriate plans to enable middle—and lower—class people to cover the rapidly increasing costs of their essential social needs. Meanwhile, government controls over the cost of medical care are diminishing under the new international regulations of the General Agreement on Trade in Services (GATS), and the General Agreement on Tariffs and Trade (GATT), and the growing influence of transnational companies (UNCTAD 1998; WHO 2000).

In addition to other social difficulties, such as the increased rate of unemployment and deterioration of public education, individuals are caught between the inability of governments to continue public health service functions and the failure of individuals to cover the soaring costs of basic health care (WHO 2000).

To limit the scope of this paper to a manageable degree, the following two main assumptions will be analyzed:

1. Economic policies and practices have a significant impact on the health status and services of any community.
2. Globalization forces developing countries to reduce government spending on social sector programs. If not counterbalanced, this aspect of globalization has detrimental effects on health status.

Due to the limitations of space, this essay will not include any information from field-studies or provide an analysis of a representative sample of countries. The author's experiential frame of reference is the Islamic countries (see Appendix B for data on basic health and social indicators for various Islamic countries). Because of the substantial theoretical, methodological, and empirical problems involved in assessing the consequences of such a complex and all-embracing phenomenon as globalization, this essay will not attempt to assess the impact of globalization on the social sector in specific countries or regions; instead, it will raise a number of important considerations related to the above-mentioned two assumptions.

## The New Scenario in the Health Services Sector

Developing countries' governments are faced with a complex set of factors that make it increasingly difficult to provide adequate health services to their population. Average life expectancy is on the rise, resulting in an aging population that requires increased medical interventions. The cost of medical care is also rapidly increasing under the new globalized economy. Meanwhile, ecological problems have emerged, posing continuously increased threats to health. The World Health Organization (WHO) reports that the number of poor in developing countries has increased; projections indicate that there is a great danger that the gains realized in health coverage and access over the recent past cannot be maintained in the future (WHO 2000:3). The redefinition and reduction of the role of the state is now taking place on all continents, but is most severe in the developing countries.

Health services are considered to be part of GATS, while health commodities are subject to the GATT. Many pharmaceuticals and vaccines are subject to the Agreement on Trade-Related Aspects of Intellectual Property Rights (TRIPS). The multiplicity of these kinds of agreements and the other political and social factors that contribute to health status create a complex subject for research. We will attempt to deal with the combined influences of globalization, in particular: the aforementioned agreements and the interlinked issues of health facilities, drugs, health staff, health insurance, environment, and food safety.

## Influence of Globalization on Health Facilities

Many developing countries are "selling" their public institutions to the private sector. While this approach may have been successful in the developed countries, the ability of the developing countries to steer and regulate the health sector with large private providers is questionable (UNCTAD 1998). The benefits that may accrue from privatization must be weighted against the potential negative effects. Concerns about equity and access to services, especially for those with the most need among the population, have to be addressed. The development of private facilities, with state-of-the-art technology, to serve the wealthy increases available technology in the local health sector. However, unless the government succeeds in arranging for a certain proportion of the beds or services to be made available to the public sector, it is unlikely this development will benefit the neediest members of the population.

Another issue at hand is the commercial presence of foreign health institutions from developed countries that enter the markets of developing countries to provide health-related services. This presence can take the form of the operation/management of locally owned health facilities, joint ventures, and the provision of health insurance and health education. As a promising field of investment, hospital management, often attracts companies whose traditional business lies outside the field of health care services. The direct impact of this type of foreign presence can be the deterioration of the level of services provided. In some cases, the foreign partner combines management of health facilities with health insurance, and this can create a type of monopoly.

In contrast, all the member governments of the European Union (EU) maintain some form of economic-need limitations on the establishment of new hospital facilities (ILO 2001c:22). Moreover, almost every EU government favors local, over foreign interests, in the establishment of a commercial presence in these facilities. Less favorable treatment may be given to foreign persons or entities with respect to acquiring real estate or investing in health care concerns. Japan limits ownership of hospitals and clinics to nationally licensed physicians, or groups of persons of whom at least one member is a Japanese-licensed doctor. Similar regulations apply for many other developed countries.

For the developing countries, the commercialization of health services raises the following questions: How can public and private health services coexist in the same market, benefiting from each other's presence? Can the price of quality services in the private facilities be controlled so that more people will opt to use them, leaving the limited public funds for the neediest members of the population? Can telemedicine, including the diagnosis, treatment, consultation, education, and transfer of data using interactive audio and visual media, help to cut the cost of quality health service? Can ethical and professional standards, as well as legal liability, be maintained with the growth of telemedicine networks?

In view of a well-developed global transportation system, and readily available information on health facilities and professionals abroad through the Internet, developed countries are in a better position to attract patients from developing countries than vice versa. "Overcapacity" in health facilities in some developed countries, notably the United States, has prompted major marketing efforts on the part of some developing countries to attract potential foreign patients. Developing countries, with state-of-the-art technology and reputable professionals, are able to offer the same services for lower prices. Penetrating the international health services markets could be achieved based on their comparative advantages, such as cultural, linguistic, geographic, and highly specialized services. Some examples worth studying in this regard are Australia's establishment of a National Health Industry Development Forum (HIDF), the National Health System Overseas Enterprise (NHSOE) in the United Kingdom, and Parkway Health Group in Singapore (UNCTAD 1998).

Another problem is protecting the indigenous germ pool and medicinal plants from foreign commercial exploitation. This should be a priority for all developing countries. Appropriate regulations and better marketing of available health facilities and staff can empower the national facilities of developing countries so that they can successfully confront the giant transnational companies who are threatening to undermine their national assets. The alternative is simply to leave the citizenry subject to the monopoly of these giant corporations.

## Influence of Globalization on Accessibility of and Trade in Essential Drugs

Studies on the trade in health commodities are scant, and the role of ministries of health in developing trade policy is almost nonexistent. Access to low-cost, safe, and effective essential drugs is largely threatened by the agreement on Trade-Related Aspects of Intellectual Property Rights (TRIPS). The WTO agreement allows the owners of new know-how, in the pharmaceutical field, a 20-year monopoly over this know-how (WHO 2000). In spite of providing two means for obtaining exceptions and limiting the exclusive rights of the patent holders, experts from both the developed and developing countries fear that there will be a substantial increase in drug prices in those countries (most of the developing countries and the former socialist countries) that did not grant patents in the past. While protection and enforcement of intellectual property rights is intended to contribute to the promotion of technology innovation, it should also enhance the transfer and dissemination of technology to developing countries. A balance of rights and obligations, in a manner conducive to social and economic welfare is needed to ensure that there is a mutual advantage for both producers and users.

Given the lack of systematic data collection and analysis in most of the developing countries, the impact of trade in health services on public health cannot currently be determined (UNCTAD 1998). The impact should include benefiting the technological and skills base, fulfilling market needs, creating job opportunities, and possible accentuation of inequalities in the developing countries.

The developing countries may be able to make use of the flexibility of some articles of the TRIPS agreement. When reasons of national interest justify it, national public authorities may allow the exploitation of a patent by a third person without the owner's consent. Compulsory licenses (provided for in TRIPS) provide a mechanism by which the patented objects such as drugs can be used without the permission of the patent owner, after unsuccessful attempts to obtain a voluntary license to produce the object. Many developed countries are already using these rights. For example, French law authorizes applying the regime of compulsory licenses. Some international conventions (e.g., the Paris Convention) leave states free to counterbalance, through the use of compulsory licenses, possible abuses and monopolies. The following five main types, not inclusive, of use without authorization of the right holder are possible:

1. Licenses for public non-commercial uses by the government.
2. Licenses granted to third parties, authorized by the government for public non-commercial use.
3. Licenses granted in conditions of emergency.
4. Licenses granted to remedy a practice, which has been determined, after administrative or judicial process, to be anti-competitive.
5. Licenses arising from a dependant patent.

Developing countries should establish by legislation "Sectors of Vital Importance" (as provided for in TRIPS) that include the health sector, to allow them to ensure improved supply of vital drugs to their domestic market and to ensure appropriate price conditions prevail in this sector. If the patent holder does not manufacture the product locally and is still only importing after three years, he or she should be required to grant a compulsory license for local manufacture. Economies of scale and well-established know-how should be studied in these cases.

Developing countries need to negotiate concessions for their particular needs during the WTO rounds. They should optimize their utilization of the flexibility in the existing trade agreements to control drug prices in their respective low purchasing power countries using the lever of "Preferential Pricing." Rapid production of generic products and compulsory licensing should remain a priority to prevent possible abuses connected with monopoly control of the market. Technology transfer, production, and global movement of health commodities are presently threatened by monopoly control (WHO 2000).

## Influence of Globalization on Health Staff

Most of the developing countries do certify diplomas obtained from developed countries and license their holders to practice in their country. This is not the case for developed countries dealing with diplomas from the developing countries. Disparities of curricula and the resistance of professional associations are among the main reasons for this unequal treatment. Medical education in many developing countries is quite reputable. Moreover, better marketing is required to minimize the brain drain of health professionals from the developing countries.

Research and Development (R&D) represent an important vehicle to achieve a better place in today's fiercely competitive world market. Health staff in developing countries must be well prepared to undertake this responsibility. The development of research facilities should represent a priority for investment. Research to develop new essential drugs is threatened by the market failures resulting from globalization. South-South cooperation is needed to offset the impact of these failures on investment in R&D.

Health professionals should not be denied the right to seek improved living and working conditions. More lucrative remuneration is one of the incentives for the movement of health staff from developing to developed countries, but acquiring higher professional qualifications and exposure to new technologies are some of the other benefits associated with this movement of health professionals. Moving from the public to the private sector, as well as temporary movement outside the home country, can benefit the health staff as well as the local health sector. However, permanent emigration of health personnel can result in a brain drain. It is estimated that the developing countries supply 56 percent of all migrant physicians and receive less than 11 percent (ILO 2001c:7).

In some cases, arrangements are made to allow health professionals to work for a limited duration in developed countries, both to supplement their income and upgrade their professional skills. Restrictions in developed countries may arise from the lack of recognition of professional qualifications and residency requirements. Professional associations often attempt to dampen price competition and restrict new entrants.

## The Influence of Globalization on Health Insurance

With the diminishing role of governments in health care, health insurance has become the option for an increasing proportion of individuals in developing countries. However, individuals seeking health insurance need to be protected against misuse and "cream skimming." Experience gained from countries that have privatized health insurance indicates the need for clear public health guidelines for domestic and foreign insurers (ILO 2001a). National policy needs to address equity issues, and minimize the selective insurance approach to make sure coverage is equitable.

Bearing in mind that many health care facilities in developing countries are reputable and could offer quality treatment for competitive prices, the portability of public health care insurance and other health insurance systems in developed countries would promote treatment of their citizens in developing countries. Negotiations on this topic should be initiated. Developing countries should also promote traditional medicine and focus on their comparative advantage to attract patients from developed countries interested in this type of medicine (Eastwood 2002).

## Environmental Impact of Globalization

With the opening of their borders to the movement of technology, capital, goods and services, and in some cases, workers, the environment in developing countries is being threatened. Developed countries have restricted many industries that they consider environment-unfriendly, and many of these industries have moved to the developing countries, with far-reaching impact on their ecological balance. International investors are usually not concerned with the health hazards caused by the technology used, or the lack of safeguards in these industries. Some developing countries have accepted the dumping of dangerous health-threatening wastes from the developed countries in their soil, as a part of economic development deals (Millen and Holtz 2000:202-203).

The developing countries are facing the full range of global environmental problems faced by developed countries; but in addition, they have extra problems to solve. Exploitation of fishing rights, deforestation, industrial wastes, and dumping of health-hazardous material are just part of a long list of items faced by the developing countries (Millen and Holtz 2000). Scientists and environmentalists in developing countries need to be well trained and given the opportunity to participate in decisions related to the movement of goods and services across their borders.

## Impact on Food Safety

The quantity and types of food moving in the international market are growing and becoming more diversified. The developing countries are receiving a wide range of technologically manipulated foods, while their national capacity for testing the hazards of this food is humbly limited. Genetically modified organisms, microbiological pathogens, and hazards in animal production could represent a real health risk for developing countries. Some of the hazards of technologically manipulated foods are yet to be known, even in the developed countries. These hazards could require decades or centuries before being discovered. Developing countries must be able to assess the health impact of imported foods, and their decisions on the application of health protection measures must be science-based. The Agreement on the Application of Sanitary and Phytosanitary Measures deals with health and safety requirements for food movement in international commerce. The agreement recognizes the set of standards, guidelines, and recommendations representing the international consensus (Sullivan and Shainblum 2001).

Developing countries are in need of up-to-date scientific advice on health hazards of imported foods. They are also in need of assistance to build their own national capacity in setting, evaluating, and establishing appropriate standards. Research and testing facilities, as well as well-trained and informed staff, are basic requirements for developing countries.

International trade is also opening the doors of developing countries for products with proven negative health impact. Consumption of tobacco and similar products is on the rise in most developing countries, while declining in the developed communities. Giant tobacco companies are doing all that they can to replace their declining market in the developed countries by increasing markets in developing countries (Bettcher et al. 2001).

## What Can Be Done?

In the aforementioned discussion, this paper has attempted to address the possible effects of globalization on several health-related issues. Each one of these issues has, in turn, its impact on the individual. To avoid redundancy, this paper will not attempt to report on the possible impact of these issues on the individual. Rather, following the identification of the present scene, the proceeding will seek a way out of the current situation.

Some encouraging indicators can be reported. The Group of Eight (G8) declaration of Köln in 1999 stressed the need to give globalization a "human face" (Ministry of Foreign Affairs of Japan 2003). They encouraged all members of the WTO to make proposals for progress, where developing countries can make solid and substantial gains. Some of the proposed actions here could help developing countries foster their proposals. The main three groups addressed separately by the proposals are developing countries; developed countries; and the international, regional, and other concerned organizations.

## The Role of Developing Countries

Let us, from the very beginning, agree that insufficient financing is a major issue hindering the capacity of developing countries in dealing with many issues, including globalization. Nevertheless, let us also agree that good management and setting appropriate controls are equally important to optimize utilization of the available limited resources. Developing countries should not await actions to be taken by developed countries on their behalf, without playing an active role in mining for solutions. We should agree that potential gains from globalization are neither automatic nor painless. Equally right is that negative impacts of globalization are neither automatic nor unavoidable. What makes the difference is how developing countries are going to deal with the consequences of globalization.

Unfortunately, WTO agreements are not well studied by specialists and policy makers in developing countries. Some of these agreements could have a significant impact on the health sector, particularly health and health-related industry, including the drug industry. Developing countries need to build their own national capacity to be able to negotiate and play an active role in the WTO decisions. These capacities should not be limited to specialists and data on the economy, but must be diversified to include health and other social fields. It is proposed to form "A National Multi-Disciplinary Study and Negotiations Team," including specialists from the health sector (services, manufacturing, training, etc.). The team should be well prepared to undertake necessary studies to assess the impact of every article of the WTO agreements on social aspects in general and health services in particular. The members of the team should command the skills necessary for "expert reading" of articles of agreements, with possible cooperation from the UN concerned agencies. They should also be able to formulate an appropriate perspective of the social dimension and to come up with "informed recommendations" for each round of the WTO negotiations. Developing countries should also cooperate and consult with other developing and developed countries to influence decision-making, including, interalia, formulation of economic blocks, and multilateral and bilateral agreements. They are also urged to insist on the active role of WHO, other UN and Regional Organizations, and other concerned organizations in trade and services negotiations within WTO.

Developing countries must make use of the main articles of WTO agreements (GATT, GATS, Technical Barrier to Trade [TBT], Anti-Dumping (AD) and safeguard agreement), which allow for special and transitional arrangements. They should devise suitable export strategies based on comparative advantage and gaining improved access to markets with potential. Governmental programs could include compensatory actions, allowed under the agreements, to limit the possible negative effects on their markets.

To face health hazards of imported food, developing countries must build their capacity to assess, on a scientific basis, possible health risks, and to strengthen national food safety infrastructure. Human and material capacity in this domain is not easy to build; thus, in the absence of such capacity, developing countries could become a "test big" for technologically manipulated food.

With the importance of health services to the development of countries and the need for softer conditions to deal with the costly health sector, governments should seek concessions from international companies that strengthen the health sector as a trade-off for market entry into other related sectors, such as insurance. Policies and programs for this trade-off necessitate a sound base of the know-how. Building reliable information systems, based on continuously updated studies, in order to provide support to decision-makers is a crucial component of the know-how.

Contrary to the prevailing feeling that governments have lost control of their own mandate, developing countries must formulate or amend laws and regulations to adopt measures necessary to protect the public interests in environment, public health, and nutrition. They could also formulate regulation of insurance by domestic and foreign insurers to cover health insurance schemes, rather than letting these companies focus on easy profit through "cream skimming" in more profitable sectors. Appropriate regulation of health staff movement would minimize brain drain and maximize benefits to developing countries, without hurting the individual.

## Role of the Developed Countries

The rich industrial countries have repeatedly declared their support for developing countries in order to benefit from the expansion of international trade. The G8 Köln declaration of 1999 encourages developing countries to bring forward proposals that could be of their interest (Ministry of Foreign Affairs of Japan). In addition, several declarations have shown commitment to some measures that would assist developing countries in maximizing their benefit from international free trade agreements and policies. Most of these economic measures focus on two-fold actions by the developed countries: reduction of the debt of the developing countries and removal of the barriers and entrance measures so that the share of developing countries in the global open market can be increased. The economic and monetary measures to bridge the gap between these declarations and the commitments are numerous, but so far few of the commitments have been realized.

Several of the proposed actions by the developed countries could be used as mechanisms to minimize the negative impact of globalization on developing countries. These proposals are based on WHO concerns and agreements. The WHO has urged the developed countries to ease the rules for transfer of technology and drug patents, take effective action against the anti-competitive practices of the giant transnational companies, and encourage them to offer voluntary licenses to the developing countries that most need these drugs. Governments and professional associations have also been urged to remove barriers to the movement and fair treatment of health personnel from developing countries.

The developed countries need to be reminded that genuine free trade tends to improve the living conditions and increase the real income for all countries and communities involved. World experience has shown that poverty and low standards of living represent a threat to international peace everywhere. Recent events show that the negative impacts of poverty in the developing countries, including the denial of access to appropriate health services, are not limited to the developing countries. They can also affect the developed countries.

## International, Regional, and Other Organizations

International, regional, and other organizations concerned with the social dimension have an important role to play in defending the interests of their member states, particularly in the developing countries. Their role in this regard is not only essential to the developing countries, but it is also crucial for the continuation of international peace. Experience through the years has proven that strengthening the social pillar of society contributes to maintaining civil and international peace (ILO 2001b). Giving globalization a "human face" is increasingly becoming a major global issue, and all concerned countries and organizations must share the responsibility in carrying out this task.

A good example in this regard is the decision by the Governing Body of the International Labor Organization (ILO) in 1994 to establish a "Working Party on the Social Dimension of Liberalization of International Trade" (ILO 2001c). Members of this working party were selected from employers, labor organizations, and governments from the developing as well as the developed countries. The achievements of this working party were numerous and gradually built a consensus on the need for an authoritative report on the social dimension of globalization (ILO 2001b).

As a result of recent developments in the international scene, the Governing Body of the ILO initiated the process of establishing a 25 member World Commission on the Social Dimension of Globalization to produce a blueprint for reducing inequality in the global economic system (ILO Press Release March 22, 2002) and with the aim of building a consensus on a model of globalization that reduces poverty and insecurity, and increases opportunities for all (ILO Press Release February 14, 2003). The Commission emphasizes the importance of close collaboration with the international community, the UN system, and with the Bretton Woods' institutions (the IMF and World Bank). In that connection, the Commission has held important sessions with the Managing Director of the IMF and the Director General of the WTO to discuss the social dimension of globalization and how the benefits of globalization can be made more inclusive.

Many governments, employers' and labor organizations have already submitted ideas and proposals, or provided support in other ways, to the Commission. The Commission is building a broad constituency and has benefited from the important opportunity for dialogue on the social dimension of globalization provided by the 2002 World Summit on Sustainable Development held in Johannesburg, South Africa. A series of national and regional dialogues in different geographic regions took place in early 2003. The Commission aims at helping countries and regions to achieve their social objectives within the context of the global economy.

The Commission is preparing a major authoritative report based on its fourth meeting on February 16-18 2003 in Geneva (ILO Press Release February 14, 2003). The Commission's report will provide an in-depth analysis of the social dimension of globalization and the implications of this analysis on decent work, poverty reduction and development. This will include examining the impact of trade, foreign direct investment, foreign aid, and other factors on employment and poverty reduction. The report is intended to produce political solutions to resolve the complex question of how to create sustainable employment so that the benefits of economic globalization can be shared more broadly, particularly in developing countries.

## Conclusion

Although the effects of globalization are influencing the daily life of each one of us, more efforts have been devoted to denouncing it than to mitigating its effects. The impact of globalization differs from one country to the other and among different groups within the same country. Much work is needed in order to identify areas that could potentially benefit from the increased liberalization of international trade. Meanwhile, adjustments will not be painless. In real life, economic and social phenomena are interrelated and should be treated as complementary. Strengthening the social pillar of globalization will contribute to increasing its economic benefits. It is a basic right of all developing countries to denounce what they think is unjust in their dealings with other countries; however, proactive measures have proven to be more effective than passive ones. This essay has attempted to offer some guidance with regard to the specific actions that can be taken by the developing countries, the developed countries, and concerned organizations at the international, regional, and other levels to address the social effects of globalization. The proposed actions are neither comprehensive nor conclusive. They represent a starting point of a long journey towards more gains and less pain from globalization in the developing countries.

## References

BETTCHER, DOUGLAS ET AL.
2001     *Confronting the Tobacco Epidemic in an Era of Trade Liberalization.* Geneva, Switzerland: World Health Organization.

EASTWOOD, HEATHER
2002        "Globalization, Complementary Medicine, and Australian Health Policy: The Role of Consumerism." Pp. 222-245 in *Health Policy in Australia*, edited by Heather Gardner and Simon Barraclough. Melbourne, Australia: Oxford University Press.
INTERNATIONAL LABOR ORGANIZATION (ILO)
2001a       Studies on the Social Dimensions of Globalization: Chile. Geneva, Switzerland: ILO.
2001b       Towards a Socially Sustainable World Economy: An Analysis of the Social Pillars of Globalization. Geneva, Switzerland: ILO.
2001c       Trade Liberalization and Employment. Retrieved March 16, 2002 (www.ilo. org/public/english/standards/relm/gb/docs/gb282/pdf/sdg-2.pdf).
2002        Press Release March 22, 2002 "ILO's World Commission on Globalization begins work." Retrieved July 21, 2003 http://www.ilo.org/ public/english/bureau/pr/2002/12.htm.
2003        Press Release February 14, 2003 "Fourth Meeting of the World Commission on Social Dimension of Globalization." Retrieved July 21, 2003 http://www. ilo.org/public/english/bureau/pr/2003/5.htm.
MILLEN, JOYCE AND TIMOTHY HOLTZ
2000        "Dying for Growth, Part I: Transnational Corporations and the Health of the Poor." Pp. 177-224 in *Dying for Growth: Global Inequality and the Health of the Poor*, edited by Kim, Jim Yong et al. Monroe, Maine: Common Courage Press.
MINISTRY OF FOREIGN AFFAIRS OF JAPAN
            "G8 Communiqué Köln 1999." Retrieved July 21, 2003 http://www.mofa.go. jp/policy/economy/summit/1999/communique.html.
SULLIVAN, TERRENCE AND ESTHER SHAINBLUM
2001        "Summary of the WTO Symposium on Issues Confronting the World Trading System." *Sustainable Development* 55.
UNITED NATIONS CONFERENCE ON TRADE AND DEVELOPMENT (UNCTAD)
1998        International Trade in Health Services: a Development Prospective. Geneva, Switzerland: UNCTAD.
UNITED NATIONS DEVELOPMENT PROGRAM (UNDP)
1993-1997, 2001   Human Development Reports 1993-1997, 2001. New York, NY: Oxford University Press.
WORLD HEALTH ORGANIZATION (WHO)
2000        "The Implications of GATT and WTO agreements on Health in General." Background document for item three of the 24th meeting of Consultative Committee, EMRO. May 7-8, Alexandria.

# Appendix A

## Operational Definitions

**Globalization** is the "proces" by which persons, concepts, images, ideas, values, and capital and traded goods diffuse across national boundaries, thus steadily increasing global socioeconomic and political interdependence and integration (ILO 2001).

**Health Services** include the general and specialized services of medical doctors, deliveries and related services, nursing services, physiotherapeutic and paramedical services, all hospital services, ambulance services, residential health facilities services, and services provided by medical and dental laboratories.

**Social Dimension** is the extent to which globalization influences the level and quality of social protection and social services granted by the government.

# Appendix B

## Table 1

Basic Health Indicators for Some Developing Islamic Countries[*]

| Country | Basic health related indices | | | | Year[**] |
|---|---|---|---|---|---|
| | Life expectancy | Access to health services/ essential drugs | Access to safe water | Access to sanitation | |
| Kuwait | 73.4 | 100 | 100 | 98 | 1993 |
| | 75.2 | 100 | n.a. | n.a. | 1997 |
| | 75.9 | 99 | n.a. | n.a. | 2001 |
| Qatar | 69.2 | 100 | 91` | 97 | 1993 |
| | 70.9 | n.a. | n.a. | n.a. | 1997 |
| | 68.9 | 99 | n.a. | n.a. | 2001 |
| Malaysia | 70.1 | 88 | 78 | 94 | 1993 |
| | 71.2 | n.a. | 78 | 94 | 1997 |
| | 71.9 | 70 | 95 | 98 | 2001 |
| UAE | 70.5 | 90 | 100 | 95 | 1993 |
| | 74.2 | 99 | 95 | 77 | 1997 |
| | 74.6 | 99 | n.a. | n.a. | 2001 |
| Turkey | 65.1 | n.a. | 92 | n.a. | 1993 |
| | 68.2 | n.a. | 80 | n.a. | 1997 |
| | 69.0 | 99 | 83 | 91 | 2001 |
| Saudi | 64.5 | 98 | 95 | 86 | 1993 |
| | 70.3 | 97 | 95 | 86 | 1997 |
| | 68.4 | 99 | 95 | 100 | 2001 |
| Tunis | 66.7 | 91 | 65 | 45 | 1993 |
| | 68.4 | n.a. | 98 | 80 | 1997 |
| | 69.5 | 51 | n.a. | n.a. | 2001 |
| Iran | 66.2 | 73 | 89 | 71 | 1993 |
| | 68.2 | 88 | 90 | 81 | 1997 |
| | 68.0 | 85 | 95 | 81 | 2001 |
| Indonesia | 61.5 | 43 | 42 | 44 | 1993 |
| | 63.5 | 93 | 62 | 51 | 1997 |
| | 65.1 | 80 | 76 | 66 | 2001 |
| Sudan | 50.8 | 70 | n.a. | 12 | 1993 |
| | 51.0 | 70 | 60 | 22 | 1997 |
| | 55.0 | 15 | 75 | 62 | 2001 |
| Average developing countries | 62.8 | 72 | 68 | 55 | 1993 |
| | 61.8 | 80 | 71 | 39 | |
| | 64.1 | n.a. | | | |

[*] Reference: UNDP, Human Development Report 1993, 1997 and 2001.
[**] Year of the report.

# Table 2

## Further Health Indicators for Some Developing Islamic Countries[*]

| Country | Further health related indices | | | | | Year[**] |
|---|---|---|---|---|---|---|
| | Infant mortality rate 1991 | Maternal mortality 1988 | Vaccination 89-91 | Population/ doctoral 84-89 | Expenditures 88-90 (%GDP) | |
| Kuwait | 14 | 30 | 95 | 145 | n.a. | 1993 |
| | 17 | 29 | 93 | n.a. | n.a. | 1997 |
| | 11 | 5 | 96 | 189 | n.a. | 2001 |
| Qatar | 28 | 140 | 85 | 188.7 | 3.1 | 1993 |
| | 19 | n.a. | n.a. | n.a. | n.a. | 1997 |
| | 12 | 10 | 95 | 126 | n.a. | 2001 |
| Malaysia | 15 | 120 | 92 | 51.5 | 1.6 | 1993 |
| | 12 | 80 | 86 | 40 | 1.3 | 1997 |
| | 8 | 39 | 93 | 66 | 1.4 | 2001 |
| UAE | 23 | 120 | 85 | 98 | 9.0 | 1993 |
| | 17 | 26 | 94 | 96 | n.a. | 1997 |
| | 8 | 3 | 97 | 181 | 0.8 | 2001 |
| Turkey | 60 | 200 | 82 | 73 | 2.8 | 1993 |
| | 44 | 180 | 42 | 85 | n.a. | 1997 |
| | 40 | 60 | 79 | 121 | n.a. | 2001 |
| Saudi | 33 | 220 | 94 | 135 | 2.1 | 1993 |
| | 27 | 130 | 93 | 142 | 3.1 | 1997 |
| | 20 | 38 | 92 | 166 | n.a. | 2001 |
| Tunis | 45 | 200 | 92 | 46.3 | 2.4 | 1993 |
| | 41 | 170 | 90 | 54 | 3.3 | 1997 |
| | 24 | 70 | 92 | 70 | 2.2 | 2001 |
| Iran | 44 | 250 | 91 | 33.9 | 3.2 | 1993 |
| | 40 | 120 | 97 | n.a. | 1.5 | 1997 |
| | 37 | 37 | 99 | 85 | 1.7 | 2001 |
| Indonesia | 68 | 300 | 89 | 10.6 | 2.5 | 1993 |
| | 53 | 650 | 78 | 14 | 0.7 | 1997 |
| | 38 | 450 | 84 | 16 | 0.7 | 2001 |
| Sudan | 102 | 700 | 64 | 9 | 0.3 | 1993 |
| | 86 | 660 | 81 | 11.4 | 0.5 | 1997 |
| | 67 | 550 | 94 | 9 | n.a. | 2001 |
| Average developing countries | 71 | 420 | n.a. | 20 | 3.7 | 1993 |
| | 64 | 471 | 81.5 | 17 | 2.1 | 1997 |
| | 61 | n.a. | n.a. | n.a. | n.a. | 2001 |

[*] Reference: UNDP, Human Development Report 1993, 1997 and 2001.
[**] Year of the report.

# Globalization and Health:
# The Paradox of the Periphery

## Christine McMurray[*]

### ABSTRACT

The impact of globalization on health is complex, both positively and negatively. Benefits include improved medical technology and services, but globalization also has promoted patterns of dependency, development, settlement, and lifestyles that have been detrimental to health. This paper draws examples from the small island nations of the Pacific to show how globalization impacts environmental health, health service delivery, and lifestyles. It shows that, paradoxically, in the smallest and most remote nations the negative impacts of globalization are felt most strongly in urban areas where living standards might appear to be highest.

## Introduction

The impact of globalization on health is complex, having both positive and negative aspects. There is no doubt that the spread of Western medicine throughout the world and the implementations of global health programs have brought enormous benefits. At the same time, globalization has promoted patterns of dependency, development, settlement, and lifestyles that have been detrimental to health.

A key characteristic of globalization is that it promotes uneven development. All places become "core" or "peripheral" in relation to other places, as they become increasingly interconnected by trade, international flows of capital and investments, and by media promotion of the values, lifestyles,

[*]Australian Centre for Population Research, The Australian National University, Canberra, Australia. Institute of Island Studies, University of Prince Edward Island, Charlottetown, Prince Edward Island, Canada.

and material goods of the more-developed countries. [1] Although there is perhaps a hierarchy of core countries, it is more useful from a health perspective to think of all of the more-developed countries as the global core, where the best health services and greatest range of lifestyle options are available. The periphery comprises the less-developed nations that have a dependent relationship with developed nations, but are unable to offer a comparable range of services and lifestyle options. Most peripheral of all are the poorest countries of Africa and Asia and the remote island nations of the Pacific.

The core/periphery pattern promotes both benefits and disparities in health. On the one hand, linkages between core and peripheral places facilitate the spread of knowledge about medicine and good health. On the other hand, global forces concentrate the best facilities in core places and reduce the options and choices available in the periphery. Although disparities in the general health of countries and regions and between individuals in a single society have always existed, globalisation intensifies disparities and increases the difficulty of achieving equity in health.

This core/periphery pattern is replicated within every nation, with each having its own core where the best services and most lifestyle options are to be found. Other places that are peripheral in relation to this core exist in a state of dependency that determines the services and lifestyle options available in outer areas. While wealthy countries may have the resources to ensure that health services in peripheral areas are of a high standard, less-developed countries tend to concentrate most of their resources in their core and offer only rudimentary services in peripheral areas.

The nature and pattern of disparities between core and peripheral areas, however, is sometimes unexpected and paradoxical. In particular, disadvantaged groups can be found within the most highly developed core areas, while the health of residents of the core areas of the most peripheral nations may be inferior to that of those residing outside their cores. This paper examines the mechanisms through which globalization intensifies disparities in health between and within nations, and shows how it may create a paradoxical situation on the periphery.

## The Epidemiological Transition

To understand the manner in which globalization impacts on health it is necessary to consider the general improvements in population health

---

[1] Throughout this article the United Nations terms "more-developed," "less-developed," and "least-developed" will be used to refer to groupings of nations according to their economic level. Where "less developed" is used alone it refers to both less- and least-developed nations.

that occurred during the nineteenth and twentieth centuries. One of the most important benefits of modernization has been the Epidemiological Transition. This refers to the transition from a state of relatively high mortality from infectious diseases to a state where most infectious diseases are controlled and the main causes of death are non-communicable diseases occurring in old age (Frenk et al. 1989). It occurs largely as a result of improved sanitation and hygiene, immunization, antibiotics, and surgical advances. These improvements are complementary in their impact on health.

The essential process of the Epidemiological Transition is that the general reduction in the prevalence of infectious diseases leads to a consequent increase in life expectancy. In the post transition phase, infectious diseases are controlled, and most people die in their seventies or eighties from non-communicable diseases (NCDs), such as coronary malfunctions and cancer (Frenk et al. 1989). The Epidemiological Transition began in the early nineteenth century in Europe, and subsequently spread to other industrialized countries. Its progress across the world can be tracked by the dates when various countries achieved major increases in longevity (United Nations 1982).

The benefits of modern medicine and disease control have now spread throughout the entire world to some extent. Although the quality of care and service delivery, affordability and availability of medicine and treatments may vary, some form of modern medical care is now available virtually everywhere. In addition, mass disease control campaigns, such as the World Health Organization's Expanded Programme of Immunization (EPI), have reached the world's poorest countries (Henderson 1984).

In the last few decades, however, a new variant of the Epidemiological Transition has emerged. Although this variant still brings a general reduction in infectious diseases and increased life expectancy, the general improvement in population health is less than was experienced by industrialized countries during the twentieth century. Its main features are a slower decline in life expectancy, and a dramatic increase in the prevalence of NCDs among adults at increasingly younger ages, so extensive that it can be thought of as a "second wave" of disease (Coyne 2000:6). The most common early-onset NCDs are diabetes mellitus, coronary and vascular diseases, and obesity. All are related to lifestyle. At the same time, infectious diseases are less well controlled than in the classic Epidemiological Transition model. This new variant is usually found in "the less- and least-developed countries," as opposed to the "more developed countries" and is largely a consequence of globalization.

## How Globalization Impacts Health

In the preglobalized world, disparities in health were usually a consequence of differences in wealth and living standards and geographical variations in the risk of infectious disease. There is no question that this remains the case today, with a close positive association of health indicators and life expectancy at both the national and individual levels. It is overly simplistic, however, to explain differences in health primarily as differences between rich and poor nations, because such an approach fails to take account of the specific mechanisms through which globalization impacts health, both positively, by increasing the availability of health care, and negatively, by intensifying disparities in health. The three main mechanisms through which globalization operates are, first, its impact on environmental quality; second, its impact on the quality and accessibility of health services; and third, its promotion of unhealthy lifestyles.

The following sections examine these mechanisms. Most of the examples relating to peripheral countries are drawn from the small island nations and territories of the Pacific, since they are strongly influenced by the forces of globalization and because their small size and isolation enable the effects of globalization to be seen very clearly. Similar patterns of disadvantage, however, can be seen in peripheral countries and communities everywhere.

## Globalization and Environmental Health

As discussed above, safe water and sanitation, in addition to medical advances and health service delivery were an essential part of the improvements in population health associated with the Epidemiological Transition in the more-developed countries. The extent to which they are available in any particular place depends primarily on national resources, but also on the advice received and the strategy adopted. As centers of innovation and technology, the global cores set the technical standards for the rest of the world. An obvious manifestation of this is the use of the word "alternative" to describe any technology that differs from these global standards. For example, "alternative medicine" is used to describe traditional as opposed to modern medicine, and "alternative energy" is used for renewable energy as opposed to fossil fuel and large-scale hydro-electricity.

In thinly populated rural areas, where populations are sparse, the traditional use of the bush and ocean as toilets and for garbage disposal does not necessarily lead to dangerous levels of contamination, and surface water may be potable. As population densities increase, however, systems of waste management are essential to ensure safe water and prevent environmental contamination. Modernization has led to the development of urban centers in virtually all nations. Initially centers of culture and government, urban centers evolved into centers of trade and commerce (McGee 1967). The international forces of globalization have concentrated settlement in urban areas in most countries. Most developed countries now have 70% or more of their population in urban areas, and the percentage of population in urban areas is increasing in most less-developed countries (UNFPA 1999:25).

The global standards for water and sanitation were established in the most-developed countries: high cost networks piped to or from a central source. This is a very costly model, and less- and least-developed countries are generally able to provide such services only in their main urban areas. Many date from colonial times, or have been constructed with development assistance. Since there is often a shortage of resources and technology to maintain them, they are subject to breakdown and contamination.

In the early 1990s, for example, lack of maintenance caused the water supply in Majuro in the Marshall Islands, total population around 50,000, to become contaminated with seepage from adjacent sewage pipes and nitrates leached from human graves. Another Pacific nation, Kiribati, is experiencing severe environmental contamination in its main center, South Tarawa. Although Kiribati has only 90,000 people and comprises 33 coral atolls scattered across a vast expanse of the Pacific Ocean, around 35,000 people live on a 100-200 metre wide, 30 kilometre long coral strip on the rim of shallow, sandy, Tarawa Lagoon. Some South Tarawa houses and public buildings are connected to piped water and sewage systems, but many are not, while the services that do exist often malfunction. Refuse disposal services are inadequate and infrequent, and some areas of the beachfront are piled high with household waste. As a consequence, Tarawa Lagoon is severely contaminated, and outbreaks of diarrhoeal disease are common.

While there is no doubt that the more-developed country model of water and sanitation infrastructure can be extremely efficient and is desirable, the point to be made here is that, because of globalization, it tends to be accepted without question by less- and least-developed countries. Often it was simply a case of colonial powers installing the type of infrastructure to which they were accustomed, without thinking of the long-term affordability and sustainability. In much of the Pacific, water and sanitation infrastructure dates from colonial times or was funded by external donors, who assumed that recipient countries would take responsibility for maintenance. Small island nations, however, may lack the resources and expertise to maintain such facilities, or simply have other priorities for their limited budgets (SPC 2001).

In recent decades, more attention has been given to sustainability, but new solutions still tend to be perceived as "alternative" or "appropriate technology" because they differ from the standard set by globalization. In the Pacific, it is becoming more common to use roofs of houses for water catchment, but uptake of even this simple and obvious technology has been slow because storage tanks, metal roofs and gutters are expensive, and the costs must be borne by individual household owners rather than municipal authorities. In the Marshall Islands, the water contamination problem was solved by a major donor project to re-lay the pipes; similar projects are planned for Kiribati. In other countries, such as Papua New Guinea, the scale is larger and the costs of providing reliable services much greater. In 1992 a doctor working in Port Moresby Public Hospital, Papua New Guinea, remarked to the author that, until the local city council makes the water supply safe and reliable, his efforts to treat children with diarrhoea was nothing more than a "bandaid" solution to the problem. Although there have since been major upgrades to Port Moresby's water and sewerage services (Inter Financial, 1999), access to safe water in rural areas is probably still close to the UNFPA estimate of 31% (UNFPA 1999:71).

The paradox of the periphery is evident in the case of environmental health. In the less-developed, peripheral nations, environmental health is often better in the thinly settled areas outside the national core, even if no special services are provided. This is because there tends to be less crowding in rural areas than in urban areas, so reliance on streams and simple waste disposal methods is adequate, while the infrastructure in urban areas is likely to be inadequate and a greater source of contamination than are the rudimentary facilities.

## Globalization and Health Services

As stated at the beginning of this paper, modern Western medicine has spread throughout the world, and is available virtually everywhere, although the level of service available varies. Medical services in less- and least-developed countries are generally limited and vastly inferior to those in more-developed countries. It is interesting to consider that few people, in either more- or less developed nations, would expect them to be otherwise. While this is largely a perceived difference between rich and poor, the role of globalization as a determinant of health services is sometimes overlooked.

Since Western medicine has been adopted as the universal standard, most less-developed countries receive development assistance to help support their health programmes. In most cases, their health programs are determined by global health policies, set by the World Health Organization and other health sector donors. This can lead to management conflicts and can also compromise the appropriateness of health service delivery. Donor assistance fosters dependency and imposes conditions such as requirements that donor policies are adopted and drugs and consultants are sourced from donor countries. It also contributes to fragmentation of activities and conflict in health policies and programmes due to different political and financial agendas. Some countries may have in excess of 100 donor projects operating outside the national health management structure, with the poorest countries tending to have the most fragmentation and the least sustainable systems (Berer 2002:10).

Core/periphery relations also influence the choice of health care model adopted by less-developed countries. Since the evolution of Western curative health care played a pivotal role in the health transition in industrialized countries, it was widely assumed by colonial powers that this was the best model of health care for developing countries, including small island nations such as those of the Pacific. The more-developed countries set international health policy and standards, and provide significant amounts of health assistance, so the Western medical package tended to be accepted uncritically by health officials in the Pacific. For example, a distinctive feature of the US-designed health systems introduced to the Northern Pacific was a sharp division into preventive and curative services. Although this ensured that at least some attention was given to preventive medicine, the rigid separation of function led to inefficiencies in the provision of health care, especially since there were few trained personnel. Opportunities to provide preventive care, such as advice on nutrition or disease prevention or counselling in family planning for high-parity mothers, were lost because such care was outside the brief of those providing curative services (McMurray and Smith 2001).

While this separation has become less rigid since the mid-1980s, when the importance of primary health care was officially recognized and promoted throughout the world (World Health Organization 1978), countries still face the problem of how to share scarce resources between potentially high-cost but necessary curative services and low-cost but vastly more cost-effective preventive strategies.

Most Pacific nations have very small populations with low percentages of the labor force in formal employment. Limited revenue from taxation means few resources to devote to health and insufficient numbers to support health insurance schemes. One very positive aspect of globalization is that most Pacific nations receive substantial amounts of development assistance to supplement their health budgets. Usually this comes from the countries with which they had or have a colonial or economic relationship, or from multilateral agencies funded by such countries.

Because of their close connections with other countries, however, self-sufficiency in medicine has never really been contemplated for these peripheral nations. Most small Pacific countries have an internal hierarchy of medical facilities, with hospitals based in main centres, while outer areas are served by health centres and aid posts, the latter often little more than a first-aid kit or treatments administered by someone with only a few weeks training. The general aim is to provide basic services to the level national resources permit, and to rely on developed countries for any advanced treatment. Each nation determines the allocation of resources between in-country facilities and evacuations. Even one of the most highly developed in the Pacific region, the French overseas territory of New Caledonia, evacuates chronic cases and those requiring advanced treatment, most to Australia or France. Although this strategy does give some people access to higher-level medicine, it inevitably means that the poorest countries and poor and remote residents within countries are disadvantaged. Those living in remote or outlying regions, especially, are unlikely to receive adequate health care when it is needed urgently because they may be unable to afford or survive a trip to a main center.

Whereas some Pacific countries such as Papua New Guinea and the Fiji Islands are large enough and sufficiently well resourced to offer a reasonable standard of hospital services, if only basic surgery, others are less fortunate. For example, despite its remoteness, Kiribati has only the most basic medical capability, and most resources are at the Tarawa hospital, which is readily accessible to only around 40% of the population. An Australian specialist who visited Tarawa in 2001 to train nurses in emergency care informed the author that the only emergency equipment at the hospital was one respirator, which was not operational at the time. Evacuations are mostly via the twice-weekly commercial flights, since the cost of chartering a plane from a neighboring country such as the Fiji Islands is prohibitive, and medical insurance is unavailable. In view of these conditions, it is hardly surprising that in Kiribati most major injuries are fatal, and generally only expatriates and politicians are evacuated for medical treatment.

Similarly, although the Marshall Islands are much better off because of substantial inflows of US aid, and equipped with two hospitals to serve a smaller and more concentrated population, medical evacuations absorb a significant amount of the annual health budget. The dilemma of how to allocate scarce resources so as to achieve optimum health care is a major issue for Pacific health managers. Although it may seem a very harsh view, it is not hard to understand the comment of a Nauruan official who remarked to the author that palliative care is a luxury Nauru cannot afford, and terminally ill people should not receive any medical treatment.[2]

In addition to the limited nature of facilities, an ongoing problem in all peripheral countries, including those of the Pacific, and in peripheral areas within countries, is the loss of skilled health personnel. Migration of skilled personnel in the health sector from peripheral to core areas is a worldwide problem. This is largely a consequence of global forces that concentrate opportunities in core areas. These factors affect most professions, including teaching, as well as the medical professions (Connell 2001; Voigt-Graf 2002). Lower salaries, inferior working conditions, smaller facilities with fewer opportunities for promotion, and increased responsibility are some of the many factors that encourage skilled migration from peripheral to core areas. Core places offer better career opportunities, better facilities in the workplace, and more lifestyle options. Of particular importance is that health professionals receive more support from colleagues in core areas, whereas in peripheral areas they may be obliged to work alone, offer a wide range of services, and be held solely responsibility for patient care. Often, however, the motive for migration of health professionals is simply a desire to live where their children can receive the best education and their spouse can find employment (Connell 2001).

Although virtually all Pacific countries have shortages of trained health professionals, migration of health professionals occurs both internationally and intra-nationally. The international flow is mainly to Pacific Rim countries and also from low income to higher-income countries within the Pacific. For example, Fijian nurses migrate to Northern Pacific countries to obtain higher salaries. This is paralleled by intranational movements to core areas because of the difficulty of retaining staff in underdeveloped peripheral areas (SPC 2001:21).

Shortages of trained personnel mean that lower level facilities have more untrained or informally trained staff. Although this is intended as an efficiency measure, it can contribute to misuse of skilled personnel. In Papua New Guinea, for example, a frequently mentioned problem during the early 1990s was that the hierarchical nature of medical training contributed to wastage rather than efficiency. Because of the wide disparity in skills between fully trained health professionals and aid post and clinic staff, clients attending clinics insisted on being treated by

---

[2] Although it had one of the world's highest per capita incomes during the 1980s, Nauru has almost exhausted the phosphate reserves that made it wealthy, while provision for the future was generally inadequate. At the time of this writing, Nauru was having extreme difficulty meeting the cost of basic services: health, education, water, sanitation, and energy generation.

the most highly trained practitioner, refusing services from less qualified personnel. Although trained doctors were in short supply, they had difficulty delegating even minor procedures, such as dressing small wounds, even though the National Health Plan stipulated that "no person should be engaged to perform a task if a lesser trained, lesser paid worker could be employed to carry out that task adequately" (Papua New Guinea 1986:258).

Another consequence of the globalization of health is that senior health officials in peripheral countries are constantly travelling overseas to attend meetings. In small countries, the most qualified professionals are likely to be drafted into management, which itself contributes to wastage of skills. When, in addition to this wastage, they are frequently away from their desks participating in regional policy meetings on a wide range of subjects, in-country management capacity may be compromised.

The impact of globalization is also evident in the management of infectious disease in peripheral countries. One very positive impact has been global intervention programs such as Oral Rehydration Salts to prevent fatal dehydration of children with diarrhoeal infections, HIV/AIDS prevention programs and the Expanded Programme of Immunisation, mentioned in the introduction to this paper. This program, initially to immunize children against six major diseases (TB, measles, polio, diphtheria, tetanus, and pertussis) was possibly the most cost-effective primary healthcare intervention ever devised. It came about because of worldwide concern about infant and child mortality in less-developed countries, and although funded by more-developed countries, was delivered to children in both more- and less-developed countries. In Papua New Guinea, however, where pneumonia is a major cause of infant mortality, doctors had difficulty persuading local authorities to add the *Haemophilus influenza* B (Hib) vaccine to the program, because at that time the global standard was presumed to be sufficient (personal communication, Goroka Hospital medical staff, April 1998).

## Impact of Globalization on Lifestyles

The third major mechanism through which globalization impacts health is its promotion of particular lifestyles and lifestyle habits that increase the risk of noncommunicable diseases. Modernization has brought new technologies and a wider range of goods to peripheral countries, as well as urban lifestyles and wage employment. The polarizing forces of globalization, however, mean that in most peripheral countries the demand for modern sector employment exceeds the availability of jobs (McMurray and Smith 2001). This means that not all people have the option of enjoying the benefits of modernization. Many, especially those in urban environments, have access only to inferior goods and limited opportunities, and experience more of the unhealthy aspects of modernization than its benefits. This includes consuming poor diets because healthy diets are unavailable or unaffordable, taking insufficient exercise, smoking and drinking to excess. While such lifestyle habits are by no means unique to peripheral areas, peripheral groups in both more- and less-developed countries are especially likely to adopt them. Coyne (2001) writes of Pacific urban dwellers that they live "an infectious lifestyle ... indirect, insidious and generational, slowly transmitted and resulting in equally slow morbidity and incessant mortality" (p. 6).

It is widely recognized in developed countries that economically and socially disadvantaged people are more likely to have unhealthy lifestyles, whereas educated people are more likely to be aware of health risks and live a healthier lifestyle (Hetzel and McMichael 1987). It is not just education *per se* that makes the difference, but the capacity to live a healthy lifestyle. Since the educated are more likely to be employed or to have other economic advantages, they have a wider range of lifestyle options. Heavy drinking, smoking, overeating, underexercising, and unsafe sexual activity occur among both privileged and disadvantaged groups, in both more- and less-developed countries. The privileged have a greater capacity to choose, however, even if they do not always make the wisest choices.

The factors affecting lifestyle choice are numerous and complex and include both social and psychological factors. Even when their circumstances appear optimum, some people may adopt unhealthy lifestyle habits. From the perspective of globalization, however, two factors emerge as the most important determinants of lifestyle among peripheral groups: urbanization and changing food choices. The impact of these factors can be seen clearly in the Pacific.

## Urbanization

Urban poverty and displacement from the means of subsistence production is a worldwide phenomenon. The consequences for those who are marginalized by globalization, however, are very different for urban dwellers who have sufficient income to purchase all their needs. In developing countries, populations who migrate to urban areas for various reasons, whether to find wage jobs, to share in the benefits of modernization or even simply to flee political unrest, are at risk of poor nutrition, substandard housing and unsanitary surroundings. Their capacity to live a healthy lifestyle is largely determined by their ability to earn cash incomes. When their incomes are low, people have no choice but to purchase the cheapest food, which tends to be the least nutritious.

The burgeoning of urban areas is one of the most obvious manifestations of globalization in the Pacific. The main cause is the demand for wage employment to enable the purchase of modern goods, and the attraction of a busy and exciting urban lifestyle. While there is also increasing population pressure in rural areas, urban pull factors are much stronger than rural push factors. In most Pacific countries, urban populations are increasing at least twice as fast as rural populations (SPC 2000). Despite this, employment opportunities are growing only slowly in urban areas in most of the Pacific, so labor force participation rates are low and unemployment rates are high. In the Fiji Islands, for example, in 2000, there were five people of working age for every formal sector job, and in the Solomon Islands, 7.9 (UNDP 2001). In Papua New Guinea, only 270,000 out of about 3 million people of working age are in formal wage employment (Hess and Imbun 2002).

School dropouts in particular have difficulty finding employment. In Samoa, it is estimated that around 4,500 students leave school each year, of whom about 1000 find work or continue to higher education, while the rest are employed in subsistence work or unemployed (Government of Western Samoa 1997). In Papua New Guinea around 40,000 students leave the education system each year, while another 10,000 or more who did not get into the education system at all reach working age. Only about 5,000 find wage employment (Tautea 1997:185).

The health implications of urbanization without equivalent growth in employment opportunities are far-reaching for both young and old. Poverty and lack of purchasing power, combined with changing dietary patterns, described below, have major implications for health. Unemployment and poverty are widely recognized as causes of stress, and stress is associated with smoking, drinking to excess, and substance abuse. Smoking and drinking to excess are common in disadvantaged communities everywhere, including the Pacific.

Although some people strictly refrain from drinking and smoking, and leading religious denominations, including Church of the Latter Day Saints and Seventh Day Adventists, oppose these habits, smoking and drinking to excess are common in Pacific countries (Coyne 2001). Although adult Pacific women are less likely than men to drink in excess, smoking is increasingly acceptable and common among women. Studies of Tonga and Vanuatu, for example, have shown that smoking, alcohol abuse, and use of narcotics is widespread among both male and female adolescents (UNICEF 2000, 2001), despite social condemnation of such behaviour and numerous health campaigns to discourage it. In-depth research in these countries showed that a major cause of this behavior is scarcity of employment opportunities for school dropouts. Even though they are well aware of the harmful effects of substance abuse, young people have little incentive to take a long-term view of their health and welfare when their future appears uncertain and insecure. Risk-taking with substances, sometimes extremely toxic substances such as methylated spirits, datura, and psylocibin, has become the accepted way of building self-esteem in the absence of other avenues. For some, brewing alcohol has become a time-filling activity that substitutes for employment, with peer groups meeting early in the day to spend many hours brewing yeast-based concoctions before drinking copious amounts (McMurray 2001, 2002).

An associated problem arising from lack of opportunity is crime, especially in peripheral countries that have also experienced political instability, such as Fiji, Papua New Guinea, the Solomon Islands, and Vanuatu. In Papua New Guinea urban areas, where substance abuse is also rife, substantial numbers of those who cannot find work have turned to crime as a substitute for employment. In addition to housebreaking and robbery, violent crime, including murder, assault and rape and pack rape are endemic in urban areas (Chand and Levantis 1998). Many of the perpetrators are youths working in gangs organized by older crime bosses. Crime increases the risk of injury and sexually transmitted infections (STIs) and also inhibits the development of business and tourism that could increase employment opportunities.

## Changing Food Preferences and Options

An important aspect of globalization has been the promotion and marketing of foods from abroad, especially Western foods. Imported food is widely available in the Pacific, and Western methods of cooking, especially frying, have become very popular. For some, Western food is a treat or a luxury, but urban dwellers who have become separated from traditional lifestyles and displaced from the means of subsistence rely to a considerable extent on imported food. Since incomes tend to be low, most families subsist on the cheapest food items. In the Pacific, this means white bread or polished white rice as the staple food, supplemented with low-grade fatty cuts of meat such as frozen turkey tails and mutton flaps. Sugary soft drinks and sweet biscuits are relatively cheap and ubiquitous. In atoll countries, especially, perishables that are not produced locally, including meat, fresh fruit and vegetables, are shipped or air-freighted, so retailers sell them for high prices and stock only small quantities to minimize spoilage.

The following extracts from focus group discussions with Marshallese urban residents conducted in 1997 show how urban living has affected their diets and health.

> Woman (aged 30-40): Marshallese eat mainly rice, bread, chicken, beef, tuna, and other canned meats. These are the cause of our health problems today,

the reason for so many types of illnesses. A typical Marshallese meal consists of boiled rice, meat, and perhaps a pot of tea. Not many people think or bother to add other food items such as cabbage or papaya. Sometimes it may be that they have not acquired a taste for cabbage and sometimes they cannot afford the cost of cabbage.

Woman (aged 30-40): Residing on Majuro (the atoll on which the seat of government is located) prevents our having access to suitable traditional food. Sometimes traditional foods may be found in the stores, but we do not possess the financial means to purchase them. While prices in stores are continually going up, the minimum wage has remained constant. This is another problem. Now our government has been reducing the work force.

Woman (aged 50+): A place like Rita (a densely settled urban district of Majuro) has no pandanus, and very few coconuts or breadfruit trees. There are not enough places to grow these plants. People on the outer islands have healthy skins from the food they eat. But people on Majuro have scabies and other skin diseases and many are also night-blind.

Man (aged 30-40): We not only consume only imported food stuffs, but are restricted to consuming only what we can afford. But now the information we are getting from the Ministries of Health and Social Welfare is that these types of food are not only non-nutritious, but can also lead to health problems if consumed in large amounts. But what are we to do if these are all we can afford?

Woman (aged 50+): When we get sick we go to see the doctor and are told we need to eat cabbages and other greens to help us control our diabetes, but the problem is, where do we get the money to buy the cabbage and other greens? And where can one find space to plant on Majuro? If we were living on our own island, then we could plant a garden. People on the outer islands do not have such high rates of diabetes and cancer as we on Majuro, and they live longer.

Woman (aged 50+): Even if you do have a place to grow these foods in Majuro, people steal what you plant. That's how much people realize our own foods are better for us than foreign food.

Man (aged 50+): Living in the urban centres is difficult because you need money to survive. I cannot get what I need to survive if I do not have a job. And since I do not own the property I live on, if I want a coconut, I need money to buy it. If I lived on my own island I would not need money to survive. In the urban areas, if you have only one person employed in say, a household of 15 people, about the only thing that person can buy is rice. A small amount can feed all members of the household. In order to buy better food, that person would have to earn more money.

Woman (aged 50+): Money, or the lack of it, is the root of all our social problems today. If people had enough money they would not have to worry so much and would be able to buy all the healthy and nutritious food their bodies require. This is why we have so many murder cases, especially among young, unemployed men. They may want something but do not have the means to obtain it so they get drunk and kill and rob someone, so they can buy whatever they want.

(McMurray and Smith 2001)

Even in countries where abundant local produce is grown and sold at local markets, such as the small Pacific nation of Tonga, urban families may not have the means to purchase a good diet. In February 2003, for example, high school graduate clerks in the Tongan public earned in the range P2,000-P5,000 [3] annually, with the graduate entry salary around P7,000, and middle-level managers earning perhaps P10,000. In the Nuku'alofa market, fruit and vegetables were not cheap, with taro P1.00 per kilo and yams and sweet potatoes up to P3.00 per kilo. Tomatoes cost P2.00 per kilo, a very small cabbage P2.00 each, and pawpaw P1.00 each. In the supermarket, uncooked white rice cost P2.20 per kilo, white bread P1.00 per loaf, and fatty mutton flaps and turkey tails P4.90 and P4.40 per kilo, while minced beef and lean meat cost P11.00 per kilo and upward. Tinned goods and other foodstuffs had prices comparable to those in Australia and New Zealand, where incomes are at least four times those in Tonga. While families with several wage earners, or a home garden and a small fishing dinghy had the means to live well, urban families depending on a single pay packet were obliged to select the cheapest food items.

Consumption of diets high in fat and sugar contributes to obesity and diabetes mellitus (Coyne 2001). This is exacerbated by lack of exercise, especially in adults. Pacific society generally requires women to move sedately and wear modest clothing at all times, so most women get little exercise when they are no longer required to perform the work associated with growing, gathering, and catching food. Moreover, although daytime temperatures are usually uncomfortably high, access to indoor exercise facilities is extremely limited or nonexistent, and even walking along the road in urban areas is difficult when there are few footpaths and heavy traffic. This manifests as a high prevalence of obesity, among women especially. Studies carried out in the Fiji Islands, Marshall Islands, New Caledonia, Cook Islands, French Polynesia, Tonga, Samoa, American Samoa, and Nauru during the 1990s found from 30% (Fiji Islands) to 80% (Nauru) of women were obese, and from 20% (Cook Islands) to 80% (Nauru) of men (Coyne 2001).

The negative impact of urban lifestyles on health is clearly evident in that the incidence of early onset NCDs is lower in the outer islands and remote areas within Pacific Island nations where traditional foods are consumed and people are engaged in subsistence agriculture and food

---

[3] In February 2003, one painga = approximately 50 cents US.

gathering (Coyne 2001). On the other hand, those living outside urban areas may have inferior access to health services. The extent to which this offsets the advantages varies from country to country and depends on living standards and the level of development of health infrastructure. In Papua New Guinea, for example, health services are very limited and even inaccessible for many in remote and isolated villages, while NCDs are only just becoming a concern in urban areas. Since death from infectious diseases and untreated injury and trauma tends to be more prevalent in rural than in urban areas, in that country health is generally better in urban than in rural areas. In contrast, in Marshall Islands, there is less risk of infectious disease. Although health services are generally rudimentary in outer atolls, most people can access them and can be taken to urban health facilities if necessary, while most children are immunized. As a consequence, health is generally better outside urban areas where people consume traditional diets and practice traditional lifestyles. This is even truer of Samoa and Tonga, where health infrastructures are more developed and more accessible and living conditions generally better, but the major negative impacts on health are lifestyle factors associated with urban living.

## Conclusion

The preceding discussion has shown that while globalization has had a substantial positive impact on population by fostering improvements in environmental health and the spread of modern medicine, these benefits are not uniform or universal. Health facilities tend to be inferior in peripheral areas and peripheral populations are less likely to have access to good medical care. Moreover, globalization has reduced the capacity of peripheral people to live a healthy lifestyle. In many peripheral societies, urbanization without industrialization or substantial employment generation has resulted in displacement from the means of subsistence production, coupled with an increasing lack of capacity to purchase nutritious foods. This has had very substantial negative impacts on lifestyles, especially in urban areas.

It is widely recognized by health authorities everywhere that most early-onset NCDs are readily preventable if healthy diets are consumed, smoking avoided, alcohol consumption kept to safe levels, and adequate exercise is obtained. For many, however, traditional foods have become difficult to obtain or less affordable than cheaper, less nutritious modern food, while the stress of living in an urban environment supports smoking and high levels of alcohol consumption. In addition, opportunities for exercise may be restricted by custom and by certain types of urban environment. These factors have resulted in a burgeoning of noncommunicable diseases in peripheral areas such as those of the Pacific.

It is clear from research focusing on young people in Kiribati, Vanuatu, and Tonga and from the comments of Marshallese residents that lack of knowledge about healthy lifestyle practices is not the main cause of high levels of noncommunicable diseases in these Pacific countries. Respondents in all age groups have been found to have a good understanding of the relationship of lifestyle and health. Despite this, in Pacific countries the efforts of national health programs and many donors to reduce adolescent and adult substance abuse have achieved relatively little so far. It is increasingly recognised by the people, by governments, and by donors that this situation exists because a major underlying cause is lack of opportunity, especially lack of opportunity to obtain satisfying employment. This is a direct consequence of the economic structure that has arisen as a consequence of globalization.

Although this paper has focused on examples from the small island nations of the Pacific, similar patterns can be observed in peripheral areas everywhere, including remote and economically depressed areas within the most industrialized countries. A distinctive feature of peripheral nations, however, is that because traditional lifestyles tend to persist in rural areas, health is sometimes better outside urban areas. This paradox is a direct consequence of global forces that have led to urbanization without industrialization, idealization of Western lifestyles, and imports of cheap food, alcohol, and cigarettes. No matter how much is invested in health infrastructure, substantial improvements in the health of peripheral nations cannot be expected until their people are empowered and have the means to choose healthy lifestyles.

# References

BERER, MARGE
2002       "Health Sector Reforms: Implications for Sexual and Reproductive Health Services." *Reproductive Health Matters* 10:6-15.
CHAND, SATISH AND THEODORE LEVANTIS
1998       "The Nexus Between Crime and Productivity in Papua New Guinea." Pp. 33-46 in *Productivity Performance in the South Pacific*, edited by S. Chand. National Centre for Development Studies. (Pacific Policy Paper 31). Canberra: Asia Pacific Press.
CONNELL, JOHN
2001       "The Migration of Skilled Health Personnel in the Pacific Region." Study commissioned by the World Health Organization, Western Pacific Regional Office, Manila, Phillipines.
FRENK, JULIO, THOMAS FREJKA, JOSE L. BOBADILLA, CLAUDIO STERN, JAIME SEPULVEDA AND MARCO JOSE
1989       "The Epidemiologic Transition in Latin America." Paper presented at the International Union for the Scientific Study of Population meeting, September 20-27, New Delhi, India.

GOVERNMENT OF WESTERN SAMOA
1997    *Western Samoa Population Policy*. Apia: Population Policy Technical Committee.
HENDERSON, R.H.
1984    "The Expanded Programme on Immunization of the World Health Organiza-
        tion." *Reviews of Infectious Diseases* 6:475-479.
HESS, MICHAEL AND BENEDICT IMBUN
2002    "Papua New Guinea Human Resources Management Country Paper." Singa-
        pore: APEC Secretariat.
HETZEL, BASIL AND TONY MCMICHAEL
1987    *The LS Factor: Lifestyle and Health*. Ringwood, Australia: Penguin.
INTER FINANCIAL
1999    "Port Moresby Water Supply Upgrade Company Funded." *PacNews*, June 22,
        p. 71.
KINSELLA, KEVIN
1992    "Population and Health Transitions." International Population Reports.
        P95/92-2, Washington: US Department of Commerce.
MCGEE, TERRENCE G.
1967    *The Southeast Asian City*. London: Bell.
MCMURRAY, CHRISTINE
2002    "Report on Qualitative Research on Substance Abuse Among Young People
        in Kiribati." Pacific Action for Health Project. Secretariat of the Pacific
        Community, Noumea, New Caledonia. Unpublished report.
MCMURRAY, CHRISTINE AND ROY H. SMITH
2001    *Diseases of Globalization*. London: Earthscan.
MINISTRY OF SOCIAL POLICY
2001a   *The Social Report*. Wellington, New Zealand: Ministry of Social Policy.
PAPUA NEW GUINEA
1986    *Papua New Guinea National Health Plan 1986-1990*. Port Moresby: Department of
        Health.
SPC (SECRETARIAT OF THE PACIFIC COMMUNITY)
2000a   "Oceania Population 2000 (wall poster)." Noumea: Demography/Population
        Programme, Secretariat of the Pacific Community.
2001b   *Population and Development in the Pacific*. Report on the Seminar on Population and
        Development, March 26-30, Demography/Population Programme Noumea,
        New Caledonia: Secretariat of the Pacific Community.
TAUTEA, LAUATU
1997    "Human Resource Dilemma: The Missing Link?" Pp. 176-187 in *Papua New
        Guinea: A 20/20 Vision*, edited by I. Temu. National Centre for Development
        Studies. (Pacific Policy Paper 20). Canberra: The Australian National Univer-
        sity.
VOIGT-GRAF, CARMEN AND KERRY LYONS
2002    "The Migration of Secondary School Teachers in Fiji: Taking Stock and
        Introducing a Research Agenda." Pp. 33-42 in *International APMRN Conference,
        Fiji 2002: Selected Papers Australia, Fiji, India, Indonesia, Japan, Korea, New Zealand,
        and Taiwan*, edited by K. Lyon and C. Voigt-Graf. Asia-Pacific Migration
        Research Network (Working Paper No. 12). Wollongong, Australia: APMRN,
        University of Wollongong.
UNICEF (UNITED NATIONS CHILDREN'S FUND)
2000    *The State of Health Behaviour and Lifestyle of Pacific Youth: Vanuatu Report*. Suva, Fiji:
        UNICEF Pacific.
2001    *The State of Health Behaviour and Lifestyle of Pacific Youth: Kingdom of Tonga Report*.
        Suva, Fiji: UNICEF Pacific.
UNITED NATIONS
1982    *Levels and Trends in Mortality Since 1950*. New York: Department of International
        Economic and Social Affairs.
UNDP (UNITED NATIONS DEVELOPMENT PROGRAMME)
1999    *Pacific Human Development Report 1999, Creating Opportunities*. Suva, Fiji: UNDP.
2001    *Sustainable Livelihoods*. (http://www.undp.com.fj).
UNFPA (UNITED NATIONS POPULATION FUND)
1999    *State of the World's Population*. New York.

# Health Transition and Globalization in the Pacific: Vestiges of Colonialism?

SITALEKI A. FINAU[*], IRIS L. WAINIQOLO[*]
AND GIUSEPPE G. CUBONI[*]

## ABSTRACT

This paper disaggregates the various transitions that led to the so-called health transition in the Pacific. It challenges the notion of unified health transition and looks at changes that shaped the health of Pacificans. It examines the velocity (speed and direction) and the framework with which contemporary discussions of health transition in the Pacific have taken place. This is an effort to look at how health transition is more about power imbalance than about morbidity and mortality. We argue, first, that changes in the health of Pacificans are about power imbalances brought about by globalization, imperialism, and colonialism. We also describe the multiple transitions that need to be taken into account in understanding the health changes among Pacificans. In the end, we suggest a range of alternate ways of viewing the processes of change in the Pacific.

## Introduction

Health transition and globalization are assimilative frameworks. They imply a change from a Beginning, "alpha," to an End, "omega": the transition points are all those between "alpha" and "omega."

There are multiple stages in the health transition for different populations and places. What these populations have in common is that they are

[*] The School of Public Health and Primary Care, Fiji School of Medicine, Suva, Fiji.

in transit. However, the health of all populations, unavoidably, changes with time, but, in some countries, such changes are called transitions, while, in others, such changes have no special name. What is not certain is whether the transition is for the better or for the worse. It is also uncertain how a population may recognize that it has transited, that is, it has reached "omega." These considerations suggest that the linear model for explaining the cause of changes in human well-being may be false.

## Health and the Pacific

Health has been defined in the Pacific, largely as the World Health Organization (WHO) has promoted it as the "world's consensus": "Health is a state of complete physical, mental and social well being, and not merely the absence of or disease infirmity" (Finau, Tukuitonga, and Finau 2000). This ideal state is akin to happiness. Some Pacificans, in their definition, have included relationship with the environment, people and their ancestors (Finau 1996). The inclusion of ancestors challenges the medical notion that death is the end. The Pacific notion is that death may be seen as transitional, and more a translocation to another level of being. Therefore, to measure health transition in terms of mortality will reflect terminally and negatively on death and transition per se. It does not address Pacificans' quality of life.

The Pacific is multicultural, multiethnic, and comprises a multitude of small populations in ecological microcosms (Crocombe 2000; World Bank 1993). Each population group is unique in language, physique, culture, and lifestyle. Therefore, the pan-pacific notions of Pacific peoples, Pacific islanders and, lately, Pacificans, in general, have attempted to assimilate all peoples from the Pacific islands to the prevailing economy of scale (Finau, Tukuitonga, and Finau 2000). This assumes that a defined minimum scale exists for economic efficiency. Whatever that may be, it is undefined and especially so for dispersed small islands. This smallness, isolation, and uniqueness have not been protective towards health transition and globalization.

Changing health status, mostly measured in morbidity and mortality, is inevitable over time and during the life span (Lewis and Rapaport 1995; Taylor, Lewis, and Levy 1989). This change varies with the variable risks and vulnerabilities, at personal and community levels, and how they interact with the physical, social, mental, and spiritual environments. Changing health status not only should include morbidity and mortality, but also should measure wellness, satisfaction with life, and happiness. Similarly, health transition should include these living dimensions, not just count the sick and the dead.

Health transition is a framework that was developed for describing and explaining the shifts in the patterns and causes of death due to interactions with the above dimensions of health (Beaglehole and Bonita 1997). It is based on the measurement of death and the reasons for such deaths. It is not based on health, well-being and happiness. Therefore, some have called this framework mortality, demographic, or epidemiological transition. These definitions were given a sectorial direction as "the change from high fertility and high mortality, from mostly infectious diseases in traditional societies to low fertility, and low mortality from mostly non-communicable diseases in modern societies." The speed of this change has not been specified.

This definition of health transition has basically stated that traditional societies must be modernized (Lewis and Rapaport 1995). This concept has become synonymous with occidentalization, even though some oriental countries (e.g., Japan) have had accelerated transit to the modern pattern of death (Beaglehole and Bonita 1997). Pacificans, apparently, have to follow these steps or periods of health transition (Oman 1971), which are as follows:

- Era of pestilence and famine, with high mortality especially among the young.
- Era of receding pandemics, with mixed causes of mortality among the middle-age groups (<50 yrs).
- Era of non-communicable diseases, with chronic problems and death at old age (>55 yrs).

These stages have not taken into account the current substantial youth mortality from war, suicide, violence, and injuries (Beaglehole and Bonita 1997; Kassalow 2001). The health transition framework cannot account for the reemergence of infectious diseases in modern societies (e.g., tuberculosis, cholera, diphtheria), and the increase of drug resistant infections (e.g., Gonorrhea, MRSA infections, malaria) (Kassalow 2001).

## Imperialism and the Pacific

In the last four or five centuries, imperialism has been one of the most powerful forces in operation: exploiting colonies, oppressing indigenous populations, and compromising native civilizations. Imperialism is the process where the dominant politicoeconomic interests of one nation are lauded over those of another country or people. The dominant nation penetrates and transforms the land, labor, raw materials and markets of another people for its own enrichment (Parenti 1995). The subject of imperialism is one that is ignored and, thus, seldom addressed in any serious manner. According to Parenti (1995), imperialism, when not ignored, has been put forward in a very "sanitized" or cushioned manner.

For example, empires are labeled as commonwealths; colonies become territories; and military interventions and invasions are seen as issues of national security, all for the maintenance of stability in a country or region.

Imperialism and colonialism involve the systematic accumulation of capital or wealth through organized exploitation of labor and penetration of overseas markets. It must be noted that the central theme of imperialism is always to expand and accumulate capital. Such expansionism has been described as a "bourgeoisie that chases the whole surface of the globe. It must nestle everywhere, settle everywhere, establish connections everywhere ... it creates a world after its own image" (Parenti 1995). The expansionists forcibly fragment, change, and assimilate the colonized with a foreign paradigm. This amounts to be transition from self-sufficiency to employer-controlled wage earners; from localized subsistence economies to the global market economy; from self-employed to foreign-controlled employment; and from autonomous regions to centralized autocracies (Carew-Reid 1989; World Bank 1993).

Prior to colonial contact, the traditional Pacific cultures were mainly subsistence-based, as determined by their local environments. The cultures, beliefs, and practices were focused mainly on meeting their basic needs for survival and maintaining social cohesion within their communal settings. Pacificans were not individualistic but, rather, they depended on each other for their survival and for security. Accumulation of wealth was discouraged, and equitable distribution of goods and services through sharing and reciprocal giving was encouraged. The capital goods and sacred treasures were the land and the people. The Pacificans believed that they were the guardians of the land, and that the land was the source of their very being, identity, and history. Therefore, the land was held in high regard, as being as sacred as the gods they worshipped (Ravuvu 1995).

The first contact of the Pacificans with European imperialism took place in the early nineteenth century, with the "colonialization" of most Pacific territories (Bellwood 1979; Denoon et al. 1997). The accepted European ideology of colonial rule in the 1920s and 1930s was that their work brought huge benefits to the islanders. Colonial officials believed that they had a duty to take control of islanders' affairs for their own good, thus the proverbial "white man's burden." Understanding colonial government policies in the Pacific requires, first, a grasp of the ideological foundations that led to the formulation and implementation of those colonial policies.

The colonizers invented the concept of "the Native," a category embracing all those who were non-Europeans. According to the colonizers, the Native lacked "European virtues," such as application of foresight. A native's mind worked in mysterious ways. For example, the Methodist mission chairman in Fiji, in 1923, cautioned a colleague to "take the native mind into consideration" when attempting to give responsibilities to Fijians (Denoon et al. 1997). The same attitude is seen in the case of a governor of New Guinea, who put his fears on paper in 1919, in defense of corporal punishment (Johnstone 1920). The statements below demonstrates the prejudices of the time:

1. The Native is a primitive being, with no well-developed sense of duty or responsibility. A full belly and comfortable bed are his two chief pre-occupations.
2. On most plantations and centers of native labor, there is an enormous preponderance of males who are, on the whole, well fed and in robust health. Where there are the white women and children, this is a danger.
3. The Native frequently mistakes kindness for weakness.
4. Corporal punishment does not have any brutalizing effect on natives, any more than the average schoolboy. With a native, as an animal, correction must be of a deterrent nature. Would a man imprison his horse for offering to bite him?
5. Calaboose (jail) is the native's paradise, especially the calaboose run by humane officials (Lewis and Rapaport 1995).

There were many other self-serving imperialist theories that were put forth, all belittling the indigenous people and promoting the idea of "cultural backwardness." They also used this notion in order to justify their act of enslaving and assimilating indigenous people (Parenti 1995).

Based on these colonial policies, transition and globalization were rampant even then. Only now it is globally legitimized and more organized. It is still beyond the power and influence of Pacificans. The fact that the developed nations are still dictating to Pacificans how to live in the Pacific demonstrates the arrogance of imperialism.

## Globalization and the Pacific Economics

Colonialism and capitalism focus on mass-production with an export emphasis. The two forces regulated and promoted the incorporation of small Pacific economies into the global economy. This meant that localized village economies, which sustained the majority of Pacificans, needed to change to an emphasis on cash and export. These same villages were required to supply labor and cash crops, and the imperialists decided and dictated how these sectors should interact. They took over the decisions on the following questions:

- Who was to own the land?
- Who was to do the work?
- Who was to supply the capital?

- What was to be the balance between the interests of the indigenes and those of settlers?
- Were the villages to be sources of wage labor, or places of direct export production?
- How far was tradition to be preserved?
- Where would the labor be deployed?

These questions demonstrate not only colonial imperialism but also, the expansion of a capitalist economic order (Denoon et al. 1997). Globalization is the latest label for capitalism, colonialism, and imperialism expansions combined. Commentators of the Western world view this as "a new era of unprecedented opportunity," opening up for the world capitalist class. The main idea behind globalization is that, the world becomes a global village, under the doctrines and practices of capitalism. This means that capital flow would transfer, with technology and the teaching of proper work habits, to the "poor, backward nations" that will thus be made rich. This is an updated version of the "white man's burden" (*What is Globalization?* 2002).

According to the Western world's "development theory" or "modernization theory," the introduction of Western investments to backward economic sectors of poor nations will, eventually, create a more prosperous economy. However, in reality, the opposite has been happening in that there has been no convergence between rich and poor nations. What has emerged is an intensely exploitative form of capitalism, where a relatively small, elite network of international corporations dominate the global economy and make huge profits in the face of worsening economic conditions in "Third World" countries or the "global South" (Parenti 1995). The two agents of globalization, the World Bank (WB) and the International Monetary Fund (IMF), demonstrate a classical example of this exploitation. These two agencies are the chosen avenues by which the political and business elites of the Northern countries operate to rule the global economy and to dictate to the rest of the world how those countries should be run and how the indigenes should live their lives according to imperialists' paradigms.

WB and IMF, two of the worlds most powerful financial institutions, are empowered and led, by the U.S.A, United Kingdom, Japan, Germany, France, Canada, and Italy (the so-called G7). They function as financial bodies to "revive and help pay off" outstanding debts, and to fund infrastructural projects of countries, so as to sustain economic growth and to alleviate poverty. In 1992, the President of the World Bank, Lewis Preston said that the main challenge of the World Bank is sustainable poverty reduction. He went on to note that this challenge is identified as the benchmark by which the institution's performance will be measured. It is the benchmark by which our performance, as a development institution, will be measured" (Madeley, Sullivan, and Woodroffe 1994). However, the extent to which this benchmark is achieved is a matter of concern to most developing countries that have sought their assistances.

For example, in order to access funds from WB and IMF, a country requesting a loan must first agree to policy changes and economic system restructuring by adopting Structural Adjustment Programs (SAPs). These SAPs, by orienting economies toward generating foreign exchange, are designed to ensure that debtor countries pay up, often at the expense of local programs. The outcomes of this SAP approach have not been favorable in most of the countries where they have been applied. SAP activities have increased poverty; have exacerbated the suffering of millions; and have created a net flow of wealth from the developing world to the industrialized countries, further enriching them and their multinational corporations. Table 1 shows the SAPs and their impacts that have reinforced the current trend of maintaining the rich at the expense of the poor (Global Exchange 2002).

## Transitions in the Pacific

Health transitions are a framework based on the outcomes of living (Lewis and Rapaport 1995; Taylor, Lewis, and Levy 1989). Therefore, for an understanding of the determinants and effects of health transition, the events preceding mortality need to be identified and discussed. Such an analysis will help to address the following questions:
- Is health transition inevitable?
- Can the velocity of health transition be changed?
- What are the determinants of health transition?

In the Pacific, many accelerated changes are taking place. Many of these contribute to health in different ways for different Pacificans. However, there are common themes that run through these societies in transition. These include the following:

**Economic transition:** The fundamental change here is the monetization of the economy, translating subsistence into globalization (Siwatibau 1995). Table 2 shows the variables that have changed, over time, at different velocities between different Pacificans (Delailomoloma et al. 1982; Hempenstall and Rutherford 1998; King 1991). These changes have taken place with interaction involving foreign imperial powers.

The emphasis on the economy of scale buried the interests of Pacificans through the law of averages. That is, the average reflects the most numerous rather than the minority. In addition, the expected trickle-down effect from the economy of scale assumes a finite absorptive capacity

# Table 1

## Impact of World Bank (WB) and International Monetary Fund (IMF) Policies on Poor Populations

| STRUCTURAL ADJUST-MENT PROGRAMS (IMF; WB) | IMPACT ON ELITE (Corporations, Investors, the Wealthy) | IMPACT ON POOR POPULATIONS |
|---|---|---|
| **Cut Social Spending:** Reduce expenditures on health, education, social services, etc. [IMF claims it is now making sure such spending goes up, but often claims that it is to put in place systems to collect fees.] | More debts are repaid, including those to WB and IMF. | Increased school fees force parents to pull children—usually girls—from school. Literacy rates go down. Poorly educated generations are not equipped for skilled jobs. Higher fees for medical services mean less treatment, more suffering, needless deaths. Women, already overburdened, must provide health care and look after family members. |
| **Shrink Government:** Reduce budget expense by trimming payrolls and programs. | Fewer government employees mean less capacity to monitor businesses' adherence to labor, environmental, and financial regulations. This frees up cash for debt service. | Massive layoffs occur in countries where government is often the largest employer. Makes people desperate to work at any wage. |
| **Increase Interest Rates:** to combat inflation, increase interest charged for credit and awarded savings. | Investors find such countries a profitable place to park cash, though they may pull it out at any moment. | Small farmers and businesses can't get capital to stay afloat. Small farmers sell land, work as tenants or move to worse lands. Businesses shut down, leaving workers unemployed. |
| **Eliminate Regulations on Foreign Ownership of Resources and Businesses.** | Multinational corporations can purchase, or start enterprises easily. Countries compete for foreign investments, by offering tax breaks, low wages, free trade zones, etc. Once in the country, corporations can turn to WTO for enforcement of "rights." | Control of entire sectors of economy can shift to foreign hands. Governments offer implicit pledges not to enforce labor and environmental laws. |

## Table 1

### (Continued)

| STRUCTURAL ADJUST-MENT PROGRAMS (IMF; WB) | IMPACT ON ELITE (Corporations, Investors, the Wealthy) | IMPACT ON POOR POPULATIONS |
|---|---|---|
| ***Cut Subsidies for Basic Goods:*** Reduce government spending to support reduced cost of bread, petroleum, etc. | Frees up money for debt payments. | Cost of items needed to survive is raised. Most frequent flashpoint for civil unrest. |
| ***Re-orient Economies from Subsistence to Exports:*** Give incentives for farmers to produce cash crops (coffee, cotton, etc.) for foreign markets, rather than food for domestic ones; encourage manufacturing to focus on simple assembly (often clothing) for export rather than manufacturing for own country; encourage extraction of valuable mineral resources. | Produces hard currency to pay off more debts. Law of supply and demand pushes down price of commodities, as more countries produce more, guaranteeing supply of low-cost products to export markets. Local competition is eliminated for multinational corporations. Availability of low-cost labor is increased. | Law of supply and demand pushes down price of commodities as more countries produce more, meaning local producers often lose money. Best lands are devoted to cash crops; poorer land is used for food crops, leading to soil erosion. Food security is threatened. Women are often relegated to gathering all food for family, while men work for cash. Country is made more dependent on imported food and manufactured goods. Forests and mineral resources (oil, copper, etc.) are over-exploited, leading to environmental destruction and displacement. |

Source: Global Economy Web page. (http://www.globalexchange.org/wbimf/facts.html).

for wealth of the bourgeoisie. However, the latter's large and expanding capacity to accumulate wealth minimizes the trickle down to Pacificans and the working class, thus creating the gap between the poor and the rich.

**Religious transition:** A major transition in the Pacific is the conversion of the islands to Christianity (Munro and Thornley 1996). The spread of this new religion in the early nineteenth century was one way in which colonialism penetrated the Pacific. Global Christianity brought Christian morality; trained the natives in the use of European technology; and helped the islanders to deal with the debasing influences of contact with

# Table 2

Economic Changes of Pacific Society from Traditional to Modern

| Specific Economic Element | Traditional Pacific Society | Modern Pacific Society |
| --- | --- | --- |
| Economic Basis | Subsistence | Cash Cropping, Export Emphasis |
| Primary Industries | Agriculture/Fishing | Industrialization |
| Food/Service Exchange | Bartering | Monetization |
| Use of Product | Localized | Market Economy |
| Use of Manpower | Manual Labor | Globalization/Mechanized |
| Physical Impact of Work | Active Occupation | Sedentary Occupation |
| Work Organization | Small, Local, Family-Based | Large, Bureaucratic, Foreign |
| Workforce | Self-employed | Foreign-Employed |

the early European traders. The vigorous application of the Christian principles resulted in lifestyle changes varying from clothes, food, and cooking, to suppression of local religions and Pacific cultural practices that were unacceptable to the imperialists. This repeatedly undermined the islanders' self-respect and confidence in their own cultures (e.g., denouncing native gods and traditional worship), thus affecting the way the people interacted with each other and fragmenting the social fabric of the island communities.

Today, Christianity has been joined by a multitude of other religions (Kila et al. 1985), sects, and denominations, which dominate the lives of the Islanders and have subtly recreated Pacificans in the image of foreign deities (Finau, Ieuti, and Langi 1992). Some have even become fanatical, and for most, it has become difficult to tell where religions and cultures begin or end. With this religious transition come negative and positive changes, nonetheless changing Pacific societies forever. Will that transition ever end?

The case of the Solomon Islands South Seas Evangelical Church is one of many examples of how an introduced religion disturbed culturally significant acts that served to strengthen social ties and kinship among families. The use of "bride price" gifts during a traditional wedding ceremony among the "Are'are" people was frowned upon and discouraged by the Australian evangelists who came to Malaita in the 1930s. They repeatedly told the natives that "God did not sell Eve to Adam, and therefore the human body, especially that of a woman, cannot be sold like a commodity" (Pollard 2000).

While the Western-styled "free marriage" movement that was encouraged by the Church promoted individualism, bride price marriages were communal affairs requiring collective decision-making, gift exchanges, and rituals that served to strengthen family cohesiveness. "Free marriage" fostered the presentation of gifts useful for the newlyweds, bride price marriages involved the presentation of the traditional shell money and other gifts that are not merely for the generation of wealth but the strengthening of social relations, which were achieved through the reciprocal sharing of resources. In addition, the "Are'are" offering of gifts recognized the value of the bride socially, biologically, and economically, emphasizing that she would be the reproducer, the teacher, and manager for her family and the next generation. The bride price marriage is not seen as the union of just the newlyweds but the union also of two separate kin-based social groups. "Free marriage" fostered the idea that children were solely the responsibility of the parents, whereas for children born to couples whose union was confirmed through bride price, the nurturing of children was seen as a communal obligation on both the maternal and paternal sides. There are many such examples in the Pacific where subtle and yet rich cultural messages have been superficially judged or ignored by colonialists. The bride price marriage debate has not been resolved but has led to divisions, confusions and loss of cultural mores among the "Are'are" people (Pollard 2000).

**Environmental transition:** With cash cropping, mining, mechanization, and industrialization, the fragile Pacific environment has become very vulnerable (South Pacific Environment Programme 1992a). The "green house effect" and the rising sea levels caused by metropolitan modern societies' efforts to maintain their consumption level are threatening the Pacificans' habitat (Jokhan et al. 1993). In addition, the environments have become obesogenic (Swinburn, Egger, and Raza 1999); toxic (South Pacific Environment Programme 1992a, 1992b); and insecure, due to crime and violence. The new environment has also generated motor vehicles, wars, and serious injuries. The environmental transition not only brought physical and social changes, but also developed uncertainty and stress in the Pacific psyche.

**Social transition:** The most fundamental social change is the occidentalization and orientalization of lifestyle and values of the Pacificans (South Pacific Commission 1995). In search of progress, many have traded traditional values for imported ones. Global crime syndicates now operate and trade in illicit commodities in the Pacific. There is an increased focus in women and feminist advocacy (Emberson-Bain 1994; Thomas 1986); men-generated violence and neglect (Emberson-Bain 1994); delinquencies and youth alcoholism (Finau 1999); and migration and social dislocation

(Connell 1990). The basic unit of Pacific societies, the family, is breaking down, and is redefined, narrowly, to emphasize individuals, rather than the family unit and its basic tenet of reciprocity and common good.

**Political transition:** The traditional forms of government are being replaced by a search for democracy (Tagaloa et al. 1992). This transformation and migration have led to a transition in leadership from the traditional leaders to a new elite of Western-educated men and women (Ghai and Cottrell 1990; Kamikamica et al. 1988). The traditional social structure is adjusting to the new leadership with foreign ideologies (Latukefu et al. 1985). These ideologies and their practices (e.g., democracy, globalization, capitalism) are lulling the masses to believe that they are part of government and therefore, in control, when, in fact, the focus of control is elsewhere (e.g., multinational companies, local business, media, foreign government (Crocombe 1995; Finau 1999). Many of the new leaders are on a string (e.g., aid and defense), and are slaves of inappropriate ideologies and are second-class protagonists of foreign models.

The continuance of colonialism and imperialism in different forms (e.g., education, trade, technology) (Wickham et al. 2000) ensures that inequality and inequity persist. Even the notion of political independence of Pacific countries is doubtful, with aid strings and MIRAB economies being the order of the day (Bertram and Watters 1985). There cannot be political independence without, at least, economic autonomy.

**Food and nutrition transition:** This started when the missionaries' wives began having special classes, for the natives, on "baking cakes" to supply modern-day upper-class restaurants (Schoeffel 1987). The classes both teach and subtly imply that native food is no longer classy and good and that the new foods have status. In addition, other changes (e.g. cash cropping and sedentary labor) have also affected food production and the variety of food available. A society in a hurry needs fast foods, while in transition. Therefore, there is a high consumption of processed and caloric-dense foods (Coyne 2000). Even the definition of a meal is changing from a social occasion to an individual consumption of food and drinks. A recent study demonstrated the deleterious effect of globalization on people's diet in Tonga (Evans, Sinclair, Fusimalohi and Liava'a 2001).

**Health services transition:** The production and management of health have been drastically changed (Finau 1987). The environment, food, politics, economics, and social trends have generated new diseases. The health services are sluggishly responding to diseases, rather than health (Finau 1993). The health services are becoming bureaucratic, specialized, technology-dependent, professionalized, and Westernized. All these changes have not stopped the reemergence and persistence of infectious diseases and new threats, for example, from AIDS, alcohol, drugs, smoking, and bacterial drug resistance.

There has been improvement in the information systems, but the counting of the sick and the dead, let alone the accuracy of diagnosis, is incomplete (Finau 1994). One analysis based on mortality has shown that what the health services in the Pacific need are more doctors (Taylor, Lewis, and Levy 1989), contrary to evidence that the most effective health intervention is by other health categories (e.g., environmental health workers) and other sectors (e.g., agriculture) (Finau 1987). In most Pacific countries, the health expenditure is almost entirely (70-90%) spent on diseases, rather than on health (Taste 1998). It has been suggested that Ministries of Health should be renamed Ministries of Disease, because of this overwhelming focus (Finau, Tukuitonga, and Finau 2000).

**Demographic transition:** This is very much a function of death, fertility, and birth rates (Taylor 1990). The ideal demographic change is low fertility and low birthrates, the argument being that high birth rates lead to lack of resources and poverty (Haberkorn 1995). The reproductive behavior has been attacked to hasten the demographic transition towards those of the "modern societies." However, there has been no concomitant effort to improve the flow of resources to poor counties. The effect has been that the number of diners has been curbed, rather than the production of more dinners being increased, in order to control the high mortality common in money-poor countries (Navarro 1979). In "modern societies," populations in old age increase, resulting in an increased incidence of chronic diseases and disabilities of the old. These aged persons have to die, and the cause of death has been attributed mostly to non-communicable diseases.

**Mortality transition:** It is assumed that enumeration of mortality and morbidity is accurate (Finau 1994). This varies from country to country. As previously alluded to, mortality does not reflect quality of life. For many Pacificans, the quality of life, due to various transitions, may as well mean that they are dead long before the certification of the expiry of life (Finau 1995). The data quality, in most Pacific countries, is such that information on cause of death, age, religion, residence, and other factors is compromised. Has the system properly counted and diagnosed the dead? This question leads to the question: How much of the mortality transition is due to non-communicable diseases? This is an especially important question because of emerging evidence that non-communicable diseases have underlying infectious risk factors, such as peptic ulceration and cancer with *Helicobacter pylori* (NIH 1994); cardiovascular disease with *Chlamydia pneumoniae* and *Helicobacter pylori* (Strachan, Carrington and Mendall et al. 1999); renal disease with *streptococcal infections* and hepatitis

B virus (Brazosko, Krawczynski, Nazarewicz et al. 1974); bacterial oral diseases with coronary heart disease (Mattila, Nieminen, Rasi et al. 1989).

## Health Transition and the Pacificans

Health transition in the Pacific is mortality transition, because there is no health parameter involved. Fertility is the other variable included in the definition of health transition. The effect of fertility on mortality is reflected only if the health services, food availability and use, and environmental and other transitions in the community lead to the death of the mother and child. So, when we talk of health transition in the Pacific, all other forms of transition must be included, for the so-called health transition is one particular outcome among many other forms of transition.

The notion that the Pacific societies must be occidentalized in order to transit to modernity suggests that being a foreigner is the way the Pacific should be. Studies on migrants have shown this to be a move that results only in the change of the cause of death, without concomitant improvement in health, happiness, and the quality of life (Finau 1993). This notion condones the suggestion that the solution to diabetes in Nauru, for example, is to inter-marry Nauruans with shiploads of white Australians or refugees rejected by Australia. It is also arrogant and assimilative to suggest that Pacificans' ways of life need to be discarded, perhaps, for foreign ones. Maybe, the current mortality state is ideal for Pacificans; perhaps they are not transiting anywhere. With the emergence of infectious diseases, mortality in "modern societies" is changing to the so-called transitional state. In developed countries, like New Zealand and Australia, we find rather large third-world populations, due to power imbalances.

Health transition in its present form is not inevitable. The speed can be controlled, as has been shown by countries like Japan (Beaglehole and Bonita 1997). It can be reversed, as is happening to "modern societies" with the reemergence of infectious diseases. If health is the focus, then health transition may be a desirable state to be at, and die quickly from infectious diseases rather than to wilt and die after a prolonged life with chronic diseases (e.g., diabetes, stroke). If quality of life is the chosen indicator, then an early, quick transitional translocation to another level may be a better option, rather than prolonged suffering and infirmity due to chronic non-communicable diseases.

The present knowledge and technology of health problems are not fully accessible, available, affordable, and acceptable to Pacificans (Finau 1987; Finau, Tukuitonga, and Finau 2000). If they were, then the health transitions of Pacificans would be different. Knowledge and technologies will decrease death rates due to both infectious and non-communicable diseases, without necessarily changing fertility. This, of course, is an untenable situation for an imperialist regime, where population increases in "traditional societies" are a threat to the security of "modern societies."

The Pacific countries are still, practically, colonies (Crocombe 1992, 1995; Hempenstall and Rutherford 1998; Taste 1998). The imperialists control all phases and determinants of the health transition. Pacificans are aspiring to political independence, struggling with democracy, accepting economic dependence, and searching for an identity (Neemia-Mackenzie 1986; Thomas et al. 1990). In New Zealand, the debate on "New Zealand-born or raised" versus "Pacific-born or raised" rages, while groups are trying to redefine their ethnicity and resident status in New Zealand. This red herring is a diversion away from the Pacificans claiming their rightful share of New Zealand and its wealth.

The socialization of Pacificans, through foreign education, is another imperialist tool to enhance control (Kin et al. 1995; Wickham et al. 2000). A Western education is status and livelihood wrapped in one. Trained health personnel train, reflect, and promote the Western disease emphasis. Many of the scholarships and training opportunities are for doctors and nurses, as disease fighters (saving individuals) rather then as health promoters (saving communities). The latter could drive health transition faster, or halt it altogether, at a stage more conducive to being Pacificans.

Imperialist control through knowledge and technology transfer is also common (Illich 1975; Navarro 1979). These forces are often assumed to be neutral. However, knowledge perpetuates ideology and logic, on which power imbalance is based. It has been shown, many times, that technologies and ideologies contribute to the reproduction and the strengthening of the pattern of power relation that feeds imperialism.

## Models for Pacific Health Transition

It is obvious that health transition is more about control over the determinants of health than about the treatment of diseases that kill. Health and disease are generated by the transition in other spheres. Health transition is merely a count of dead casualties and their reproductive habits. Therefore, we propose an alternative way of viewing the health changes of Pacificans. We address the oppression and assimilations borne by imperialism through globalization. It has been shown that "community-based" health activities (including ethnic-specific efforts) have improved access, acceptability, availability, and affordability of service for the target populations. The effectiveness, efficiency, efficacy, and equitability of health services have also improved in this model. In addition, it is accepted that those who oppress do not know how to release oppression. This shows that power relationships need to be resolved. We support viewing health in a way that addresses power relationships. Some of the alternative strategies may include the following, individually or in combination:

**Mountain Model:** This model suggests that Pacificans aspire to be like Palangis, and focus on the economic pathway of accumulation of wealth, high consumption, and increasing Gross Domestic Product (GDP). For example, build more hospitals and focus on disease management, while health spending during the last year of life is approaching 50%.

**Valley model:** This model suggests total descending to traditionalism, and lower productivity, to the level that maintains traditional living. This would mean re-tracking, for many Pacificans, "who have started the good life and have seen the bright lights." However, attempts towards traditional living for health are being made by some indigenous societies, such as the New Zealand Maori, Hawaiians and some Australian Aborigines. The evidence from these approaches has been positive for some health aspects. The control of non-communicable diseases has improved within traditional lifestyles.

**Bridge model:** This suggests selective adaptation of traditional and cultural aspects during transition. The model includes commercializing the subsistence mode; the use of traditional medicine alongside Western medicine; and the taking of the best packages from the "noble savage" and the carrying of these through time. Many healthy practices are integrated and inherent in the cultures of traditional communities, like the separation of the partners immediately after the birth of a child.

**Tunnel model:** This suggests selective adoption of the new lifestyle. A selection of ideas, technology, and values may enhance traditionalism. For example, introduction of selected fishing and agricultural methods may boost production. The use of scientific methods in health (e.g., microbial sterility techniques); the taking of the best packages for the "noble savage"; and the adaptation of these for use in combination with traditional know-how may boost health status and quality of life.

**Red Sea model:** This suggests a removal of obstacles to usual practice and its development. This is tantamount to removal of oppression, thus, imperialism. This approach suggests revolution, not evolution; confrontation, not diplomacy; and management of conflict, rather than a reception for negotiation. This model is based on the notion that power is to be taken from the powerful, as it will not be given by them. The model is consistent with the religious notion of "onward Christian soldiers, marching on to war...." This model needs to be championed by Pacificans at all levels without prejudice. However, the Pacific false modesty has made Pacificans vulnerable to foreign influences and the comfort of imported friends.

These models assume that changes are inevitable, over time. They provide strategies for the management of change, rather than a resolution of the problems of and for change. The models may be used individually or in combination, but the ultimate aim will have to be the resolution of power imbalances, rather than being civil and maintaining the Pacific false modesty.

It is anticipated and indeed, desirable, that considerable debate be evoked by the theses expressed thus far. Historians, to begin with, would pose, perhaps, the question: "What would the Pacific's situation be had there not been a 'Western,' or 'imperialistic' intervention?" And only conjecture or possibly partisan viewpoints are likely answers to this question, as history cannot be rolled back, but only studied and interpreted.

Researchers, partial to strict methodological approaches, may well argue that "evidence" or substantial data do not form part of this discussion. But one could also counter this by asking whether tools, measurements, or methods exist that would assess happiness and life fulfillment in a non-Western way.

Eventually, the pragmatists will clear the ground and will propose to focus on the following:

1. How best can lessons be learned from history? And, as a corollary to this is the question of whether the "Bridge Model" or, perhaps, its more "tradition-leaning" parallel, the "Tunnel Model," the most viable way forward.

2. Can damage that has been historically recognized and identified be remedied, or, at least, contained as time goes by?

At the end of the day, we all must wonder: Can the "Red Sea Model" be used, when all else fails, in a way that respects the Pacificans and imperialists alike?

## Conclusions

Health transition theory reflects the power imbalances that mark imperialism, globalization, and their consequences. These include the physical, social, mental, and spiritual dominance of "modern society" over "traditional society." The main driving force for health transition is its definition and the identification of the changes in the other sectors, rather than the causes of mortality.

Pacificans need not transit to the mortality and fertility patterns of "modern societies" in order to be healthy and happy. Perhaps the "modern societies" may consider a transition to a healthier state and the management of change before they are forced to it by reemerging and new infectious diseases; by a geriatric population, with high consumption and low productivity; by high technology, replacing and devaluing people; by energy source depletion; and by a competitive, fluctuating, and highly stressed market economy, with accumulation of wealth without social conscience (Bell and Reich 1986).

These strategies are for Pacificans to maintain their integrity and to demonstrate the way the world should be. To exercise these, Pacificans need to take matters into their own hands and "modern society" should make a concerted effort to curb interference at all levels of Pacific societies. These include the cessation of imperialism, and the assimilative processes that create subtle oppression and power imbalances. This is not as complex as it is made out to be if there is a will (e.g., removal of non-Pacificans from Pacific regional organizations; research of Pacificans and their environment to be controlled by Pacificans; and removal of heavy handedness from aid). All these actions should have been done yesterday, and if they had been, the process outcomes would have been different. However, these outcomes are not as important as they have always been emphasized. The ultimate and essential measures of success for the models suggested are the answers to the following questions:

- Are Pacificans endangering other societies?
- Are Pacificans healthy and happy?

This is alpha to omega, not some transitional state copying assimilation of death and births.

# References

ANONYMOUS
2002        *What is Globalization?* (http://www/marxist.com/economy/what is globaliza-tion.mb.html).
BEAGLEHOLE, R. AND R. BONITA
1997        *Public Health at the Crossroads.* Cambridge, United Kingdom: Cambridge University Press.
BELL, D.E. AND M.R. REICH
1986        *Health, Nutrition and Economic Crises: Approaches to Policy in the Third World.* Dover, MA: Auburn House Publishing Company.
BELLWOOD, P.
1979        *Man's Conquest of Pacific: The Pre-History of South East Asia and Oceania.* New York, NY: Oxford University Press.
BERTRAM, I.G. AND R.F. WATTERS
1985        "The MIRAB Economy in the South Pacific Microstates." *Pacific Viewpoint* 27: 47-59.
BRAZOSKO, W.J., K. KRAWCZYNSKI, T. NAZAREWICZ ET AL.
1974        "Glomerulonephritis Associated with Hepatitis B Surface Antigen Immune Complex in Children." *Lancet* 2: 477-481.
CAREW-REID, J.
1989        *Environment, Aid and Regionalism in the South Pacific.* Monograph No. 22. Canberra, Australia: National Centre for Development Studies.
CONNELL, J., ED.
1990        *Migration and Development in the South Pacific.* National Centre for Development Studies. Canberra, Australia: ANU.

COYNE, T.
2000    *Lifestyle Diseases in Pacific Communities.* Noumea, New Caledonia: Secretariat of the Pacific Community.
CROCOMBE, R.
2000    *The South Pacific.* Institute of the Pacific Studies. Suva, Fiji: University of the South Pacific.
1995    *The Pacific Islands and the USA.* Suva, Fiji: Institute of Pacific Studies.
1992    *Pacific Neighbours.* Suva, Fiji: Institute of Pacific Studies.
DELAILOMOLOMA, N.H. ET AL.
1982    *Pacific Youth: Youth and Development in the South Pacific.* Suva, Fiji: Institute of Pacific Studies.
DENOON, D. ET AL.
1997    *The Cambridge History of Pacific Islanders.* Cambridge, United Kingdom: Cambridge Press.
EMBERSON-BAIN A., ED.
1994    *Sustainable Development or Malignant Growth? Perspectives of Pacific Island Women.* Suva, Fiji: Marama Publications.
EVANS, M.R., C. SINCLAIR, C. FUSIMALOHI AND W. LIAVA'A
2001    "Globalization, Diet and Health: An Example From Tonga." *Bulletin of the World Health Organization* 79: 856-862.
FINAU, M., T. IEUTI AND J. LANGI
1992    *Island Churches: Challenge and Change.* Suva, Fiji: Institute of Pacific Studies.
FINAU, S.A., C. TUKUITONGA AND E. FINAU
2000    *Health and Pacificans.* Tongan Health Society, Inc. Onehunga, New Zealand: Masilamea Press.
FINAU, S.A.
1999    "The experience of Tongan Youths with Alcohol: A FOBI Perspective." *Pacific Health Dialog* 6: 120-131.
1996    "Health, Environment and Development: Towards a Pacific Paradigm." *Pacific Health Dialog* 3: 266-278.
1995    "Pacific Women: Development for Better Health." *Pacific Health Dialog* 2: 98-103.
1994    "National Health Information Systems in the Pacific: In Search of a Future." *Health Planning and Policy* 9: 161-170.
1993    "Development and Health in the Pacific: Which Way to Die?" *Papua New Guinea Medical Journal* 36: 324-336.
1987    *Management of Pacific Health Services.* University of the South Pacific Extension Course Book. Suva, Fiji.
GHAI, Y. AND J. COTTRELL
1990    *Heads of State in the Pacific: A Legal and Constitutional Analysis.* Suva, Fiji: Institute of Pacific Studies.
GLOBAL EXCHANGE WEB PAGE
2002    http://www.globalexchange.org/wbifm/faq.html.
HABERKORN, G.
1995    "Fertility and Mortality in the Pacific Islands." *Pacific Health Dialog* 2: 104-112.
HEMPENSTALL, P. AND N. RUTHERFORD
1998    *Protest & Dissent in the Colonial Pacific.* Suva, Fiji: Institute of Pacific Studies.
ILLICH, I.
1975    *Medical Nemesis: The Expropriation of Health.* London, United Kingdom: Marion Boyars.
JOHNSTONE
1920    to Secretary, Department of Defense, 14 March 1919, Australian War Memorial, *Ex-German New Guinea Miscellaneous Reports, Jan-Feb 1920.*
JOKHAN, A. ET AL.
1993    *Climate & Agriculture in the Pacific Islands: Future Perspectives.* Fiji: Institute of Pacific Studies.
KAMIKAMICA, J.N. ET AL.
1988    *Law, Politics and the Government in the Pacific Island State.* Suva, Fiji: Institute of Pacific Studies.

KASSALOW, J.S.
2001        "Why Health Is Important to U.S. Foreign Policy." New York, NY: Millbank
            Memorial Fund.
KILA, T.A. ET AL.
1985        *New Religions Movements in Melanesia*. Suva, Fiji: Institute of Pacific Studies.
KIN, H. ET AL.
1995        *South Pacific Women in Distance Education: Studies From Countries of the University of
            the South Pacific*. Suva, Fiji: Institute of Pacific Studies.
KING, M.G.
1991        *Fisheries in the Economy of the South Pacific*. Suva, Fiji: Institute of Pacific Studies
            and the Forum Fisheries.
LATUKEFU, S. ET AL.
1985        "Further Thoughts on Pacific Constitutions." *Pacific Perspective* 13(2).
LEWIS, N.D. AND M. RAPAPORT
1995        "In a Sea of Change: Health Transitions in the Pacific." *Health & Place* 1:
            211-226.
MADELEY, J., D. SULLIVAN AND J. WOODROFFE
1994        *Who Runs the World?* London, United Kingdom: Christian Aid.
MATTILA, K.J., M.S. NIEMINEN, V.P. RASI ET AL.
1989        "Association Between Dental Health and Acute Myocardial Infarction." *British
            Medical Journal* 298: 779-781.
MUNRO, D. AND A. THORNLEY
1996        *The Covenant Makers: Islander Missionaries in the Pacific*. Suva, Fiji: Institute of
            Pacific Studies.
NAVARRO, V.
1979        "The Nature of Imperialism and Its Implications in Health and Medicine."
            Pp. 5-9 in *Imperialism, Health and Medicine*, edited by V. Navarro. New York,
            NY: Baywood Publishing Company.
NEEMIA-MACKENZIE, U.
1986        *Cooperation and Conflict. Costs, Benefits and National Interests in Pacific Regional
            Cooperation*. Suva, Fiji: Institute of Pacific Studies.
NIH CONSENSUS DEVELOPMENT CONFERENCE
1994        "*Helicobacter* in Peptic Ulcer Disease." *Journal of the American Medical Association*
            275: 65-69.
OMRAN, A.R.
1971        "The Epidemiology Transition: A Theory of the Epidemiology of Population
            Change." *Milbank Memorial Fund Quarterly* 49: 509-539.
PARENTI, M.
1995        *Against Empire*. New York, NY: City Light Books.
POLLARD, A.A.
2000        *Givers of Wisdom, Labourers Without Gain—Essays on Women in Solomon Islands*. Suva,
            Fiji: Bluebird Printery Ltd.
RAVUVU, A.
1995        "Cultural Heritage and Healthy Development." *Pacific Health Dialog* 2: 90-97.
SCHOEFFEL, P.
1987        "The Rice Pudding Syndrome: Women's Advancement and the Economic
            Training in the South Pacific." In *Development in the Pacific: What Women Say*.
            Canberra Development Dossier No. 18. Australia Council for Overseas Aid.
SIWATIBAU, S.
1995        "Pacific Youth in a Changing World: What of Health?" *Pacific Health Dialog* 2:
            84-89.
SOUTH PACIFIC COMMISSION
1995        *Pacific Islands Social and Human Development*. Report for the World Summit for
            Social Development. Noumea, New Caledonia: SPC.
SOUTH PACIFIC ENVIRONMENT PROGRAMME
1992a       *Environment and Development: A Pacific Island Perspective*. Manila, Philippines: Asia
            Development Bank.
1992b       *The Pacific Way: Pacific Island Countries' Report to the United Nations Conference on
            Environment and Development*. Manila, Philippines: Asian Development Bank.

STRACHAN, D.P., D. CARRINGTON, M.A. MENDALL ET AL.
1999      "Relation of *Chlamydia pneumoniae* Serology to Mortality and Incidence of Ischaemic Heart Disease Over 13 Years in the Caerphilly Prospective Heart Disease Study." *British Medical Journal* 318: 1035-1040.

SWINBURN, B.A., G. EGGER AND F. RAZA
1999      "Dissecting Obesogenic Environments: The Development and Application of Environmental Interventions for Obesity." *Preventive Medicine* 29: 563-570.

TAGALOA, A.F.L. ET AL.
1992      *Culture and Democracy in the South Pacific.* Suva, Fiji: Institute of Pacific Studies.

TASTE, S.
1998      *Japan's Aid Diplomacy and the Pacific Islands.* Suva, Fiji: Institute of Pacific Studies.

TAYLOR, R.
1990      "Economics of Public Health in the South Pacific." (Islands/Australia Working Paper No. 90/8). National Centre for Development Studies, ANU, Canberra: Australia.

TAYLOR, R., N.D. LEWIS AND S. LEVY
1989      "Societies in Transition: Mortality Patterns in Pacific Island Populations." *International Journal of Epidemiology* 18: 634-646.

THOMAS, P.
1986      "Pacific Women on the Move." *Pacific Perspectives* 11(2).

THOMAS, P. ET AL.
1990      *Public Administration and Management in Small States: Pacific Experiences.* Suva, Fiji: Institute of Pacific Studies.

WICKHAM, A. ET AL.
2000      *Distance Education in the South Pacific: Nets and Voyages.* Suva, Fiji: Institute of Pacific Studies.

WORLD BANK
1993      *Pacific Island Economics: Towards Efficient and Sustainable Growth (Volume 1: Overview).* Report No. 11351-EAP. Washington, DC: World Bank.

# Globalization and Health Policy in South Africa

## DI MCINTYRE[*], STEPHEN THOMAS[*] AND SUSAN CLEARY[*]

### ABSTRACT

This paper considers influences of globalization on three relevant health policy issues in South Africa, namely, private health sector growth, health professional migration, and pharmaceutical policy. It considers the relative role of key domestic and global actors in health policy development around these issues. While South Africa has not been subject to the overt health policy pressure from international organizations experienced by governments in many other low- and middle-income countries, global influence on South Africa's macroeconomic policy has had a profound, albeit indirect, effect on our health policies. Ultimately, this has constrained South Africa's ability to achieve its national health goals.

## Introduction

The apartheid era left a legacy of massive inequalities in income, health status, and access to health and other social services (Gilson and McIntyre 2001; McIntyre and Gilson 2000, 2002). The government that came to power in the first democratic elections, held in 1994, committed itself to redressing these inequities. The health policy of the new government explicitly aimed to improve access to health care, noting that "emphasis should be placed on reaching ... the most vulnerable" (Department of Health 1997:13). The health department had to do this within the

[*] Health Economics Unit, School of Public Health, University of Cape Town, South Africa.

context of an exploding HIV/AIDS epidemic and its associated health care demands.

This paper considers recent health policy developments in some key areas, in an effort to assess the extent to which the South African health department has been able to meet these challenges within the context of globalization. In this paper, globalization is taken to mean the "process of increasing economic, political and social interdependence and global integration that takes place as capital, traded goods, persons, concepts, images, ideas, and values diffuse across state boundaries" (Hurrell and Woods 1995:447).

The paper begins by outlining a conceptual framework, which highlights the key actors who are likely to impact health policy formulation and implementation. Three case studies, focusing on the growth of the private health sector, health personnel migration issues, and drug policy, are then presented, with a particular focus on exploring the relative influence of various domestic and global actors. These case studies enable us to draw some conclusions on how globalization has impacted South African health policy development in recent years, which are likely to be of relevance to other low- and middle-income countries facing similar challenges to South Africa.

## Conceptual Framework

The conceptual framework attempts to explain the derivation of health policy in South Africa by understanding the relative influence of domestic and global actors (see Table 1 for an overview). It highlights the realms of influence of different South African public sector actors in health policy development and the potential for conflict between these actors. More importantly, it examines the degree to which external forces constrain, and even determine, the behavior of each of these actors and through what mechanism this leverage operates. Thus, the conceptual framework proposes that the key determinants of health policy legislation and regulation are the interactions of local ministries and global players, often multilateral institutions. This is an abstraction, as other actors, local and foreign, public and private, will exert pressure on the state to change, or keep intact, health policies.

## Realms of Influence of Different Domestic Actors Over Health Sector Policy

*National Treasury*
The national Treasury is responsible for setting the macroeconomic agenda and controlling the government budget, making it probably the most

powerful government Ministry (see Table 1). In 1996, it introduced the Government's macroeconomic policy, GEAR (Growth Employment and Redistribution) (Department of Finance 1996). The foundation of GEAR is the promotion of business confidence to catalyze foreign investment and growth. GEAR also imposes constraints on the resources flowing to the health sector, in that it requires that public expenditure growth is lower than overall economic growth in order to demonstrate fiscal probity (McIntyre et al. 1999). In addition, it is the role of the national Treasury to exercise coordination of the budget process and determine general resource allocations across different spheres of government and between provinces. Again the national Treasury's decisions about general resource allocation have implications for available finances for health care.

*Department of Trade and Industry*
The formal roles of the Department of Trade and Industry involve policy development for international trade as well as industrial development and investment in South Africa (Department of Trade and Industry 2002b). It governs international trade relations, including conducting multinational trade negotiations and cooperating with the World Trade Organization (WTO). This includes trade agreements that impact health service provision: TRIPS covers trade in drugs, while GATS affects trade in health services, including health professionals (see Table 1).

**Table 1**

Actors, Influence, and External Leverage in South African Health Policy

| Key domestic actors that shape the health sector | National Treasury | Department of Trade and Industry | National Department of Health |
|---|---|---|---|
| Realm of Influence (in terms of health care financing and provision) | • Financing (Budget ceilings, resource allocation) | • Provision (Drugs and personnel) | • Financing<br>• Provision |
| External Actors and Leverage | IMF/World Bank and financial markets exerting need for fiscal discipline, liberal orthodox policies and sound basis for foreign investment | World Trade Organization through commitments to TRIPS and GATS which promote increased liberalization of markets and interests of multinationals | Donors do not exert much leverage because of South Africa's relatively large domestic resource base |

IMF = International Monetary Fund.
TRIPS = Trade Related Aspects of International Property Rights.
GATS = General Agreement on Trade in Services.

*National Department of Health*
The draft National Health Bill (Department of Health 2001a) states that, *inter alia*, the functions of the national Department of Health are to:
- formulate national health policy;
- determine standards for health care provision;
- plan, develop, and regulate human resources for health care;
- participate in the planning and evaluation of the financing of health services; and
- regulate, control and evaluate medicines.

Hence, the national Department of Health has a key role in shaping issues concerning public health and the financing and provision of health care.

As highlighted in Table 1, there is an overlap between the national Department of Health on the one hand, and the national Treasury and the Department of Trade and Industry on the other, in the realms of financing and provision of health care, respectively.

## External Leverage on Domestic Actors

*National Treasury*
In many ways, GEAR represents a fairly orthodox, if "self-imposed," structural adjustment program. A team of South African treasury officials, supported by technical experts from the World Bank and academic institutions, hastily developed this neoliberal macroeconomic policy, which was adopted in June 1996 (Department of Finance 1996). This policy development followed a 25% fall in the South African currency in the first 4 months of 1996 (Bond et al. 1997). This decrease was seen as a signal from global powers that a firm commitment to strict monetary and fiscal control, and to creating "a favorable environment for market-led economic growth" (Marais 2001:161), was required from South Africa.

Thus, the achievement of macroeconomic stability was seen as vital to encourage foreign investment. Further, the national Treasury's commitment to dealing with debt, inherited from the apartheid era, is in large part an attempt to demonstrate fiscal prudence to foreign investors. Indeed, the government's macroeconomic strategy is reliant on investor and market sentiment. Thus, while the national Treasury has few contractual obligations to multilateral donors and banks, its economic performance depends on their approval and that of the markets. This exercises a very real constraint on the freedom of action of the national Treasury, which must always look over its shoulder to evaluate the reaction of the market (see Table 1). Yet, as the volatility of the South African currency in recent years may indicate, this strategy can be unstable and unpredictable.

## Department of Trade and Industry (DTI)

The main emphasis of the South African government's manufacturing strategy involves opening up the economy and enhancing competitiveness and growth (Department of Trade and Industry 2002a). DTI relies on stakeholder support from the business community (Department of Trade and Industry 2002a) and must therefore promote access to profitable markets to encourage growth. Nevertheless, DTI does acknowledge that the "current global economy is inherently risky" (Department of Trade and Industry 2002a:23) and that trade and investment have not been properly governed, resulting in "imbalanced" trade between North and South. Its response is to be "engaged in various bilateral and multilateral trade negotiations to lower tariff barriers and remove ... barriers to trade" (p. 45) in general.[1] This response has included multilateral negotiations in the WTO (see Table 1). Its commitments to these agreements are binding, opening up the potential for punitive action if the agreements are not honored. From a health sector perspective, such agreements will particularly impact on the supply of, and demand for, health professionals and pharmaceuticals.

## National Department of Health

The vision of the national Department of Health embraces a unified health system where all actors (including the private sector) are coordinated in pursuit of the fundamental goal of *equity* (Gilson et al. 1999). Concurrently, the national Department of Health has undertaken a range of commitments on public health matters through international treaties and agreements. Nevertheless, the Strategic Planning Framework allows the national Department of Health freedom to "consolidate" and "revisit" them "in line with the changing needs of the South African health service" (Department of Health 1999:18). Hence, as long as these agreements help achieve domestic health sector goals, they will be honored. Part of the autonomy enjoyed by the national Department of Health may be due to its lack of donor-dependence. As noted recently on the financing of the public health system, "Donors, which are so important in other Sub-Saharan African countries, account for less than 1% or only R2 for every person in South Africa in 1998/99" (Thomas et al. 2000:133). Effectively donor funds are insignificant. International agencies are thus denied a key point of leverage: finance.

---

[1] The DTI does not include health as one of the five sectors of the economy having the most or "considerable" potential for increased outputs, exports, and employment creation (Department of Trade and Industry 2002a). Nevertheless, any attempts to lower tariffs generally will impact on the health sector.

## Implications of Conceptual Framework

One direct implication of the conceptual framework is that the power of the state to set health care policy independently is severely curtailed. The national Department of Health is but one player among many and is far from being the most powerful. In a globalizing world, the market has long tentacles. While multilateral institutions such as the IMF or the WTO often directly wield leverage on the state, the agenda is that of big business, access to markets, and ultimately profits.

Further, the conceptual framework highlights that there will be conflict in health policy development in relation to health care financing and provision. Actors with different perspectives and interests perceive these areas to be within their realms of influence. This conflict has both international and local dimensions. First, leverage is exerted by global actors on the objectives of the national Treasury and the Department of Trade and Industry. The perceived costs of not toeing the line may be quite high and guarantee that the national Treasury and the Department of Trade and Industry comply. The "growth through foreign investment" principle underlying GEAR requires South Africa to be perceived as "investor-friendly" by the international community. The perceived threat for the national Treasury of not meeting the macroeconomic targets specified in GEAR is low-investment and no employment creation. For the Department of Trade and Industry, the commitments of the South African government to different international agreements are many. They impose the threat of removal of privileged trading status and punitive action for noncompliance.

However, much of the actual conflict in health policymaking will most likely happen between domestic actors. This means that the effective influence of global institutions on health policy is masked by the policy conflict between local institutions. The effect of globalization may well be to stoke up domestic conflict over health policy development, specifically in the realms of financing and provision. The resolution of such conflict will have much to do with the exertion of power and authority (Lukes 1974). Nevertheless, the conceptual framework cannot predict who will win the battles and effectively take the lead in health policy development in a particular realm. Further, the relative power of the three domestic actors noted in Table 1 might not necessarily determine who wins. There are other actors in the policy arena that may get involved in policy conflict.

In the next sections, we consider three case studies of health sector policy issues in South Africa: private sector growth and the resulting public-private mix, human resources, and drugs. The conceptual framework informs the exploration of these case studies.

## A Case Study of Private Health Sector Growth

*Brief Historical Context—The pre-1994 Situation*
The private sector has played a role in health care provision and financing in South Africa since the late nineteenth century (Naylor 1988; van den Heever 1997). However, there has been a particularly rapid growth in the private health sector since the mid-1980s. Until that time, there had been a small, gradual increase in both public and private health care expenditure (McIntyre and Dorrington 1990). Private sector expenditure, especially that by medical schemes (as private health insurance organizations are termed in South Africa), increased dramatically and considerably faster than public sector expenditure from the mid-1980s (McIntyre et al. 1995). By the late 1980s, increases in medical scheme expenditure, and hence in contribution rates, were of the order of 30% per annum.

Increases in private expenditure were mirrored by changes in private health care provision. For example, by 1990, 62% of general doctors and 66% of specialists were in private practice (Rispel and Behr 1992) compared with only 40% in the early 1980s (Naylor 1988). The number of for-profit general hospital beds nearly doubled between 1988 and 1993 (McIntyre et al. 1995).

A range of factors contributed to the rapid private health sector growth during this period. Of particular importance was the government policy of privatization and deregulation. While a key reason for embarking on this policy was that of a growing government budget deficit, the policy document also explicitly motivated the policy on the basis of international trends towards an increasing role for the private sector (South Africa [Republic] 1987). In addition to a general privatization policy, there was also a specific health sector privatization policy (Working Group on Privatisation and Deregulation 1986).

A key component of this policy was that of encouraging the growth and use of private providers: "Health authorities must not be seen as an infinite source of health facilities and medical care. More people should be able to make use of private health facilities" (Ross 1982:32). While some of this use could be funded "out-of-pocket," the growth of medical scheme membership was seen as particularly important in expanding the use of private providers (Price 1989).

At the same time, medical schemes were successful in pushing for deregulation. Of particular importance is that, until 1989, medical schemes used community-rated contribution scales.[2] Regulation changes allowed schemes to use a wider range of variables in determining contributions

---

[2] An individual's or specific group's risk of illness is not taken into account in calculating contributions or premiums. Instead, contributions are based on the average expected cost

and effectively allowed for risk-rating along the lines of private health insurance in the United States (van den Heever 1997). This undermined the principle of cross-subsidization that was central to the initial design of schemes.

Another way in which the government attempted to privatize the financing of health care was by levying user fees at public sector facilities. The privatization policy stated: "The Government endorses the principle of user charges, in terms of which the full cost of a service is, where applicable and possible, recovered from the user" (South Africa [Republic] 1987:7). This policy was introduced at a time when international organizations were strongly advocating for user fees for social services (Akin et al. 1987; de Ferranti 1985; Jimenez 1987).

Although there was little overt pressure from international organizations to pursue these privatization policies, due mainly to South Africa's relative international isolation during the apartheid era, there were two ways in which there were indirect global influences. First, the neoliberal policies of the South African government in the 1980s had much in common with "Thatcherite" policies and "Reagonomics." Commentators have noted that these policies were based on a perceived need to introduce "a set of 'normalizing' adjustments that would bring the economy in line with 'the global consensus'" (Marais 2001:105-106). Second, medical scheme administrators and private providers looked to the USA as their model, and pushed for changes in regulation that would enable them to operate under similar conditions to their American counterparts. These factors illustrate how globalization, through the diffusion of ideas and values across state boundaries, has impacted South Africa even since the 1980s. The end result is that the government that came to power in 1994 inherited a substantial and powerful private sector, which was very weakly regulated.

*Post-1994 Developments*

Despite dramatic changes in many spheres after 1994, the rapid growth of private sector health care financing and provision continued. Annual increases in medical scheme expenditure and contributions continued to far outstrip general inflation levels in the mid-to-late 1990s (Cornell et al. 2001). It is becoming increasingly unaffordable for South Africans to belong to medical schemes (Doherty et al. 2002b).

Once again, growth in private health care provision accompanied these expenditure increases. By 1999, 73% of general doctors and 75% of specialists were in private practice (van Rensburg and van Rensburg 1999).

---

of health service use for the entire insured group and are only differentiated by income level (and sometimes the number of dependents).

The number of for-profit general private hospital beds increased by nearly 10% per annum between 1994 and 1999 (Cornell et al. 2001).

In addition to the continued growth in private health care expenditure and provision, health service privatization entered a new phase after the 1994 elections. Although there has been a certain amount of health and support service outsourcing for many years, there is growing pressure for engaging in "public-private partnerships" (PPPs). A PPP Task Team, therefore was established by the national Department of Health in 1999. The policy recommendations of this group were that there should be increased efforts to purchase certain services and skills from existing private providers, outsource nonclinical services and certain diagnostic services, engage in joint ventures (e.g., leasing underutilized space in public facilities to private providers) and enter into private finance initiatives for large capital projects (Department of Health 2000).

Once again, there was limited overt pressure from international organizations on South African health policymakers to pursue this path. However, the global trend towards the marketization and commercialization of health care has undoubtedly impacted policy processes in South Africa, as in other countries (Lee et al. 2002). Of even greater importance is the indirect impact of global actors on the health sector via their influence on macroeconomic policy, as outlined previously.

In line with the GEAR policy of limiting government activities and encouraging economic growth primarily through private sector activities, the national Treasury developed a PPP unit with technical support and funding from USAID. There are PPP managers for each of the key sectors, including health, within this unit. At a time when the private health sector is under considerable pressure due to its increasing unaffordability for middle-income groups, PPPs are seen by private sector actors as a mechanism for ensuring their continued expansion. Treasury support for PPPs is key in opening up these opportunities for the private sector.

A factor of considerable importance in understanding the growth of the private health sector is the lack of comprehensive and coherent Department of Health policy for this sector (McIntyre and Gilson 2002). Although certain policies relating to the private health sector have been developed, particularly the reregulation of the medical schemes industry and regulation of pharmaceutical products (see later section), these policies have been developed by different groups of officials with no acknowledgment of the interrelationship between various private health sector actors. In addition, there are considerable policy gaps, with very little regulation aimed at private provision (such as independent practitioners, private hospitals, and the purchase of sophisticated equipment).

The only area where the Department of Health took a firm stand against the global trend, and was able to avoid conflict with other domestic actors, relates to reversing some of the previous government's privatization of health care financing initiatives. A policy of free health care for pregnant women and children was one of the first reforms announced and implemented by the government following the democratic transition in 1994. There are various explanations as to why the Health Department was able to pursue this policy relatively unhindered. First, the national Treasury was not yet active in its current form; its power was to wax later. Second, powerful political figures, including the President, backed the reform, giving it a strong base of support. Third, given the pressing need for redistribution and improved access to health care, few could argue with the principles of the reform.

## Implications of Private Sector Growth

The rapid and uncontrolled growth of the private sector has contributed to disparities in health service access and the health of South Africans. On the one hand, a minority elite (less than 20% of the population) has access to over 60% of the financial resources for health care while the historically disadvantaged majority has less than 40% of financial resources devoted to its health care needs (Doherty et al. 2002a). It is not only financial resources that are maldistributed; only a quarter of doctors work in the public sector, attempting to serve over 80% of the population (van Rensburg and van Rensburg 1999).

The inequitable public-private health sector mix has been identified as a key reason for South Africa's relatively poor health status indicators (e.g., IMR > 50 per 1,000 live births and average life expectancy of < 60 years), despite its high level of overall health care expenditure (8.5% of GDP) (McIntyre et al. 1995). It has also contributed to the massive disparities between different groups in South Africa; the IMR of the African[3] population is nearly six times greater than that of the white population (Gilson and McIntyre 2001).

The disparities in the public-private mix have worsened since the 1994 elections. While private sector expenditure increased rapidly, public sector health care expenditure was stagnating in real terms, due largely to the GEAR policy of tight constraints on government expenditure. Annual

---

[3] South Africa's population was previously categorized into African, Colored, Indian, and White, and corresponded to a historical gradient of access to wealth and power. Data are presented here for these groups to demonstrate the degree of inequity in South Africa. This does not in any way imply endorsement of racist terms or their unsubstantiated use in health research.

expenditure per medical scheme beneficiary rose from 4.7 times that spent by national and provincial government health departments per person dependent on the public sector in the 1996/97 financial year to 5.8 times in 1998/99 (Doherty et al. 2002a). While private sector expenditure has been increasing rapidly, medical scheme population coverage has declined (Cornell et al. 2001). In addition, with scheme benefit packages being constantly reduced, more and more scheme members are becoming dependent on the public sector for uncovered services and are "dumped" on the public sector when their annual benefits are exhausted (Gilson et al. 1999). The government expenditure trend, combined with growing demands on publicly provided health care, not least of all as a result of the HIV/AIDS epidemic, is adversely influencing the availability and quality of public sector services.

It is also of considerable concern that the medical scheme expenditure and contribution spiral is adversely impacting the availability of government resources. First, private employer medical scheme contributions on behalf of employees are tax deductible. Second, most civil servants are members of medical schemes and government pays two thirds of their contributions. Thus, scarce tax funds are being used to purchase health insurance cover for civil servants at a much higher cost than that of public sector care. The monthly government subsidy for medical scheme contributions per civil servant were twelve times what the government spent per person dependent on public sector services (i.e., those without medical scheme cover) in 1998/99 (Doherty et al. 2002a).

The end results of inadequate Department of Health policy direction in relation to the private sector, combined with fiscal constraints arising from the Treasury's neoliberal macro-economic policy, are growing disparities in health service access between different socio-economic groups and hence lack of significant progress in addressing disparities in health status. There have been minor interventions to address public-private mix disparities, particularly new regulation of medical schemes to attempt to limit the "dumping" of members on the public sector when benefits are exhausted (Cornell et al. 2001). The only attempt to systematically address the inequitable public-private mix, namely, the proposal to introduce a progressively financed social health insurance, was thwarted by the national Treasury (Gilson et al. 1999; McIntyre et al. 2003).

The growing private health sector and deteriorating public-private mix in South Africa has, thus, been heavily influenced, on the one hand, by weak policy action by the Department of Health and the indirect impact of global trends towards commercialization of health services. On the other hand, there have been strong indirect influences from the national

Treasury, who in turn was subject to some pressure from global actors in developing its macroeconomic policy and market-led growth strategies.

## A Case Study of Health Personnel Migration Issues

Globalization increases the mobility of people: improved transport, tele-communications, accessibility of information, and portability of skills all contribute to making the world a smaller place to work in. This is a very serious issue for low- and middle-income countries, who increasingly feel that they are losing more and more of their skilled health personnel. While not the only contributing factor, the World Trade Organization's General Agreement on Trade in Services (GATS) will certainly enhance future migration.

## GATS' Effect on Health Professional Migration

The GATS is the World Trade Organization agreement governing the liberalization of trade in services. Services differ from goods, as their trade is mainly controlled through domestic laws, regulations, norms, and standards. The GATS applies to all services, except those "supplied in the exercise of government authority" (Article 1:3 b and c). These are defined as services not supplied on a commercial basis or in competition with other service suppliers. The implication of this definition is that privately delivered health services are subject to the GATS, but also, potentially, services offered to private patients in the public sector. Although the GATS offers countries a choice of which service sectors they wish to liberalize, it also has a built-in agenda to move towards greater overall liberalization of trade in services (WTO Secretariat 1999).

The GATS identifies different modes of supply of services. The services offered by health professionals would mainly be supplied through the mode termed "the movement of natural persons," which relates to temporary movement rather than permanent migration. South Africa has not yet committed to liberalizing the services of health professionals via "the movement of natural persons." Liberalization would imply that the nationals of all GATS signatories would need to be treated equally.

While the GATS may not directly lead to increased loss of health professionals, by its encouraging mutual recognition of qualifications and temporary movements of professionals, permanent migration is enhanced. As noted by others, "The loss of health personnel from needy countries to wealthier ones is already a serious problem. If barriers to this type of movement are reduced without an appropriate regulatory framework and/or improvement in working and income conditions in the domestic health system, equity, quality and efficiency will all suffer" (Adams and Kinnon 1998:39).

## South Africa's Response

The South African Department of Health is deeply concerned about all forms of professional migration. The draft National Health Bill states that "South Africa invests large amounts of public funds in the schooling and tertiary education of health professionals, only to see its efforts to accelerate equitable delivery of quality health services stifled by three forms of professional migration: from rural to urban areas, from the public to the private sector and from South Africa to highly industrialised countries" (Department of Health 2001a:54).

In order to meet the challenges of shortages of professionals, the Department has introduced one year of community service for certain categories of health professionals, including medical doctors and pharmacists. In addition, bilateral agreements with countries have been instituted; for instance, 402 Cuban doctors have been posted to public health services in poorer regions.

Mindful of the fact that it might be accused of hypocrisy by poaching skilled professionals from other low- and middle-income countries, the national Department of Health has taken steps to limit its own immigration. Indeed, it will not entertain the applications of *individual* health professionals from low- and middle-income countries (only through bilateral country agreements). There must also be a demonstrated need for such recruitment, such as in rural underserved areas. Further, subsequent migration of the incoming health professionals to the private sector is not supported (Cleary and Thomas 2002).

Clearly this unilateral move by the Department of Health is opposed to the spirit of future liberalization in the trade of health services. In contrast to the health sector's stand, the Department of Trade and Industry's position on the flow of human resources is that GATS does not favor the discrimination of foreign health professionals based on their country of origin (from Article XVII), unless this was openly listed in the GATS schedule as a limitation (Adlung and Carzaniga 2002). However, owing to the seriousness of the issue of the brain drain, the Department of Trade and Industry is choosing to focus on compliance to other areas of GATS. A debate is currently underway between the two national Departments about the free inflow of foreign health professionals and has yet to be resolved.

## A Case Study of the Impact of Globalization on the Formation of Domestic Drug Policy

The formation of domestic drug policy in South Africa is a particularly interesting case study of the potentially detrimental effects of globalization. When the South African government passed the Medicines and Related Substances Control Amendment Act, No. 90, of 1997, both domestic and international actors attempted to use their influence to modify these amendments. Much of the dispute focused on whether certain of the amendments were in contravention of South Africa's obligations in the Trade Related Aspects of International Property Rights (TRIPS) Agreement. While this was not the case, Pharmaceutical Research and Manufactures of America (PhRMA), Pharmaceutical Manufacture's Association (PMA), [4] and the United States Government nevertheless entered into a concerted campaign to induce South Africa to exclude these amendments, which were viewed as paving the way to introducing compulsory licensing and parallel importation of medicines. [5]

## The TRIPS Agreement

The TRIPS agreement prescribes a minimum standard of domestic intellectual property protection binding on all World Trade Organization members. This agreement was clearly of more benefit to industrialized countries because a significant aspect of their comparative advantage in trade lies in research and development in high technology fields. In addition, the inclusion of medicines in the TRIPS agreement was seen as a major coup for the multinational pharmaceutical companies. It is of importance that "twelve chief executive officers of US-based transnational corporations (TNCs) organized themselves in 1986 into the Intellectual Property Committee for the Uruguay Round of the General Agreement on Tariffs and Trade (GATT) negotiations, and succeeded in getting most of what they wanted from an intellectual property agreement, which now has the status of public international law" (Buse et al. 2002:261-262). Those low- and middle-income country governments that sanctioned the inclusion of TRIPS did so for the sake of the perceived compensating gains in other parts of the Uruguay package (Wolson 1997).

Under TRIPS, a patent confers on its owner exclusive rights for a period of 20 years from the time of filing of the patent. Third parties cannot make, use, offer for sale, sell, or import the product without the owner's authorization in this period. However, the TRIPS agreement does allow

---

[4] PhRMA and PMA are the pharmaceutical industry trade associations in the United States and South Africa, respectively.

[5] Compulsory licenses allow a generic manufacturer to produce a drug before the patent on the brand name drug has expired. A medicine is parallel imported into a country *a* if, once it is sold by the patent owner or a licensee in a second country *b*, a third party sells it on into *a*'s market. Parallel imports are viable and economically significant only given significant preimportation price differentials between the markets in *a* and *b*. One cannot parallel import a generic copy of a locally patented medicine without issuing a compulsory license first.

for the weakening of patent protection through parallel importation and compulsory licensing in certain circumstances.

Parallel importation, which is the purchase of branded drugs from another country at lower cost than if procured directly from the manufacturer in one's own country, is permitted under the TRIPS agreement. Compulsory licensing "allows for the legal manufacture and use of generic drugs without the agreement of the patent holder … [but with] compensation of the patent holder" (Kumaranayake and Lake 2002:86). TRIPS provides for fast tracking of compulsory licensing if the government is prepared to offer the drugs in the public sector, if a national emergency is declared or if the license is correcting for anticompetitive practice. TRIPS is therefore relatively permissive about unauthorized use of patents, especially in the case of HIV/AIDS, which is widely recognized as constituting a national emergency in South Africa (Cleary and Ross 2002; World Trade Organization 1994, 2001).

## The South African Medicines and Related Substances Control Amendment Act[6] and Global Pressures

The South African drug policy aims to improve access to essential medicines, promote the rational use of medicines and to contain the costs of medicine use (Department of Health 1996). The Medicines Act of 1997 was the key legislative tool for achieving these policy goals. In particular, it explicitly allowed for parallel importation as a measure for reducing the price of medicines. Section 15C of the Medicines Act, which gave the Minister of Health wide-ranging discretion in matters relating to parallel importation and possibly also compulsory licensing, was particularly objectionable to the transnational pharmaceutical companies. They argued that the extent of this discretion was inadequately specified and that the Minister could use these powers in contravention of the TRIPS agreement.

After the passing of the Medicines Act of 1997, there was intense pressure from the PMA at home as well as PhRMA and the US government abroad to change Section 15C. The transnational pharmaceutical companies (under their umbrella group the PMA) filed a lawsuit against the national Department of Health in February 1998, which effectively blocked the implementation of the 1997 Medicines Act. The US government applied considerable pressure, including placing South Africa on the United States Trade Representative's Special 301 Watch List in May 1998 (Consumer Project on Technology 1999; Department of Health 2001b). An

---

[6] Hereafter referred to as the Medicines Act of 1997.

example of the level of feeling against Section 15C is evident from a US Department of State report, which reads: "Since the passage of the offending amendments in December 1997, U.S. Government agencies have been engaged in a full court press with South African officials from the Department of Trade and Industry, Foreign Affairs, and Health, to convince the South African Government to withdraw or amend the offending provisions of the law, or at the very least, to ensure that the law is implemented in a manner fully consistent with South Africa's TRIPS obligations" (Consumer Project on Technology 1999).

Some have noted that transnational pharmaceutical companies, with the support of their host governments, were attempting to impose a "TRIPS-Plus" policy. In effect, they were attempting to pressurize the South African government (and governments in other low- and middle-income countries, such as Thailand) to change their domestic legislation that would restrict their ability to engage in parallel importation or to issue compulsory licenses, despite these both being TRIPS-compliant practices (Cleary 2001; Kumaranayake and Lake 2002).

By mid-1999, the issue, which was initially an intellectual property issue about increasing access to medicines, had become about HIV/AIDS. Intellectual property rights activists (such as the Consumer Project on Technology) teamed up with Médecins sans Frontières and Health Action International (as well as the leading local AIDS activist group, Treatment Action Campaign or TAC) to deliver their message via the vehicle of HIV/AIDS. After mass demonstrations by activists, particularly during the Gore presidential campaign (where Gore was accused by activists and the media of defending pharmaceutical profits at the expense of South African AIDS patients), the US government dropped its trade pressures against South Africa. A statement of agreement with the US government was issued in 1999 by the South African Department of Trade and Industry where it was agreed that "It is the expressed position of the South African Government that, in the implementation of provisions of the Medicines Act—which permits parallel importation and compulsory licensing of patents for pharmaceuticals—it will honor its obligations under the TRIPS Agreement" (Department of Trade and Industry 1999) (p. 1).

In May 2000, the United States' TRIPS-Plus policy was reversed for sub-Saharan Africa with the release of a Presidential Executive order prohibiting the US government from taking action against sub-Saharan African countries who attempt to enhance access to antiretrovirals through TRIPS-compliant means (Kumaranayake and Lake 2002).

## Impact of the Dispute on HIV/AIDS Treatment

The case between the government and the PMA eventually came to court in March 2001, but was delayed until April when South Africa's Treatment Action Campaign (TAC) was admitted to the case as *amicus curiae* (friend of the court). The TAC saw the implementation of the Medicines Act as critical to ensuring affordable access to antiretroviral treatment for South Africans. When the case returned to court in April 2001, the PMA immediately agreed to settle out of court. In their statement, the government agreed to seek measures to protect public health (including the enactment of 15C) within its TRIPS obligations, while the PMA agreed to work with the Government towards this end (African National Congress 2001). This settlement was widely hailed as a victory by the government, by AIDS activists and by almost all of the South African media.

As a result of the TAC campaign, it had become the standard interpretation by the media and others that, if the government were to win the case, it would use 15C to access generic antiretrovirals to address the HIV/AIDS crisis. However, if this ever was the government's intention, by the time the case came to court, this stance had changed. One could hypothesize that two developments contributed to this change. First, after the failure of the Seattle WTO negotiations at the end of 1999, increased attention was paid to holding high-income countries accountable to moralized standards on trade liberalization and market access; and this message regularly incorporated the claim that South Africa was an exemplary observer of Uruguay treaty commitments, including TRIPS. The South African government would, thus, not want to engage in any activity that would call this "model WTO citizen" status into question. If this is the case, globalization has impacted adversely on addressing the HIV/AIDS crisis in South Africa. The second development relates to domestic health policy and internal disputes. The TAC campaign had closely associated Section 15C of the Medicines Act with increased access to antiretrovirals in the popular media. It was possibly no longer in the Government's interests to implement compulsory licensing (to import or manufacture generics) via the Act, since the Government's opposition to enhanced access to antiretrovirals was then a dominant theme in its health policy (Cleary and Ross 2002).

Through its involvement in this dispute over medicine patents, South Africa has widely been seen as a world leader in tackling issues of more affordable access to medicines. In reality, two years after "winning this battle," South Africa has yet to use TRIPS-compliant mechanisms to address deficiencies in access to drugs, particularly for the millions of South Africans who have AIDS.

## Conclusion

As indicated in the introduction, the South African Health Department faced considerable challenges, particularly in relation to addressing massive health and health-system inequities after the change of government in 1994. The case studies highlight that many of the most pernicious inequities have not been addressed and that this lack of progress is, at least to some extent, related to the impact of globalization. In particular, the continued growth of private sector expenditure and provision, yet declining population coverage by this sector, combined with stagnating public sector resources in the face of increased health care demands, including those related to the HIV/AIDS epidemic, is resulting in deepening public-private mix inequities.

One of the justifications put forward by the South African Health Department for refusing to make antiretroviral treatments available to people living with AIDS is that they are unaffordable. It is unclear whether the motivation for not using TRIPS-compliant mechanisms to access cheaper generic antiretrovirals was that of succumbing to global pressures to be seen as a "model WTO citizen" or a result of domestic policy disputes over the safety and efficacy of antiretrovirals. However, the end result is growing health status inequities due to the HIV/AIDS epidemic, whose burden falls more heavily on the lowest socioeconomic groups.

Four broad conclusions about the relationship between globalization and domestic health policy can be drawn from the conceptual framework and its application to the three case studies. First, the South African experience highlights that the influence of global actors is not always immediately evident, as it is often obscured by the more visible engagement between domestic actors. There is sometimes a tendency to look for "obvious" global interventions, such as the introduction of structural adjustment programs through World Bank and IMF loan conditionalities. In the South African case, many of the global influences have been more subtle, such as the pressure of a dramatic and seemingly inexplicable fall in the domestic currency, which resulted in a "self-imposed" structural adjustment program, and indirect, such as the effect of GEAR on health policy directions relating to the private health sector.

Second, globalization has promoted an increasing connectedness between health and other sectors, particularly the trade and finance sectors (Buse et al. 2002). As was highlighted in the private sector case study, national Treasury policies, particularly GEAR and the PPP regulations, are significantly contributing to the exacerbation of inequities in resource availability in the public and private health sectors, relative to the population served by each. In addition, it was the Treasury that opposed proposals to introduce a Social Health Insurance when its design was such that public-private mix inequities would have been dramatically reduced. The Department of Trade and Industry is interacting with the national Department of Health around the migration of health professionals and overseeing compliance with the TRIPS agreement in the area of access to affordable medicines. The case studies suggest that the Treasury is impacting more forcefully on health policy, while the Department of Trade and Industry appears to be exercising less overt authority over health policy developments which are within its realm of influence.

Third, the global trend of ascendance of private sector actors in influencing government policy (Buse et al. 2002) is also evident in South Africa. Domestically, the private sector routinely lobbies the government to ensure that policies are favorable to their continued growth. Of equal importance is the pressure exerted by transnational companies to adopt policies that are well disposed towards them, both directly and via their host governments, as was well illustrated in the drug policy case study.

Finally, a countervailing effect on the abovementioned potentially negative effects of globalization is the growth in number, size, and power of civil society organizations combined with increased networking of these organizations across national boundaries (Buse et al. 2002). The implications of this effect were most dramatically illustrated in the drug policy case study, where South African organizations were able to secure the support of American organizations to pressurize the US government to retract its TRIPS-Plus policy.

Ultimately, there has been a global trend towards a rapid expansion in the number and range of actors engaged in health policy. While it is sometimes difficult to identify the precise role and relative influence of each domestic and global actor, there is convincing evidence that globalization has influenced the direction of health care policy in South Africa and the extent to which the nation's health objectives may be achieved.

## References

ADAMS, ORVILL AND COLETTE KINNON
1998    "A Public Health Perspective." Pp. 35-55 in *International Trade in Health Services: A Development Perspective*, edited by S. Zarrilli and C. Kinnon. Geneva: UNCTAD and World Health Organization.
ADLUNG, R. AND A. CARZANIGA
2002    "Health Services under the General Agreement on Trade Services." In *Trade in Health Services: Global, Regional and Country Perspectives*, edited by N. Droger and C. Vieira. Geneva: Pan American Health Organization and World Health Organization.
AFRICAN NATIONAL CONGRESS
2001    "Historic Agreement Lays the Basis for Co-operation Towards Health for All." Retrieved June 8, 2001 (www.anc.org.za/ancdocs/anctoday/2001/at13.htm). *ANC Today.*

AKIN, J., N. BIRDSALL AND D. DE FERRANTI
1987      "Financing Health Services in Developing Countries: An Agenda for Reform.
          A World Bank Policy Study." The World Bank, Washington, D.C.
BOND, PATRICK, YOGAN G. PILLAY AND DAVID SANDERS
1997      "The State of Neoliberalism in South Africa: Economic, Social and Health
          Transformation in Question." *International Journal of Health Services* 27:25-40.
BUSE, KENT, NICK DRAGER, SUZANNE FUSTUKIAN AND KELLEY LEE
2002      "Globalisation and Health Policy: Trends and Opportunities" in *Health Policy
          in a Globalising World*, edited by K. Lee, K. Buse and S. Fustukian. Cambridge:
          Cambridge University Press.
CLEARY, SUSAN
2001      "The South African Government, the Pharmaceutical Companies and Access
          to HIV/AIDS drugs." Masters Thesis, School of Economics, University of
          Cape Town, Cape Town.
CLEARY, SUSAN AND DON ROSS
2002      "The 1998-2001 Legal Interaction Between the South African Government
          and the International Pharmaceutical Industry: A Game-Theoretic Analysis."
          University of Cape Town, Cape Town.
CLEARY, SUSAN AND STEPHEN THOMAS
2002      "Mapping Health Services Trade in South Africa." Trade and Industrial
          Strategies, Johannesburg.
CONSUMER PROJECT ON TECHNOLOGY
1999      "US Government Efforts to Negotiate the Repeal, Termination or Withdrawal
          of Article 15(c) of the South African Medicines and Related Substances Act
          of 1965. In: Time-line of Disputes over Compulsory Licensing and Parallel
          Importation in South Africa." Retrieved June 8, 2001 (http://www.cptech.
          org/ip/health/sa/sa-timelinc.txt).
CORNELL, J., J. GOUDGE, D. MCINTYRE AND S. MBATSHA
2001      "South African National Health Accounts: The Private Sector." National
          Health Accounts Research Team and National Department of Health,
          Pretoria.
DE FERRANTI, D.
1985      "Paying for Health Services in Developing Countries: An Overview." The
          World Bank, Washington, D.C.
DEPARTMENT OF FINANCE
1996      "Growth, Employment and Redistribution: A Macro-Economic Framework."
          Department of Finance, Pretoria.
DEPARTMENT OF HEALTH
1996      "National Drug Policy for South Africa." Department of Health, Pretoria.
1997      "White Paper for the Transformation of the Health System in South Africa."
          Pretoria: Government Printer.
1999      "Health Sector Strategic Framework 1999-2004: Accelerating Quality Health
          Service Delivery." Pretoria: Department of Health.
2000      "Public/Private Partnership in Health: National Department of Health Policy
          Framework." Pretoria: Department of Health.
2001a     "National Health Bill (Draft)." Pretoria: Department of Health.
2001b     "Briefing Document: Defending the Medicines Control Amendment Act."
          Retrieved June 8, 2001 (http://www.gov.za/search97cgi/s97_cgi?action=View
          &VdkVgwKey=%2E%2E%2Fdata%2Fspeech01%2F010305945a1003%2Etxt
          &DocOffset=1&DocsFound=1&QueryZip=Medicines+Control+Amendment+
          Act&Collection=empty&Collection=speech01&SortField=TDEDate&SortOr
          der=desc&ViewTemplate=gov%2Fdocview%2Ehts&SearchUrl=http%3A%2F
          %2Fwww%2Egov%2Eza%2Fsearch97cgi%2Fs97%5Fcgi%3Faction%3D
          Search%26  QueryZip%3DMedicines%2BControl%2BAmendment%2BAct%
          26ResultTemplate%3Dgov%252Fdefault%252Ehts%26QueryText%3DMedi
          cines%2BControl%2BAmendment%2BAct%26Collection%3Dempty%26
          Collection%3Dspeech01%26SortField%3DTDEDate%26SortOrder%3Ddesc
          %26ViewTemplate%3Dgov%252Fdocview%252Ehts%26ResultStart%3D1
          %26ResultCount%3D25&).

DEPARTMENT OF TRADE AND INDUSTRY
1999        "Joint Understanding Between the Governments of South Africa and the
            United States of America." Retrieved June 8, 2001 (http://www.polity.org.za/
            govdocs/pr/1999/pr0917b.html). Pretoria: Department of Trade and Industry.
2002a       "Accelerating Growth and Development: The Contribution of an Integrated
            Manufacturing Strategy." Pretoria: Department of Trade and Industry.
2002b       "DTI Pushes into Global Economy. SouthAfrica.info." Retrieved January 20,
            2003 (http://www.safrica.info /doing_business/investment/agencies/dti.htm).
DOHERTY, JANE, STEPHEN THOMAS AND DEBBIE MUIRHEAD
2002a       "Health Care Financing and Expenditure in post-Apartheid South Africa,
            1996/97-1998/99." Pretoria: Department of Health.
DOHERTY, JANE, STEPHEN THOMAS, DEBBIE MUIRHEAD AND DI MCINTYRE
2002b       "Health Care Financing and Expenditure in the Post-Apartheid Era" in *South
            African Health Review 2002*, edited by Health Systems Trust. Durban: Health
            Systems Trust.
GILSON, LUCY, JANE DOHERTY, DI MCINTYRE, STEPHEN THOMAS, VISHAL
            BRIJLAL, CHRIS BOWA AND SANDI MBATSHA
1999        "The Dynamics of Policy Change: Health Care Financing in South Africa
            1994-99. Monograph No. 66." Johannesburg: Centre for Health Policy and
            Health Economics Unit.
GILSON, LUCY AND DI MCINTYRE
2001        "South Africa: Addressing the Legacy of Apartheid" in *Challenging Inequities in
            Health: From Ethics to Action*, edited by T. Evans, M. Whitehead, F. Diderichsen,
            A. Bhuiya and M. Wirth. New York: Oxford University Press.
HURRELL, A. AND N. WOODS
1995        "Globalization and Inequality." *Millennium Journal of International Studies* 24.
JIMENEZ, E.
1987        "Pricing Policy in the Social Sectors: Cost Recovery for Education and Health
            in Developing Countries." Baltimore: The Johns Hopkins University Press for
            the World Bank.
KUMARANAYAKE, LILANI AND SALLY LAKE
2002        "Regulation in the Context of Global Health Markets" in *Health Policy in a
            Globalising World*, edited by K. Lee, K. Buse and S. Fustukian. Cambridge:
            Cambridge University Press.
LEE, KELLEY, KENT BUSE AND SUZANNE FUSTUKIAN
2002        "Health Policy in a Globalising World." Cambridge: Cambridge University
            Press.
LUKES, S.
1974        *Power: A Radical View*. London: Macmillan.
MARAIS, HEIN
2001        *South Africa: Limits to Change: The Political Economy of Transition*. London and Cape
            Town: Zed Books and University of Cape Town Press.
MCINTYRE, D.E. AND R.E. DORRINGTON
1990        "Trends in the Distribution of South African Health Care Expenditure." *South
            African Medical Journal* 78:125-129.
MCINTYRE, DI, GERALD BLOOM, JANE DOHERTY AND PREM BRIJLAL
1995        "Health Expenditure and Finance in South Africa." Durban: Health Systems
            Trust and the World Bank.
MCINTYRE, DI, STEPHEN THOMAS, SANDI MBATSHA AND LUVUYO BABA
1999        "Equity in Public Sector Health Care Financing and Expenditure in South
            Africa." Durban: Health Systems Trust.
MCINTYRE, DIANE AND LUCY GILSON
2000        " Redressing Dis-Advantage: Promoting Vertical Equity Within South Africa."
            *Health Care Analysis* 8:235-258.
MCINTYRE, DI AND LUCY GILSON
2002        "Putting Equity in Health Back onto the Social Policy Agenda: Experience
            from South Africa." *Social Science and Medicine* 54:1637-1656.
MCINTYRE, DI, JANE DOHERTY AND LUCY GILSON
2003        "A Tale of Two Visions: The Changing Fortunes of Social Health Insurance
            in South Africa." *Health Policy and Planning* 18:47-58.

NAYLOR, C. DAVID
1988      "Private Medicine and the Privatisation of Health Care in South Africa." *Social Science and Medicine* 27:1153-1170.
PRICE, MAX
1989      "Explaining Trends in the Privatization of Health Services in South Africa." *Health Policy and Planning* 4:121-130.
RISPEL, L. AND G. BEHR
1992      "Health Indicators: Policy implications." Johannesburg: Centre for Health Policy, University of the Witwatersrand.
ROSS, M.H.
1982      "Future Provision of Health Services in the RSA." *RSA 2000* 4:32.
SOUTH AFRICA (REPUBLIC)
1987      "White Paper on Privatization and Deregulation in the Republic of South Africa." Pretoria: Government Printer.
THOMAS, S., D. MUIRHEAD, J. DOHERTY AND C. MUHEKI
2000      "Financing and Expenditure in the Post-Apartheid Public Health Sector" in *South African Health Review 2000*, edited by Health Systems Trust. Durban: Health Systems Trust.
VAN DEN HEEVER, ALEX
1997      "Regulating the Funding of Private Health Care: The South African Experience" in *Private Health Providers in Developing Countries: Serving the Public Interest?* edited by S. Bennett, B. McPake and A. Mills. London: Zed Books.
VAN RENSBURG, D. AND N. VAN RENSBURG
1999      "Distribution of Human Resources" in *South African Health Review 1999*, edited by Health Systems Trust. Durban: Health Systems Trust.
WOLSON, ROSEMARY
1997      "Intellectual Property Rights and Their Rise to Prominence in the International Trade Arena." *Trade & Industry Monitor* 2.
WORKING GROUP ON PRIVATISATION AND DEREGULATION
1986      "Privatisation and Deregulation of Health Care in South Africa." Pretoria: National Department of Health and Population Development.
WORLD TRADE ORGANIZATION
1994      "The Results of the Uruguay Round of Multilateral Trade Negotiations: The Legal Texts." Geneva: GATT Secretariat.
2001      "TRIPS and Pharmaceutical Patents: Fact Sheet." Retrieved June 8, 2001 (http://www.wto.org/english/tratop_e/trips_e/factsheet_pharm00_e.htm). Geneva: World Trade Organization.
WTO SECRETARIAT
1999      "An Introduction to the GATS." Geneva: World Trade Organization.

# Global Challenges to Equity in Safety and Health at Work: Struggles for Fair Work in Southern Africa

RENE LOEWENSON*

## ABSTRACT

Weaknesses in social protection and risk management systems within workplaces and in the wider public health environment and weak investment in health insurance and health services shift a significant share of the burden of production risks onto worker communities and under-funded public services. Inequality has been constructed by powerful economic and political interests and by weak policies for channelling the benefits of globalization to those most in need. Powerful drivers of inequity are not simply addressed through technical interventions—they demand political and economic action. This paper explores the knowledge and evidence needed to impact public policy and the approaches to building political momentum for that knowledge to be used.

## Introduction

*Equity Aspirations and Widening Inequality*

Southern Africa has become synonymous with struggles against inequality. It is a region where people have carried out acts of enormous courage to challenge unfair differences in political and economic rights on the basis of race, class and ethnic group, and to obtain basic rights to vote, and secure jobs, own land, receive health care, and attend schools. And yet it remains

---

*Training and Research Support Center (TARSC), Harare, Zimbabwe.

a region of significant and often growing inequality. Disparities in the fulfillment of basic rights persist by race, rural/urban status, socioeconomic status, and gender and geographical region. Despite strong public policy and commitment to equity in the region, public resources still do not preferentially reach those with the greatest needs. This paper draws attention to the driving forces of this inequity and explores how the driving forces for equity may be better mobilized.

## Development and Deprivation in the Lives of Workers

*Gaps Between Global Knowledge and Workplace Practice*
The first dimension of inequity lies in the gap between global knowledge and local practice in the work life of people, North and South. Workplaces in Southern Africa continue to experience work-related hazards that have long been controlled or even eliminated in high-income countries. The movement of capital, technology, and changes in work organization appears to have outpaced the systems for social protection of workers' health. Agriculture, manufacturing, and mining sector work is associated with high rates of injury from mechanical, electrical, and physical hazards (Loewenson 1998). The expansion of chemical, electronic, and biotechnology industries and of the service and transport sectors has introduced new risks, widened the spread of work-related risks and their interaction with non-work factors in ill-health, including environmental pollution. Hence, in addition to old and prevalent problems of traumatic injury, respiratory disease, occupational dermatitis, and musculo-skeletal injury, workers also now suffer new stresses such as new asthmatic disorders, psychological stress, and ergonomic and visual effects of VDUs. Work is increasingly characterized by a high level of demand, with little control over the nature and content of the work, leading to digestive disorders, sleep difficulties, and musculoskeletal problems (Fuentes and Ehrenreich 1994; Kothari et al. 1996).

## Poverty and Poor Returns from Global Integration Undermine Workers' Health

Avoidable differences in the distribution of risks and ill-health due to work in the region are often attributed to poverty within production processes, particularly in small enterprises. Workers in small enterprises and in the "informal" economy experience high rates of exposure to work- related risks, with inadequate systems for protection. Informal employment has increased as formal sectors of the economy have failed to provide adequate incomes or employment to a rapidly growing labor force (Mhone 1996). Jobs in the informal economy are often of poor quality, provide low incomes, and have low annual profits and start-up capital (USAID/Gemini 1991).

Risks in the sector include poor work organization, poor access to clean water and sanitation, ergonomic hazards, hazardous hand-tools, and exposure to dusts and chemicals. Informal workers in agriculture often apply chemicals manually, using old, poorly maintained equipment, with inadequate information to users on the risks. Workers are exposed to toxic chemicals that have been restricted or banned in the North, used in unsafe and poorly maintained application techniques—with lack of information and knowledge provided to the user—workers are also exposed to the risks of unsafe storage of chemicals and use of old chemical containers for food and water storage (Lakew and Mekonnen 1997; Loewenson and Nhachi 1996; London 1994). Hazards are poorly controlled. Even personnel protective equipment (PPE) is poorly provided and often poorly maintained where it is provided (Batino 1995; ILO 1990; Kogi 1985; Loewenson 1998). These risks spill into wider populations in home-based enterprises (Kogi 1985).

Workers in the informal sector suffer occupational injury and mortality rates similar to those of workers in the formal sector, but higher rates of occupational illness (Jinadu 1987; Loewenson 1998, 2000; Lukindo 1993; Tornberg et al. 1996). While their injuries have been found to lead to lost work time and thus to be compensable, almost none of such injuries, according to one survey in Zimbabwe, were reported or compensated (Loewenson 1998).

However, not all the differentials in occupational injury and illness can be traced to poor value added in production systems. There is in some cases an inverse relationship between returns to production and investments in safe work. Paradoxically, those workplaces most integrated into the global economy are sometimes those found to experience the highest level of risk. Export Processing Zones (EPZs) have highly liberalized tax and trade regimes to improve access to global markets for export goods. They have been associated with above average-rates of machine-related accidents, dusts, noise, poor ventilation, and toxic chemical exposure. They are also documented to expose workers to high levels of job stress. A combination of accidents, stress, and intense exposure to other common hazards is reported to arise out of unrealistic production quotas, productivity incentives, and inadequate controls on overtime, all of which create pressures for highly intense work. These stresses have been documented to produce cardiovascular and psychological disorders. It is often young women who work in low quality insecure jobs in EPZs, and they have been documented to experience additional reproductive health problems, including miscarriage, problems with pregnancies, and poor fetal health (Fuentes and Ehrenreich 1994; ILO 1988b).

Workers who migrate to areas of higher employment do not reap returns in improved social protection. While migrancy is a longstanding feature of production systems in Southern Africa, increased trade and financial flows have added new waves of migrancy, including informal sector traders. Migrant workers experience chronic occupational disease that is poorly detected, leading to unemployment and disease burdens being borne in poor households or public health systems in countries that migrants come from and producing a number of problems in detection, reporting, and compensation of illness and injury. Studies in South Africa and Botswana have indicated, for example, that there are thousands of undetected or unreported cases of occupational lung diseases in former mine workers in the rural areas of Southern Africa (Dubovsky 1993; Steen et al. 1994; Trapido et al. 1996).

## Greater Exportable Surpluses, Greater Cost Burdens of Ill-Health Borne by Workers

A further source of inequity arises in an unfair shift of the burden of injury and illness from production systems to poor workers and their families. Migrant workers with chronic occupational disease are generally absorbed back into poor rural communities, where their disease is managed in poor households and underfunded public health systems.

Shortfalls in workers' protection and compensation in informal employment shifts the burden of social protection to the workers and their families. Poor households and communities thus provide the major source of relief in such cases. Many workers in the informal economy spend large amounts on health and education, but they do so through individual out-of-pocket payments and not through collectively pooled risk schemes. This may further reduce available resources to spend on technologies or other measures for workplace safety, and further increase risk of injury.

Occupational risks spill over to non-employed populations, through home-based enterprise, air and water pollution, and through the transmission of communicable disease (Packard 1989). Sexually transmitted infections and HIV, for example, have been found to be greater in communities along transport routes, or in communities surrounding major development projects. Enterprises that provide poor living environments, as have been found in the dormitory style hostels of EPZs or agroindustries, generate public health problems that are not adequately factored into health services provided (Kamel 1990a). Such morbidity is not usually classified as "occupational" but is certainly work related (Maganu 1988).

Not only are these burdens often not borne within production systems, but also occupational morbidity may be masked by background levels of ill-health attributable to poor diet, substandard housing, overcrowding, and adverse environmental conditions.

Few workers are covered by formal health insurance, leaving individuals and public health systems with inadequate funds for a reasonable quality of medical care. Compensation systems provide extremely low benefits after injury, and in the absence of formal health insurance, injury leading to job loss can lead to the collapse of household income. Informal social protection mechanisms (extended family, local community) have been stretched to extreme limits.

The burden of ill-health borne at the household level has been exacerbated by longstanding inequities in health and access to health care, with worsening inequalities under new market reforms (EQUINET 1998; EQUINET 2001). Hence, while poor health status in the region is higher in groups that have in the past been subject to racial discrimination, it is also increased in groups with recent experience of decreased employment opportunities and/or lack of employment rights (Gilson and McIntyre 2000).

## The Driving Forces of Inequity

It has been argued that inequality is a natural consequence of economic and social life, and that equity is constructed by social action and public policy. However, it appears that within current processes of globalization, inequality is not simply happening but is being constructed by powerful economic and political interests and public policies that are not able to ensure the application of the benefits of globalization in those most who most need it.

## Poor Application of Global Knowledge

Knowledge and information have spread rapidly within recent years, but application of both in Southern Africa is undermined by the low visibility or consideration of workers' health when plans and decisions are made regarding production. Weak monitoring and regulatory systems imply that a significant share of occupational morbidity is not routinely reported, particularly chronic illness due to chemical, ergonomic, and psychosocial factors. Health problems may also be underreported due to fears of job insecurity and high labor turnover, factors that have become more pronounced under recent economic reforms. WHO/OGIEH (1996) estimates of the burden of occupational disease suggest that occupational reporting systems in Southern Africa probably underestimate the real burden of occupational disease 50-fold (Loewenson 1998). [1]

Underdetection of occupational morbidity also implies that the burden of uncertainty over the adverse health risks of production processes is usually borne by exposed workers. In industrialized countries, standard setting in unclear situations may err on the side of controlling risks, but in poorer countries this often errs on the side of continued exposure. Unfortunately, these countries also have the least human, technical, and financial resources to carry out studies needed to demonstrate the risk, a situation exacerbated by the outflow of occupational health professionals.

Improved knowledge and practice in systems for protecting workers health is poorly applied due to economic signals that factor workers' health as a *cost* rather than a contributor to production systems. Operators within the financially starved informal economy, for example, avoid regulation and try to diminish contact with administrative and enforcement systems to avoid spending on safety requirements. At the same time, they are poorly served by public information, insurance, or technical support services. With low levels of capital, informal operators may use poorly developed tools and techniques and may innovate shortcuts in production that, while necessary for economic survival, may pose serious hazards to workers. These conditions generate a number of deficits in the informal economy—a *rights gap* in relation to freedom of association, right to organize, and to collective bargaining; a *social protection gap* in terms of working conditions and social security; and *gaps in labor law and its enforcement.*

Again, the attempt to cut health and safety *costs* is not unique to sectors where productivity is low. Concessions given in EPZs to allow production without labor or health protection and without applying safety regulations signal the extent to which these inputs are regarded as "costs" to production. While ILO has carried out a significant amount of work to show the production returns from quality, secure jobs and investments in work environments and labor well-being, on the ground, these are areas commonly sacrificed by those seeking to attract investors or by companies themselves (ILO 2002).

## Losing Sight of Workers' Health in the Wider Resurgence of Disease

Work-related ill-health has become less visible in the wider resurgence of disease and reversal of health care gains in the region. Structural

---

[1] The WHO estimate is made on the basis of evidence from countries with better reporting systems, and is compared against the real reported levels from occupational injury and disease reporting systems in Southern Africa.

adjustment and liberalization of economies in Sub-Saharan Africa at the end of the last century were associated with increased infant mortality, worsening nutritional status, reduced per capita expenditure on health, reduced real earnings of health workers, and massive attrition of health sector personnel (Anyinyam 1989; Cliff 1991; Commonwealth Secretariat 1989; Cornia et al. 1987; CWGH 1997; Kalumba 1991; Kanji 1991; Lesley et al. 1986; Loewenson and Chisvo 1994; Loxley 1990).

The most marked health problem in this respect has been the HIV/AIDS epidemic, with Southern Africa being the worst affected region in the world. With adult HIV prevalence rates of 25% and more, companies that had little investment in reducing occupational risks became concerned about mitigating the impacts of HIV/AIDS on production. Such impacts cost the company about US$200/employee annually, while insurers predicted collapse of benefit schemes due to AIDS. In fact, HIV/AIDS moved through all the current equity fault lines in Southern African social and economic systems and demonstrated clearly and rapidly the extent to which production sectors were geared to shift health risks and burdens from production to poor communities.

HIV first moved through skilled, mobile, educated, and urban groups in the region, but rapidly spread to rural, lower income groups, and from adults to adolescents. The epidemic moved from more socially and economically powerful adult males to poor and economically insecure females, particularly female adolescents (ILO 1995a, 1995b, 1995c). HIV transmission was highest where income and gender inequalities coincided with movement for trade, work, food, and social support—a common pattern in the region in areas of migrant employment, along transport routes, and in urban and peri-urban areas.

Despite the increased risk emanating from production-related activities, productive and formal sectors transferred, with relative efficiency, the negative impacts of HIV-related ill-health to the household level. Some companies, despite running ad hoc HIV awareness programs, screened employees for HIV before employment, or found ways of discharging HIV-infected employees. Death, disability, and medical insurance schemes excluded people with HIV or reduced benefits, reducing coverage and household savings and shifting the costs of unsecured risks to public and household budgets. Regulatory frameworks for demanding company liabilities had been significantly weakened by liberalized labor and tax regimes under market reforms. Even where new laws were passed, under pressure from unions, to prevent HIV discrimination in employment, they were poorly implemented or enforced.

Health services, facing increased burdens from non-working ill people, promoted home- based care approaches. These have often been inadequately supported, further stressing households, and particularly women caregivers. Worker households were largely unsupported by social security after job termination due to AIDS; these households spent four times their share of annual household income on AIDS-related health costs compared with households covered by social security (Hanson 1992). The impact of AIDS has thus been to shift burdens from formal to informal economies, to precipitate deeper poverty in poor households, and to facilitate the intergenerational transmission of poverty (Loewenson and Whiteside 1996).

## Negative Terms Reinforced by Macroeconomic Reforms and Trade Systems

Globally, the incomes of a quarter of the world's population declined towards the end of the last millennium, a large share of these concentrating in Sub-Saharan Africa (UNDP 1996). Globalization has produced mixed employment outcomes, particularly in the South. On the one hand, the global spread of human rights agendas, the enhancement of equity in employment law, and the widening of employment opportunities in nontraditional spheres of employment have brought more people into the workforce. New production technology and processes have generated new forms of employment. The gains, however, have not been felt across much of Southern Africa. For the large majority of Southern African workers, liberalized trade has been accompanied by a transfer of hazardous technologies and processes, an increase in assembly line, low quality jobs with minimal options for advancement and a growth in insecure, casual and small-scale informal employment (Fuentes and Ehrenreich 1994; ILO 1998b; ILO in SATUCC 1977; McConnell 1988; Pearce et al. 1994).

Women have been particularly affected by these employment patterns. They have taken on more jobs and work longer hours. Generally, they occupy low-skill, low-paying jobs, and casual or nonpermanent forms of employment and jobs where unionization rates are low (Fuentes and Ehrenreich 1994; Johal et al. 1993; Kothari et al. 1996; Smyre 1992). Such poor quality jobs do not usually enhance social protection, while the increase in out-contracted, casual, and home-based work disguises the employment relationship and shifts liability for working conditions to the worker. It is not simply poor growth that generates these conditions: UNDP data on development indicators in SADC countries show that, even in countries experiencing economic growth or greater prosperity, economic returns are not being translated adequately into human development (UNDP 1999).

Market reforms and poor economic performance have generally led to weakened public sector services and infrastructures, reduced real public spending on health and social protection, increased competition for scarce health resources, and caused a plateau or at best reduced coverage and poorer quality of care, particularly at the primary care level (Lennock 1994; Loewenson and Chisvo 1994; Price 1997; Sahn and Bernier 1996; UNICEF MoHCW 1996).

Liberalization has enabled a wider spread of providers, with an inadequate state infrastructure to regulate quality or ensure equity in the growth of private providers. Cost escalation in the private sector has also led to a greater share of overall health resources going to a smaller and wealthier section of the population. This has exacerbated salary differentials between private and public sectors, leading to attrition of skilled health professionals from the public sector into the private sector. Declining real wages and social benefits for health professionals have also encouraged the attrition of skilled personnel to migrate to higher income countries, sometimes aided by active recruitment processes. New trade rules such as General Agreement on Trade in Service (GATS) threaten to further weaken the ability of the state to protect public sector employment or regulate private providers. The liberalized growth of private care under conditions of declining access to basic public services has led to parallel worlds, where those with wealth and connections have access to the highest technology, while many poor people cannot get or afford secure access to essential services or drugs (EQUINET 2001; Klugman and McIntyre 2000; Mutizwa, Mangisa, and Mbengwa 2000).

With few exceptions, health services in the region continue to be more accessible to social groups who experience lower levels of ill-health, even with respect to basic preventive and curative services for diseases that are more commonly experienced among the poor (World Bank 2000). It would thus appear that trends towards insecure, low-quality employment, reduced public sector capacity and professional attrition have not only increased inequalities in health, but have also enabled more powerful business, medical, and wealthy interest groups to exact health and social welfare concessions at the cost of poorer, less organized workers (Bennett et al. 1995; Kalumba 1997; Lafond 1991; Storey 1989; Van Rensburg and Fourie 1994).

## Confronting Inequity: Turning Values into Practice

How can such trends towards inequality and poverty be addressed? Such powerful drivers of inequity are not likely to be simply addressed through technical interventions, nor through applying resources to social interventions targeted at specific problems or groups. They demand a deeper level of political and economic action.

Equity assigns social value to what is considered to be unfair, avoidable and unnecessary within the spectrum of inequalities. It is thus not possible to confront inequity purely from a technical perspective: The decision on what is unfair is a social and political decision and often a site of struggle.

Further, experience of Southern Africa interventions in the late twentieth century indicates that it is difficult to sustain the implementation of equity-oriented social policies and gains when health inequalities arise from patterns of ownership of wealth, employment, trade, and political influence that are not adequately addressed. If improved equity in health demands engagement with the political and economic factors that generate unfair inequalities, then struggles around health at work are an ideal site for raising and confronting the decisions around production and employment that undermine health at national and global levels.

There are many ways of tapping this opportunity. This paper focuses on two such drivers for equity:

- The first relates to building the knowledge and evidence that can impact on public policy at global and national levels.
- The second relates to building the political momentum for that knowledge to be used.

## Knowledge and Information as a Fundamental Basis for Any Policy Shift

Occupational health risks in Southern Africa, as in other parts of Africa, have always been poorly monitored, studied, and documented. Many occupational health studies have been directed at describing occupational risks and health outcomes in groups of workers, often documenting risk-disease relationships already well documented in industrialized countries, and in some cases long controlled or eliminated (Loewenson 1998b). There is still a serious gap in the evidence base for policies on safe work in Southern Africa.

Evidence is thus needed to raise the visibility of gaps in workers' health, examine and critique the assumption that health improvements are a cost to production, and strengthen the arguments and mechanisms for improved monitoring and detection of the ill health arising from production. Information is needed on the extent to which production gains are translated into safe work investments and the manner in which shortfalls are mediated by insecure employment and wider inequalities in access to inputs to health and health care. The burden shift of injury and illness to households and poor communities needs to be made more visible, particularly where this shift is mediated by market reforms and weak public policy.

Producing this knowledge is not simple, given the manner in which economic trends have fragmented, disrupted, and moved vulnerable communities and undermined the technical and financial resources available.

## Political Momentum for Change

Southern Africa is not unique in experiencing inequities in workers health. Even within high- income countries, there are areas of employment and groups of workers that experience increased risk and poor social protection. This situation not only traces back to an absence of evidence, it also traces back to the interests and political momentum for applying knowledge in practice. Paradoxically, global knowledge is poorly applied in precisely those settings where risks are greatest.

Rather than reversing this trend, globalization has been associated with economic policies that intensify it. It is insufficient to make information on risk available to public authorities in Southern Africa. Liberalization and trade competition between poor states have been associated with deregulation of production and health laws and weakened public sector capacities, such as is described in this paper in EPZs and in declining public social protection systems. This deregulation weakens both the state systems and the strength of workers' organizations necessary to ensure that risks are recognized and standards enforced. States vulnerable to investor pressures and workers vulnerable to job insecurity and labor flexibility may themselves be unwilling to expose and deal with health problems (Packard 1989).

Confronting inequity cannot therefore be separated from the political struggle around policies and resources. As Sen (1999) puts it "Issues of social allocation of economic resources cannot be separated from the role of participatory politics and the reach of informed public discussion" (cited in WHO 1999). In workers' health, health and safety outcomes are associated with the social norms and networks within production systems, the basic rights workers have to collective organization and action, and the mechanisms for procedural justice and participation (Loewenson 1998b; Pearce et al. 1994; Wilkinson 1997).

The extent of political momentum for equity in health and safety at work is reflected therefore in the presence and application of legal frameworks of rights and obligations, in the public sector policies and capacities, in the norms that define the "safety culture" and in the effectiveness and authority of tripartite systems for reaching consensus on acceptable standards of work safety.

This site is currently one of struggle. Liberalization has been associated with deregulation of employment and health and safety laws, promotion of nontransparent self-regulation systems, often with absurdly low penalties for breach of law relative to other production costs. Declining public sector capacities, patchy law enforcement, and rare invoking of criminal sanctions for breach of law signal weak public policies. As multilateral lending agencies (and bilateral aid agencies) have become more directly involved in political and economic decision-making processes, they too have influenced the extent of state regulation of and expenditure on employment-related issues like health and safety. There are exceptions to this influence in both Zimbabwe and South Africa, where, beyond efforts at safety promotion, the state has been willing to take strong measures to enforce laws and prosecute offences.

Behind this development is the pressure from workers themselves. If equity is socially defined, then those directly influenced by the conditions of work have an important role to play in shaping the values and norms that determine what is unfair and the attendant public policy choices.

The political momentum for occupational health is stronger where workers are well organized and more informed and able to control the work process. Job and income security, literacy, information rights and access, union access, collective bargaining rights and effective union representation organization are thus fundamental to equity in health and safety at work. Conversely, current trends towards output related pay, insecure and flexible contracts, restrictions to union access, migrant and out-contracted work and proscribed collective bargaining rights fundamentally undermine the social and political resources that enable workers to achieve improved health and safety (Dreze and Sen 1995; Navarro 2002; Sen 1992).

Southern African workers seeking to address the economic, investment, employment, and public policy measures that generate inequity in workers' health quickly confront the extent to which these concepts are only partially defined, under globalization, by national policies and processes. Increasingly global institutions, policies and transnational investors and producers shape whether a worker in Malawi has a job, what type of job, and whether that worker will access medical care or drug treatments.

The success with which Southern African workers are able to resolve these problems nationally now depends on the extent to which inequity in health and safety is perceived to be a risk not only for the poor, or the unemployed, or the disabled in the South, but also for the rich, and for wider prosperity and health globally.

## Linking Knowledge to Political Momentum

Much occupational health work disregards or underplays the social production of occupational health gains, compared to the role of technical knowledge and development. In Southern Africa, as in many other parts of the world, production systems and social services have both undergone periods of radical transformation based on organized, social and political demand. As noted at the beginning of this paper, popular struggles lay behind the transformation of the state in most of the region. The central role of the state in responding to and consolidating law and services around that demand and the weak arrangements for sustaining public participation and accountability have masked the critical role that social norms and action play in shaping and realizing public policy. Whatever lies behind it, the gap between technical knowledge and organized demand, reflected in the gap between professionals and workers, undermines the ability of *both* to influence public policy.

In contrast, there have been unique moments in history when that gap has been closed, with significantly positive outcomes. For example, the use of participatory inquiry for occupational health in Italy in the 1970s brought together professionals and workers to identify risks and promote a healthy work life. This joint work created a widespread consciousness about the importance of work for health that influenced Italian public health policy and institutions in the 1970's. It not only led to a large body of new scientific literature on work-health relationships, but brought about changes at the work-place through local action, gave unions and workers greater control over work environment decisions, motivated unions to develop their own occupational health institutions, and motivated changes in labor legislation. The combined effects of these changes contributed to a decline in work-related health problems and work accidents (Berlinguer 1979; Laurell 1984). Similarly in Zimbabwe and in South Africa, there were periods of participatory and joint work between professionals and unions that raised the profile of occupational health and safety, made visible occupational health problems, led to new areas of collective bargaining in occupational health and new legal rights and services (Loewenson 1998b; ZCTU 1992, 1994). These experiences signal the type of political and technical momentum needed to face the challenges highlighted earlier to equity in health and safety and work. Such links between technical and political elements of change have been achieved where there are strong alliances between professionals and workers.

Globalization, however, adds a new dimension to these old lessons. This paper has highlighted not only the inequalities North and South, but also the global source of many challenges to equity in the healthy work life among people in the South. Global institutions such the World Trade Organization (WTO) now set terms that limit the authority of governments at the national level, while transnational corporations have more power than many states.

With this imbalance between risk and resources, addressing inequity in health and safety depends on the extent to which it is perceived to be a risk not only in those exposed, but also for wider global security, prosperity, and health. Recurring episodes of financial collapse, poverty- induced conflict, warfare, and human rights abuses have raised some awareness in the North that markets have become too dominant in human life and that poverty is a risk not only for the poor, but also for wider global security. There is a growing understanding that global security and equity cannot be built on the significant burdens of deprivation borne by communities in the South, which includes workers in Africa. What is less well appreciated is that improving conditions in Southern Africa also depends on more deliberate policies for ensuring global equity.

The current level of engagement between South and North professionals, workers, researchers, and others who could give counsel on how to deal with risks in occupational health is, however, too low and too sporadic to outpace the prescriptions emerging from powerful political and economic actors. Globalization has produced powerful tools, new communication technologies, more widely connected social movements, and an increasingly global recognition of universal rights as fundamental to policy. The full potential of these tools is still to be realized in building concerted global action for the health of workers.

# References

BATINO, J.
1995        "Snapshot of Working Conditions in the Urban Informal Sector," ILO Interdepartmental Project on the Urban Informal Sector, 2 June 1995 (Mimeo).
BENNETT, S., S. RUSSELL AND A. MILLS
1995        "Institutional and Economic Perspectives on Government Capacity to Assume New Roles in the Health Sector: A Review of Experience. In *The Role of Government in Adjusting Economies* (Paper 4). UK: University of Birmingham Series.
BELINGUER, GIOVANNI
1979        *Una Riforma per la Salute*. De Donato, Bari.
CIVIC GROUP HOUSING PROJECT
1995        "Survey of Home Based Enterprises in Zimbabwe" (Monograph). TARSC, Harare, Zimbabwe.
CLIFF, JULIE
1991        "Destabilisation, Economic Adjustment and the Impact on Women." Paper presented at the ZCTU/UZ Economics Department Workshop on Structural Adjustment and Health, February 1991, Harare, Zimbabwe.
CORNIA GIOVANNI, J. JOLLY AND F. STEWART
1987        *Adjustment with a Human Face*. Oxford: Clarendon Press.
COMMUNITY WORKING GROUP ON HEALTH
1997        Health in Zimbabwe: Community Perceptions and Views Research Report. OXFAM and TARSC, Zimbabwe. November 1997.
COMMONWEALTH SECRETARIAT
1989        *Engendering Adjustment for the 1990's*. London, UK: Commonwealth Secretariat Publications.
DREZE, J. AND AMARTYA SEN
1989        *Hunger and Public Action*. Oxford, UK: Clarendon Press.
DUBOVSKY, H.
1993        "Occupational Lung Disease." *South African Medical Journal* 83: 436.
EQUINET STEERING COMMITTEE
1998        "Equity in Health in Southern Africa: Overview and Issues from an Annotated Bibliography." EQUINET Policy Series No. 2. Harare, Zimbabwe: Benaby Printers.

EQUINET STEERING COMMITTEE
2001       "Equity in Health in Southern Africa: Turning Values into Practice."
           EQUINET Policy Series No. 7. Harare, Zimbabwe: Benaby Printers.
FUENTES, A. AND BARBARA EHRENREICH
1983       (Revised 1985) *Women in the Global Factory*. Boston, MA: South End Press.
GILSON, LUCY AND DI MCINTYRE
2000       "Experiences from South Africa: Dealing with a Poor Health Legacy of
           Apartheid." In *Challenging Inequities in Health: From Ethics to Action*, edited by
           M. Whitehead, T. Evans, F. Diderichsen, and A. Bhuiya. New York: Oxford
           University Press.
GOUDGE, JANE AND VELOSHNEE GOVENDER
2000       *A Review of Experience Concerning Household Ability to Cope with the Resource Demands
           of Ill Health and Health Care Utilization*. Harare, Zimbabwe: Equinet.
HANSON, K.
1992       "AIDS: What Does Economics Have to Offer?" Pp. 315-328 in *Health Policy
           and Planning*. London, UK: Health Policy Unit.
ILO
1988b      *Economic and Social Effects of Multinational Enterprises in Export Processing Zones*.
           Geneva, Switzerland: International Labour Organisation.
1990       *The Working Poor in Bangladesh. A Case Study on Employment Problems, Conditions of
           Work and Legal Protection of Selected Categories of Disadvantaged Workers in Bangladesh*.
           Dhaka, Bangladesh: International Labour Organisation.
1995a      "The Impact of HIV/AIDS on the Productive Labour Force in Africa"
           (Working Paper no. 1). EAMAT, Addis Ababa, Ethiopia.
1995b      "The Impact of HIV/AIDS on the Productive Labour Force in Zambia"
           (Working Paper no. 5). EAMAT, Addis Ababa, Ethiopia.
1995c      "The Impact of HIV/AIDS on the Productive Labour Force in Tanzania"
           (Working Paper no. 3). EAMAT, Addis Ababa, Ethiopia.
2002       "Decent Work and the Informal Economy." International Labour Conference
           90th Session, November 12, 2001, Geneva, Switzerland (June 2002 General
           Discussion Paper Draft 2).
JINADU, M.
1987       "Occupational Health and Safety in a Newly Industrialising Country." *Jo Royal
           Society of Health* 107(1): 8-10.
JOHAL, R., S. KEYVANSHAD AND D. LISKER
1993       "Zimbabwe Gender Issues" (Information Sheet No. 1.43). World Bank, Africa
           Region.
KALUMBA, KATELE
1991       "Impact of Structural Adjustment Programmes on Household Level, Food
           Security and Child Nutrition in Zambia." Paper presented at the ZCTU/UZ
           Economics Department Workshop on Structural Adjustment and Health,
           February 1991. Harare, Zimbabwe.
1997       "Towards an Equity-Oriented Policy of Decentralisation in Health Systems
           under Conditions of Turbulence: The Case of Zambia" (Discussion Paper
           No. 6). World Health Organisation: Zambia.
KAMEL, RACHEL
1990       *The Global Factory: Analysis and Action for a New Economic Era*. Philadelphia, PA:
           American Friends Service Committee.
KITUNGA, L.
1996       "Prevalence of Occupational Disease in Tanzania." *African Newsletter on Occupa-
           tional Health and Safety* 2: 42-45.
KOGI, K.
1985       *Improving Working Conditions in Small Enterprises in Developing Asia*. Geneva,
           Switzerland: ILO.
KOTHARI, U. AND V. NABABSING
1996       *Genders and Industrialisation*. Mauritius: Editions de l'Ocean Indien.
KLUGMAN, BARBARA AND DI MCINTYRE
2000       "From Policy Through Budgets to Implementation: Delivering Quality Health
           Care Services." In *The Fifth Womens Budget*, edited by D. Budlender. Cape
           Town, SA: IDASA.

LAFOND, A.
1995      *Sustaining Primary Health Care*. London, UK: Earthscan Publications Ltd.
LAKEW, K. AND Y. MEKONNEN
1997      "A Study among Agricultural Workers in Ethiopia." *African Newsletter on Occupational Health and Safety* 7: 68-70.
LAURELL, AUSA CHRISTINA
1984      "Ciencia y Experiencia Obrera." *Cuadernos Políticos* 41: 63-83.
LENNOCK, J.
1994      *Paying for Health: Poverty and Structural Adjustment in Zimbabwe*. Oxford, UK: OXFAM.
LESLEY, J., M. LYCETTE AND M. BUVINIC
1986      "Weathering Economic Crises: The Crucial Role of Women in Health." In *Health, Nutrition and Economic Crises*, edited by D. Bell and M. Reach. Auburn House, Ireland.
LOEWENSON, RENE
1988      "Assessment of the Health Impact of Occupational Risk in Africa: Current Situation and Methodological Issues." *Epidemiology* 10: 632-9.
1998b     "Situation Analysis of and Issues in Occupational Health and Safety in the SADC Region." Paper Prepared for the Employment and Labour Sector Meeting of the Southern African Trade Union Co-ordinating Council, April 21-23, Port Louis, Mauritius.
1993      "Safety Issues Identified in Zimbabwe." *Pesticides News* 21: 13.
1997      "Assessment of the Health Impact of Occupational Risk in Africa: Current Situation and Methodological Issues." Paper presented at the WHO/ILO Consultation on Health Impact Assessment of Occupational and Environmental Risk, July 1997, Geneva, Switzerland.
2000      "Occupational Hazards in the Informal Sector: A Global Perspective." In *Health Effects of the New Labour Market*, edited by K. Isaksson, C. Hogstedt, C. Eriksson, and T. Theorell. New York, NY: Kluwer Academic/Plenum Publishers.
LOEWENSON, RENE AND MUNHAMO CHISVO
1994      "Transforming Social Development: The Experience of Zimbabwe." UNICEF, Harare, Zimbabwe. Unpublished Report.
LOEWENSON, RENE AND CHARLES NHACHI
1996      "Epidemiology of the Health impact of Pesticide Use in Zimbabwe." Pp. 25-37 in *Pesticides in Zimbabwe: Toxicity and Health Implications*, edited by CFB Nhachi and OMJ Kasilo. Harare, Zimbabwe: University of Zimbabwe Press.
LOEWENSON, RENE AND ALAN WHITESIDE
1997      "Social and Economic Impacts of HIV/AIDS in Southern Africa." (SAfAIDS Monograph). Harare, Zimbabwe: Fontline.
LONDON, LESLIE
1994      "Agrichemical Safety Practices on Farms in the Western Cape." *South African Medical Journal* 84: 273-278.
LUKINDO, J.
1993      "Comprehensive Survey of the Informal Sector in Tanzania." *African Newsletter on Occupational Health and Safety* 3: 36-37.
MAGANU, E.
1998      "The Health Effects of Workers in Botswana: A Study on the Effects of Mining and Migration" (Working paper). ILO, Botswana.
McCONNEL, ROB
1998      "Epidemiology and Occupational Health in Developing Countries: Pesticides in Nicaragua." In *Progress in Occupational Epidemiology*, edited by C. Hogstedt and C. Reuterwall. Amsterdam, Holland: Exerpta Medica.
MHONE, GUY
1996      *The Informal Sector in Southern Africa*. Harare, Zimbabwe: SAPES Books.
MONGUTI, S.
1993      "Special Problems of Women Workers in a Developing Country." *African Newsletter on Occupational Health and Safety* 3: 63-65.

MUTIZWA MANGISA, DOROTHY AND MBENGWE ALBERT
2000 "Human Resource Policies and Equity in Health in Southern Africa." Paper presented at the EQUINET Conference, September 2000, Midrand.

NAVARRO, VINCENT
2002 *The Political Economy of Social Inequalities.* New York, NY: Baywood Publishing Co.

NOWEIR, M.
1986 "Occupational Health in Developing Countries, with Special Reference to Egypt." *American Journal of Industrial Medicine* 9: 125-141.

PACKARD, RANDALL
1989 "Industrial Production, Health and Disease in Sub-Saharan Africa." *Social Science and Medicine* 28: 475-496.

PEARCE, NEILL AND E. MATOS
 *Industrialisation and Health in Occupational Cancer in Developing Countries.* Lyon, France: IARC Publications.

PRICE, MAX
1997 "Policies for Health Sector Development—Where Does Equity Feature?" Paper presented at the Southern African Conference on Equity in Health, March 1997, Kasane, Botswana.

SAHN, D. AND R. BERNIER
1996 "Has Structural Adjustment Led to Health System Reform in Africa?" In *Health Sector Reform in Developing Countries: Making Health Sustainable*, edited by P. Berman. Cambridge, MA: Harvard University Press.

SATUCC
 "Report of the Follow-Up Regional Trade Union Workshop on Export Processing Zones, Environment and Sustainable Development" (Workshop Report). SATUCC, Pretoria, SA.

SEKIMPI, DEO ET AL.
1990 "Respiratory and Allegoric Status Assessment of Coffee Dust Exposed Workers in Uganda." (Preliminary Report). International Development Research Centre, Nairobi, Kenya.

SEN, AMARTYA
1992 *Inequality Re-Examined.* Oxford, UK: Clarendon Press.

SHUKLA, A., S. KUMAR AND F. ÖRY
1991 "Occupational Health and the Environment in an Urban Slum in India." *Social Science and Medicine* 5: 597-603.

STEEN, T. ET AL.
1994 "Prevalence of Occupational Lung Disease Amongst Botswana Men Formerly Employed in the South African Mining Industry." Unpublished data.

STOREY, P.
1989 "Health Care in South Africa: The Rights and Responsibilities of the Community." *Medicine and Law* 7: 649-655.

STRASSMAN, W.
1988 "Home Based Enterprises in Developing Countries." *Economic Development and Cultural Change* 36.

TAQI, ALI
1996 "Globalization of Economic Relations: Implications for Occupational Safety and Health." Presented at the XIV World Congress on Occupational Safety and Health, April 23, Madrid, Spain.

TORNBERG, V., V. FORASTIERI, P. RIWA AND D. SWAI
1996 "Occupational Safety and Health in the Informal Sector." *African Newsletter on Occupational Health and Safety* 6: 30-33.

TRAPIDO, A. ET AL.
1996 "Occupational Lung Disease in Ex-Mineworkers Sound a Further Alarm." *South African Medical Journal* 86: 559.

TRIPLE, A.G.
1993 "Shelter as Workplace: A Review of Home Based Enterprises in Developing Countries." *International Labour Review* 132.

UNDP
1996 *Human Development Report 1996.* New York, NY: Oxford University Press.

1999        *Human Development Report.* New York, NY: Oxford University Press.
UNICEF
1996        "District Health Service Costs, Resource Adequacy and Efficiency: A Comparison of Three Districts." Ministry of Health and Child Welfare, Harare, Zimbabwe. Mimeo.
USAID/GEMINI
1991        "Micro and Small Scale Enterprises in Zimbabwe: Results of a Country Wide Survey." Gemini USAID Technical Report No. 25.
VAN RENSBURG, H.C. AND A. FOURIE
1994        "Inequalities in South African Health Care. Part II: Setting the Record Straight." *South African Medical Journal* 84: 99-103.
VILEGAS, G.S.
1990        "Home-Work: A Case for Social Protection." *International Labour Review* 129.
WHITE, NEIL AND JONNY MYERS, N.D.
             "Agricultural Respiratory Disease in Industrialising Countries." Cape Town, South Africa: University of Cape Town. Mimeo.
WILKINSON, RICHARD G.
1997        "Income Inequality and Social Cohesion." *American Journal of Public Health* 87: 1504-6.
WORLD HEALTH ORGANIZATION/OGIEH
1996        "Global Burden of Disease and Injury Due to Occupational Factors." Geneva, Switzerland: WHO.
WORLD HEALTH ORGANIZATION (WHO)
1999        "Good Health is a Question of Priorities Not Income." WHO Newsletter, 4.
ZIMBABWE CONGRESS OF TRADE UNIONS (ZCTU).
1992        "Report of the Shopfloor Survey on Occupational Health Practices Part I." Harare, Zimbabwe. Mimeo.
1994        "Report of the Shopfloor Survey on Work Environment Hazards Part II." Harare, Zimbabwe. Mimeo.

# Reproductive Health in Post-Transition Mongolia: Global Discourses and Local Realities

## KIMBERLY RAK[*] AND CRAIG R. JANES[**]

### ABSTRACT

Global reproductive health policy is based on assumptions, couched in scientific language, that technological methods of birth control are superior to traditional methods, use of these methods is more modern and "rational" than alternatives, and abortion should not be considered a form of birth control. The authority these assumptions have achieved in global health circles prevents alternative options from being considered. Our research on women's birth control experiences in Mongolia suggests that reproductive health programs based on such global assumptions fail to consider the local cultural contexts of reproductive decision-making address women's needs, and are therefore seriously flawed.

## Introduction

Critical analysis of global discourses surrounding family planning exposes their culturally and historically constructed nature. Rabinow (1986) noted that "We need to anthropologize the West: show how exotic its constitution of reality has been; emphasize those domains most taken for granted as universal (this includes epistemology and economics); make them seem as historically peculiar as possible; show how their claims to truth are linked

[*] Department of Anthropology, University of Pittsburgh, Pittsburgh, PA, USA.

[**] Health and Behavioral Sciences and Anthropology, University of Colorado-Denver, Denver, CO, USA.

to social practices and have hence become effective forces in the social world" (p. 241).

The knowledge systems that inform the dialogues create and reinforce systems of power (Foucault 1980). The forms of knowledge and the systems of power must be seen as mutually interdependent, with each creating and recreating the other. Those in power set the "rules of the game: who can speak, from what points of view, with what authority, and according to what criteria of expertise; it sets the rules that must be followed for this or that problem, theory, or object to emerge and be named, analyzed, and eventually transformed into a policy or a plan" (Escobar 1995:41). These discourses are operationalized through the processes of labeling, monitoring, institutionalization, bureaucratization, and professionalization. However, these discourses and their practices are not hegemonic, in that "from many Third World spaces, even the most reasonable among the West's social and cultural practices might look quite peculiar, even strange" (Escobar 1995:12). These "Third World spaces" offer a site where resistance, modification, hybridization, and alternative discourses can be explored.

Our goal in this article is to explore the disjuncture between global discourses on family planning and reproductive health and the locally and culturally contingent experiences of Mongolian women in contemporary Mongolia. We find that ideas about what constitutes "modern" and "rational" birth control methods—ideas that underlie the policies of the United Nations Population Fund (UNFPA) and a host of nongovernmental organizations now operating in Mongolia—run counter to Mongolian women's beliefs, knowledge, experiences, and needs in a rapidly changing economic situation in which women are highly vulnerable to structural violence. Women in Mongolia, though highly knowledgeable of modern birth control, do not use it at the rate that such knowledge would suggest. Instead, concerned about side effects, living in a highly unpredictable socioeconomic situation which may shift the cost-benefit analysis that women use to decide on whether to have a child or not, and often experiencing difficulties accessing birth control services when they need them, Mongolian women prefer to use traditional methods over which they have control. When these fail, or when their economic circumstances change, women may consider abortion. Reproductive health programs would be in a much better position to meet women's needs if they listen to the voices of the local rather than the global, which in the case of Mongolia would be to lend support and legitimacy to women's use of traditional methods and to acknowledge the role abortion plays in women's health.

## Methods and Characteristics of the Study Population

The research upon which this article is based was conducted in Mongolia between May and September of 2002 as part of a larger study of the impact of global health reform on access to health care services by low-income Mongolians. This study surveyed members of 91 households selected at random, using a staged, cluster-type sampling routine in urban Ulaanbaatar and rural Huvsgol province in northwestern Mongolia. The surveys collected information on social and economic factors and the health experiences of individual members (Janes 2003). As part of this survey, we asked women to complete a self-administered questionnaire concerning their reproductive health. In the following pages and tables we refer to this group as the *survey sample*.

The geographical distribution of the survey sample is as follows: 79 (86.8%) were from the capital city and 12 (13.2%) were from the countryside. Of the 12 from the countryside, 2 (17%) lived in the provincial capital, 5 (41%) lived in county centers, and 5 (41%) lived in the remote countryside.

The survey sample consists of 91 women ranging in ages from 17 to 63 years old. The mean age of respondents was 30 years. Self-reported employment status was as follows: 24% are employed by a government organization, 18% are employed by a private organization, 10% are self-employed, 7% are herders, 21% are unemployed, 7% are housewives, and 14% are students. The distribution of educational status of the population was as follows: 42% have a high school level education or above, 38% have completed 10 years of high school, 17% have 8-10 years of high school, and 3% have 4-7 years of education. Based on government and United Nations criteria, approximately 28% of the women fall below the poverty line (UNDP 2000), a figure below the overall poverty rate of 36% reported by the Mongolian government in 1998 (NSO 1998).

In addition to the self-administered survey, semi-structured, face-to-face surveys were conducted with an additional group of 70 women, aged 19 to 58 years, regarding their knowledge, beliefs, and experiences with birth control and reproductive health services more generally. These women were contacted either in the course of the survey reported above or by referral from a practitioner. Interview questions overlapped the self-report questionnaires and were undertaken in part to validate the survey data. In the following pages and tables, we refer to this as the *interview sample*.

The geographic distribution of the interview sample is as follows: 40 (57%) were from the capital city and 30 (43%) were from the countryside. Of the 30 from the countryside, 23% were living in the provincial capital, 43% were living in county centers, and 33% lived in the remote countryside. The percentage of individuals represented from the countryside is over three times higher in the interview sample than in the survey sample because reading comprehension severely limited the ability of women in the countryside to complete the survey. This methodology was abandoned in favor of the interview format during the rural portion of the research.

In the interview sample, consisting of 70 women ranging in age from 19 to 58, the mean age was 31 years. Self-reported employment status is as follows: 16% are employed by a state organization, 20% are employed by a private organization, 17% are self-employed, 16% are herders, 19% are unemployed, 3% are housewives, 7% are students, and 3% are retired. The distribution of educational status of the population is as follows: 34% have above a high school level education, 49% have completed 10 years of high school, 9% have 8-10 years of high school, 7% have 4-7 years of education and only one woman reported never having attended school. The smaller percentage of women having obtained a college or university degree reflects the greater number of rural women in the interview sample; education above elementary school is presently only available in the provincial or national capitals. We did not collect detailed economic information from the women in the interview sample. Given the greater number of rural women in the interview sample, these women were more likely to be poor than women in the survey sample.

Qualitative interviews were conducted with 27 "key respondents" working as health care providers or policymakers. These individuals include physicians, representatives of organizations providing reproductive health services (local NGOs), and representatives of reproductive health policymaking bodies, ranging from the Mongolian Ministry of Health and Social Welfare, to the United Nations Population Fund. We also collected statistics on birth control usage and abortion rates from several clinical settings.

## The Global Discourse on Reproductive Health

Modern family planning policies have their roots in the post-World War II era. As the world was moving from colonialism to newly formed independent countries, the West adopted paternalistic policies to help "develop" these backward nations in the image of themselves (Escobar 1995). These dialogues and subsequent policies functioned to allow developed nations to maintain social control over developing nations without the high costs of direct military intervention. Policy planners believed that over-population was an impediment to both development and the reduction of poverty levels in these target countries. [1] Reducing fertility became an important goal for the betterment of individuals and countries alike (Hartmann 1995). The belief that development strategies, as dictated by the West, and population control could reduce poverty served to divert attention from the reality that the poverty was created by unequal access to resources aggravated by years of colonial domination. "Massive poverty in the modern sense appeared only when the spread of the market economy broke down community ties and deprived millions of people from access to land, water, and other resources. With the consolidation of capitalism, systematic pauperization became inevitable" (Escobar 1995:22). The reality has been that not only have these policies failed to reduce poverty but have exacerbated the divide between the rich and the poor. In international discourse, Third World women became a homogenized, faceless group who were visible only through their uncontrolled fertility. This had the effect of constructing a Third World "other" associated with poverty, ignorance, and an inability to control even the most basic elements of day-to-day life. The image called to mind in these discourses is of a pregnant woman, barely clothed, living in a hut or shack with a small child clinging to her side and several other children lurking in the background, thus, an image of a woman who passively keeps having more children without realizing the degree to which this impairs her "development." The opposite of this reproductive "other," which served as the benchmark against which the other was measured, was the "modern" woman of the rich northern countries. A relationship of power infused the dialogue.

In the 1970s, several social and political factors brought women to the fore in development discourses: women began to work in development organizations, women's role in economic activities began to become "visible"—especially as a source of cheap and easy to discipline wage labor—and the links between women's empowerment and lowered fertility were better understood. This new visibility resulted in the United Nations' proclamation of the *Decade for Women* (1975-1985) which generated discourses that sought to empower women and view them as more than reproductive bodies. Although this emerging view incorporated women as economic producers into development planning, they remained a largely undifferentiated other. Mueller (1987) described this reality:

> Women in development texts do not, as they claim, describe the situation of Third World women, but rather the situation of their own production.

---

[1] William H. Draper, then head of the Draper Committee that studied the U.S. Military Assistance Program and other international aid programs, told the Senate Committee on Foreign Relations in May 1959 that "The population problem, I'm afraid, is the greatest bar to our whole economic aid program and to the progress of the world" (Quoted in Hartmann 1995:105).

> The depiction of 'Third World Women' which results is one of poor women, living in hovels, having too many children, illiterate, and either dependent on a man for economic survival or impoverished because they have none. The important issue here is not whether this is a more or less accurate description of women, but who has the power to create it and make claims that it is, if not accurate, then the best available approximation. (1987:4)

"Women's rights," "Women in Development," and "Empowering Women" became familiar slogans, continuing into the present. For the most part, though, development programs focusing on women ignored local culture and voices. There was no fundamental shift in the basic elements of development discourse, just the inclusion of a new target group—women.

By identifying (labeling) women's reproductive capacity as a problem, global organizations could then bring in experts to study it. Solutions were sought in biomedical science and technology: "Technology was seen as neutral and inevitably beneficial, not as an instrument for the creation of cultural and social orders" (Escobar 1995:36). Backed by modern science and technology, policies were formulated to achieve set objectives and target goals. According to Escobar's critical analysis, the ostensible scientific basis of development transforms such objectives and goals from socially and culturally contingent processes to objectively valid technological interventions: "Much of an institution's effectiveness in producing power relations is the result of practices that are often invisible, precisely because they are seen as rational" (Escobar 1995:105). One can replace the word "development" in Escobar's discursive analysis with "family planning" to accurately describe how this operates in the context of reproductive health:

> Development was—and continues to be for the most part—a top-down, ethnocentric, and technocratic approach, which treated people and cultures as abstract concepts, statistical figures to be moved up and down in the charts of 'progress.' Development was conceived not as a cultural process (culture was a residual variable, to disappear with the advance of modernization) but instead as a system of more or less universally applicable technical interventions intended to deliver some 'badly needed' goods to a 'target' population. (Escobar 1995:44)

In poor countries, however, the inevitable inability of technologically-oriented development projects to achieve established goals (typically the benchmark of western fertility rates) does not lead to a reassessment of the project but to placing blame either on the backwardness of the local culture or the inefficiency of local institutions. Similar to Pigg's (1992) work in Nepal:

> [T]he generic village should be inhabited by generic villagers.... People in development planning 'know' that villagers have certain habits, goals, motivations and beliefs.... The ignorance of villagers is not an absence of

knowledge. Quite the contrary. It is the presence of too much locally instilled belief. . . . The problem, people working in development will tell each other and a foreign visitor, is that villagers 'don't understand things.' To speak of 'people who don't understand' is a way of identifying people as 'villagers.' As long as development aims to transform people's thinking, the villager must be someone who doesn't understand. (Pigg 1992:20)

The adherence to these discourses further serves to obscure or devalue (if not stigmatize) any alternatives that may already exist at the local level. Also, by defining "problems" (such as high fertility) as isolated features that can be abstracted from larger cultural, social, and political relations, these discourses eliminate the possibility of programs that address the more encompassing needs of an individual or community.

## Inventing Third World Women in Contemporary Mongolia

After 70 years of Soviet-style socialist development, in 1990 Mongolia elected to embrace market reforms. The sudden withdrawal of Soviet aid and the collapse of the Council for Mutual Economic Assistance left the Mongolian economy in particularly difficult circumstances. The total and per capita GDP decreased by about 20% in the period from 1990 to 1992; investment rates declined; many state enterprises and industries closed; and unemployment, virtually unknown prior to 1990, became widespread. A shrinking economy and public budget for health care led to a rapid deterioration of health services. To strengthen the economy, Mongolia embarked on a series of liberal economic reforms, including the privatization of public sector assets, trade liberalization, tight monetary policies, and a restructuring of the social welfare system. Indeed, Mongolia has become the veritable "poster-country" for neoliberal economics: nearly one-third of its GDP is presently comprised of pro-market development aid. Given such a huge input of foreign capital, it is perhaps unsurprising that these reforms have curtailed the slide of the economy, though economic growth has been modest-to-nil. Poverty has not lessened at all over the past decade, and the growth of social inequality has become quite troubling to Mongolians. The GINI index (an index of income inequality), for example, rose by nearly 20% in the five-year period between 1995 and 2000 (NSO 2000). Recent studies have shown that both the depth and severity of poverty have become more intense (Government of Mongolia National Statistics Office 1995, 1998; Oey-Gardiner [ADB] 2002). By 2000 the proportion of the working-age population actually working declined to 51%, with men suffering the highest rates of unemployment (ADB 2002).[2] In the rural countryside, rapid privatization of livestock

---

[2] A current ADB report which examined poverty in Mongolia (2002) notes that the psychological impact on men, especially given previous full employmant levels, has been

herds was accomplished without reconstructing the social and cultural institutions that for many centuries served to protect individual herding families from the vagaries of weather in this harsh climate, and also organized herding activities so as to protect vital grassland and forest environments. Probably for the first time since the reign of Chinggis Khan, Mongolian herders are now entirely independent, largely subsistence-level producers, enjoying access to what is essentially an open, unregulated commons of grazing land (Humphreys and Sneath 1999; Griffin et al. 2001). This independence, unfortunately, brings with it huge costs in terms of subsistence vulnerability, as seen in the devastating human consequences of drought and blizzards ("zuds") of the past several years. It also threatens the long-term sustainability of desert and steppe ecosystems.

Prior to the transition, Mongolia had achieved reasonably high standards of health care, given its sparse and dispersed population and largely undeveloped transportation and communications infrastructure. Investments in antenatal care, safe maternal health practices, and immunizations brought impressive gains to children under-5, and maternal mortality during the socialist period. Health facilities were distributed rationally throughout the countryside, such that even remote communities and households had access to physician and inpatient hospital services. Even today, Mongolia has one of the lowest doctor-patient ratios in Central and East Asia.

The transition brought about decay in the level and quality of services as drugs and equipment supplies disappeared, capital investments in hospitals and clinics dried up, and physicians, many not paid for months at a time, left health service. The maternity waiting homes—an innovation suited to providing safe obstetric care in sparsely settled rural areas— were left unattended or converted to storage facilities.[3] Maternal mortality

---

tremendous. There is a "reverse gender gap" in Mongolia with higher achievement and enrollment among girls at the post-elementary school level. This is a long-standing phenomenon that dates to the cohort born between 1956 and 1960, and will likely have long-term social and economic consequences. Women dominate in the white-collar occupations: they are the professionals, technicians, clerks, and service and sales workers. These are the occupations for which education is a necessity. These are also the occupations of the future in an increasingly market-oriented economy. In the long run such imbalances may not be to Mongolia's advantage, given that the social problems of alcoholism, crime, and divorce are rising as men have increasing difficulties in adjusting to conditions of unemployment and loss of self-respect. The root causes of imbalance are in the education system; unfortunately, the privatization ov university-level education and the collapse of rural education will likely make the problem worse.

[3] Although likely an apocryphal tale, one informant reported that the maternity waiting homes were dismantled at the demand of a World Bank consultant who deemed them "too expensive" and "unnecessary." A few years later another consultant encouraged the Ministry of Health to reinvest in maternity waiting hames; by this time, however, most

increased significantly and has remained high, particularly among women who are socially and economically marginal (Chuluundorj 2001; Janes and Chuluundorj 2004).[4] Public sector funding of health care has dropped significantly as a percentage of GDP during the transition period, and the solution has been to search for ways to shift funding increasingly to the private sector.

Unlike in other countries in East and Central Asia, women in Mongolia enjoyed reasonably equal access to education and jobs. Indeed, one of the crises now facing Mongolia is not the health of its women, but of its men. Surveys of school enrollment rates show that girls and women consistently out-enroll men at all grades above the elementary level (ADB 2002). During the latter years of the socialist period, and continuing to the present, women entered the professions and white-collar managerial positions at a significant rate. Most of the physicians, teachers, and mid-level managers now employed in Mongolia are women. With the collapse of the heavily subsidized industrial economy, there has been a rapid and disturbing increase in male unemployment, while women, given higher levels of education, have been positioned to move into the white-collar and service-sector positions created by the new market economy. Women's participation in the formal economy also appears linked to low and declining total fertility rate, which was 2.3 in 1999 (UNDP 2000). It is thus highly ironic that, when Mongolia made the transition to a market economy and began to accept international financial aid, so too did it become subject to all the assumptions regarding reproductive health needs in "underdeveloped" women. In fact, the problems that Mongolian women today face with regard to maternal and reproductive health are largely products of the post-socialist transition period during Western and global programs to foster "free market" development which led to the collapse of the economy. The Western force behind globalization has thus,

---

had fallen into disrepair. In the meantime, the labor and money required to bring these up to minimal standard had become considerable. Most importantly, though, is the nature of women's labor in the new countryside economy. Unlike during the socialist period, where pregnant women's domestic and animal-focused labor could be replaced by another commune member, during the present period, where families are independent subsistence producers, women's labor is essential, particularly during the spring and summer when caring for young animals and milking duties require significant labor inputs. Most likely, it is doubtful that maternity waiting homes will be used to the extent that they were prior to 1990, particularly during high-labor times.

[4] A study of maternal mortality in Mongolia (Chuluundorj 2001; Janes and Chuluundorj 2004) suggests three reasons for the rapid rise of maternal mortality, particularly in the countryside: a) transformation of the rural pastoral economy which placed significant demands on women's labor; b) the collapse of the health care system; and c) the severity and intensity of poverty.

through both discursive and political-economic efforts, created a Third World Mongolian woman, a needy target for technological intervention.

In keeping with international pressures over the last twenty years to fully recognize women's rights and needs, one of the most visible aid programs in Mongolia centers on reproductive health (RH) and family planning (FP). This focus resulted in programs that supply contraceptives at no charge to women who want them and drugs to treat sexually transmitted infections. There is no denying that these programs provide an invaluable service to Mongolian women, but how these programs are being implemented at the local level and the impact of the underlying assumptions about women's status and role that some of these programs carry with them require investigation. According to Hartmann (1995) "In the absence of real social transformation, the emphasis will probably be on 'motivational efforts' to sell the idea of small families. Many of these messages will push the consumer model: with fewer children, you can buy more and degrade the environment less, which of course is a doubtful proposition. Social marketing of contraceptives, rather than the establishment of comprehensive health services, will continue to be the priority" (p. 154). For Mongolia, in the absence of the specific concerns that have traditionally guided RH and FP programs, the current international agendas appear to be the application of generic top-down models that reproduce the need for their presence by the very failure they create by not taking into consideration the needs of the people they are designed to address (Justice 1986).

The important question here concerns the goals of international organizations' family planning programs as implemented in Mongolia. In the face of evidence that suggests that Mongolia is not experiencing any changes to its low fertility, there seems to be a rather absurd singularity of focus on increasing the rates of birth control usage among women in Mongolia. Reproductive health programs are developed on the assumption that things were not "modern" or functioning properly before the introduction of their policies and ideals, and that when these are adopted things will be improved, with no real sense of how or for whom. In essence, Mongolia has been created as a Third World country by international organizations. Once so defined, the status provides the logic for interventions, which tout "modern" and "technological" methods of birth control.

Extensive information, education, and communication (IEC) programs have been implemented, birth control has been made available free of charge, and the social marketing of contraceptives has been initiated. All practical barriers preventing access to contraceptives have been removed. Yet, and not surprisingly, the geographical, informational, and economic availability of contraceptives in Mongolia has not resulted in any substantial increase in birth control usage over the last four years.[5] It is of great concern to various governmental departments and international organizations that the introduction of free contraceptives at all levels of care in Mongolia has not resulted in lower numbers of abortions. Driven by American policies that restrict funding for international organizations that offer abortion services, it is the fact of abortion that most deeply disturbs governmental and international organizations.

Viewed through a Western lens, the availability of free birth control should allow women who do not want to have another child, or who want to delay having another one, to use contraceptives and therefore not have to turn to abortion as a "last resort" solution. Comments such as the following are common public statements: "...the reported rate of 12,870 abortions (262 per 1,000 live births) in 1997 is still unacceptably high.... It indicates that there is still a large unmet demand for family planning services" (UNFPA 2000b) and "[t]he abortion statistics would suggest there is still considerable unmet need for family planning among married, parous women, mostly for reliable, long-term protection" (UNFPA 2000a). The question for international organizations becomes one of why women who are having abortions are not using birth control to prevent unwanted pregnancies. The logical theory that access to contraceptives will lead to use, and therefore a reduction in pregnancies ending in abortion, falters in the specific cultural context of Mongolia. No one seems to have asked why.

## Mongolian Women's Perspectives on Birth Control

Family planning programs have to be understood within a context in which women actively play a role in decisions about their fertility, albeit with differing options and/or constraints defined by social and economic factors. As Lewin (1995) points out, "[M]otherhood, that presumptively 'natural' feminine accomplishment, [is] a complex array of consciously and unconsciously crafted strategies by which many women managed economic adversity and organized culturally rewarding identities" (p. 104). Family planning is not a "magic bullet" that will be universally acceptable to all women and viewed as the solution to their personal empowerment. It is easy to forget that women may want to have a baby. This is reminiscent of the "problem" of teenage pregnancy in the U.S. A staff member at a

---

[5] The 1998 Reproductive Health Survey (NSO/UNFPA 1998) found that about 44% of women are currently using a method of birdth control. A later survey, conducted in 2001, found that 45% of the sample population was currently using a form of birth control (NCHD/UNFPA, 2001).

school-based health clinic in Louisiana said "the worst problem we are having are pregnancies and repeats. I used to think it was a lack of knowledge about contraceptives; they didn't know what they were doing. But now I find the attitude has changed; they know all about birth-control pills, condoms and the other things. What's disturbing is that they're planning pregnancies now" (Ward 1995:154). The teenagers are opting to have children as a way to establish an identity for themselves, and it is the personal biases of the health care provider, not the girls, who is labeling this as deviant. Women make what they think is the best choice for their lives from the limited options presented to them: "In the global context of population policies, disease, and disasters of all kinds, local populations seek to envision continuity through children and act to ensure that continuity" (Mullings 1995:123). Family planning has to be viewed as just one option among many (one of which is to have children) and even though donor agendas dictate that it is the most appropriate course of action, women may decide differently given the specifics of their situations. The relationship between information and behavioral change is a complex one where "information plays a small, albeit vital, part in the process of behavior change and that the information must be relevant to the person's life. Attitudes, skills, and social and economic factors are equally—if not more—important in determining behavior, sexual and otherwise" (Gordon 1996:375).

Women are not passive actors, and they will resist or reject outright programs that do not address their needs: "People desire improved health but fear disruption and external control by regulatory powers that undermine both the authority of their own traditional specialists and the practices through which cultural reproduction, more broadly, is assured" (Ginsburg and Rapp 1995:21). The voices of Mongolian women are conspicuously absent from the agendas of donor agencies. As outlined by Pritchett (1994), an economist at the World Bank, it is not the availability of family planning but a woman's desire to have fewer children that reduces family size.

Women's knowledge about birth control methods is quite high in Mongolia. Our research found that 97% of women had some knowledge of birth control. This is identical to a countrywide survey conducted in 1998 concerning reproductive health issues, which found that 97% of women could name at least one method, and only 3% of women did not know of any method of birth control (NSO/UNFPA 1998). The frequencies with which women mentioned a method of birth control are shown in Table 1. It is not surprising that five of the top six most frequently mentioned methods are the "modern" ones promoted and supported by international

**Table 1**

Frequency a Method of Birth Control was Mentioned*

| Method of birth control | Number of women who mentioned | Percent of women who mentioned (out of 68 who had heard of a birth control) |
|---|---|---|
| IUD | 62 | 91.2% |
| Oral birth control | 59 | 86.8% |
| DEPO | 51 | 75.0% |
| Condom | 47 | 69.1% |
| Calendar | 33 | 48.5% |
| Norplant | 15 | 22.1% |
| Withdrawal | 3 | 4.4% |
| Temperature method | 3 | 4.4% |
| Female sterilization | 3 | 4.4% |
| Spermicide | 3 | 4.4% |
| Emergency contraception | 2 | 2.9% |
| Washing after sex | 2 | 2.9% |
| Female condom | 1 | 1.5% |
| Male sterilization | 1 | 1.5% |
| Breastfeeding | 1 | 1.5% |
| Herbal birth control | 1 | 1.5% |

*Among interview sample.

organizations. What is interesting is that nearly half the women interviewed discussed the more "traditional" calendar method of birth control.[6]

There are differing views on rates of birth control use. Official data collected by the Ministry of Health suggest that the birth control usage rate among Mongolian women was 45% in 1999, 50% in 2000, and 50% in 2002. The Mongolian Reproductive Health Survey (NSO/UNFPA1998) found that 66% of all women had ever used a method of birth control and that about 44% were currently using birth control. In our survey, we found that 45% of women were currently using birth control and 55% were not. The different methods women were currently using are given in Table 2.

The reasons women gave for not currently using birth control are given in Table 3. Nearly a quarter of the women (24%) are not using birth control because they have never had sex or are not currently having sex. Almost half of the women (49%) are not using birth control because

---

[6] The 1998 Mongolian Reproductive Health Survey (NSO/UNFPA 1998) reported that 84.0% of women knew of this method. The main difference between this result and the one reported here is that the RHS reported knowledge that if a woman knew of the method on her own of if the interviewer described it, the results above are for unsolicited responses only.

**Table 2**

Methods of Birth Control Currently Being Used[*]

| Method of birth control | Number of women using | Percent of women using |
| --- | --- | --- |
| Condoms | 22 | 37.9% |
| Oral birth control | 6 | 10.3% |
| IUD | 18 | 31.0% |
| DEPO | 5 | 8.6% |
| Calendar | 13 | 22.4% |
| Herbs | 1 | 1.7% |
| Withdrawal | 1 | 1.7% |

[*] Among combined interview and survey sample.

**Table 3**

Reasons for Not Using Birth Control[*]

| Reasons for not using birth control | Number of women | Percent of women |
| --- | --- | --- |
| Pregnant or trying to get pregnant | 22 | 48.9% |
| Not had sex | 10 | 22.2% |
| Just given birth and believes can not get pregnant yet | 5 | 11.1% |
| Believes too old to get pregnant | 5 | 11.1% |
| Planning to use in immediate future | 1 | 2.2% |
| Separated from husband | 1 | 2.2% |
| Never heard of birth control | 1 | 2.2% |

[*] Among combined interview and survey sample.

they are currently pregnant or are trying to get pregnant. Therefore the "unmet" need for family planning represents 27% of the population or less (some of the women may be delaying fertility by breastfeeding and some of the women may, in fact, be too old to have more children). What is important is that 60% of the women sampled recently had a baby, are currently pregnant, or want to become pregnant. Data gathered on ideal versus actual family size estimate that 54% of women would want to have another child sometime in the future.

Women know how many children they would like to have. Ideally, family planning in Mongolia would take into consideration the types of services women want and need in achieving their desired family size instead of focusing exclusively on the usage rates of contraceptives. With so many women in Mongolia wanting to have another child, programs focusing on appropriate birth spacing would more adequately address women's needs. This requires promotion of birth control that is easily reversible:

therefore the IUD and DEPO would not be a good choice for many women. However, the trend within contraceptive research, development, and promotion has been to increase the time period over which a method is effective and to reduce or eliminate women's capacity for voluntary termination (e.g., DEPO, Norplant, and IUD).

It is of serious concern that the reported usage rates, especially among urban women, of the calendar method is so high: 22% of the current birth control users, 30% of the women who have ever used a birth control method, and 44% of current urban birth control users have chosen this method. Statistics cited by Planned Parenthood (Parenthood Federation of America 2003) reports that, with typical use of this method, 20 out of 100 women will become pregnant and, with perfect use, 9 out of 100 women will become pregnant within the first year of use. This method is not recommended if a woman has irregular periods, their partner is unwilling to abstain or practice safe sex during the fertile periods (which is about 10 days a month), and if a woman is unable to keep careful records. Even women who experience regular menstrual cycles can be affected by stress, illness and climatic changes. Because the calendar method can be unreliable, PPO recommends that "it is best not to rely on this method alone. It is best to combine the temperature method, the cervical mucus method, and the calendar method. The combination of these methods is called the symptothermal method" (Planned Parenthood Federation of America 2003). However, the temperature method and the cervical mucus method require daily monitoring and can be quite difficult to sustain. Not one woman in the study mentioned using the temperature or cervical mucus method in conjunction with the calendar method. In fact, only one woman even mentioned the temperature method, and she asked us how it was done. This method also requires cooperation from one's spouse or partner. As one Mongolian doctor put it, "husbands' knowledge of sex is poor, for example, if a wife doesn't want sex because it is during an unsafe time but the husband doesn't care about it and wants to have sex."

Women's experiences with the different methods of birth control reveals the complexity of decision-making:

> One of the women interviewed reported having stable menstrual periods, and has been using the calendar method combined with condom use during the unsafe times. She was concerned that she might have gotten pregnant while using this method this past March and went to her family doctor where she was given emergency contraception. She did get pregnant last month when she "counted wrong" and this pregnancy ended in abortion. Another woman had used an IUD for six years and had it removed. Since she had the IUD removed she has been using the calendar method. Her period is every 21 days and she menstruates for 5 days. She divided the 21 days into three weeks, with week two considered the unsafe time during which her and her husband used condoms. She admitted that she calculated wrong and figured

her cycle from the last day of her period to the first day instead of from the first day to the first day. As a result of her miscalculations, the method did not work very well and she became pregnant four times since the IUD was removed. The first two pregnancies were aborted. The third pregnancy was miscarried, which was attributed by the woman to having had the two prior abortions. At the time of the interview she was pregnant and intending to carry it to term. Even after the first three pregnancies, this woman continued to use the calendar method. She either never asked professional advice on how to use this method or was given poor instruction.

These examples suggest that the question to ask is why women use a method of birth control that can be very unreliable if they so obviously do not want to have more children. The one thing these women have in common is that they either have personal experience with or have heard rumors about the side effects of other methods of birth control. The first woman told us that birth control pills cause stomachaches, the IUD makes your periods longer, and birth control injections lead to weight gain. The second woman had used an IUD but when she had the second one put in, she experienced abdominal pains and heavy bleeding, so she had it removed. Her sister had used NORPLANT and gained weight. She also stated that she doesn't like the injections because "they cause you to get fat." Like the findings of DeClerque et al. (1986) about birth control pill rumors in Egypt, stories about the side effects of modern methods of birth control in Mongolia compromise their acceptability to many women. Similarly, in Mongolia rumors and/or reports of others' less than salutary experiences with birth control may lead women to conclude that modern contraceptives are deleterious to health. However, counter to the Egyptian study, the rumors do not undermine the perceived effectiveness of the method: women generally acknowledge the modern methods to be highly effective. For Mongolian women, the beliefs about side effects are a stronger influence on decisions to use birth control than beliefs about the efficacy of the various methods. A World Development Report (1984) found that the main reason for women discontinuing birth control usage is the prevalence of side effects according to reports from 40 to 70% for users of pills, IUDs, or injectable forms of birth control (Hartmann 1995:273).

So how prevalent are these beliefs that various methods of birth control have side effects? Forty-three of the 70 women (61%) interviewed mentioned a side effect for at least one form of birth control; the results are shown in Table 4.[7] One doctor interviewed noted that "women

---

[7] The Reproductive Health Survey (NSO/UNFPA 1998) found that for women who are not using birth control and who do not intend to use BC in the future, 13.6% sited health concerns or side effects as the reason why. Another report (UNFPA 2000a) cites service statistics that 26% of women in Mongolia stop using a method of birth control due to health concerns and 21% discontinue usage because of dissatisfaction with the method.

## Table 4

### Side Effects Mentioned for Birth Control Methods*

| Method of birth control | Reported for calendar | Reported for DEPO | Reported for IUD | Reported for NORPLANT | Reported for oral birth control |
|---|---|---|---|---|---|
| Side effect mentioned | 11.6% | 53.5% | 58.1% | 16.3% | 55.8% |
| Weight gain | 0% | 27.9% | 16.3% | 7% | 7% |
| Harmful to body | 0% | 11.6% | 9.3% | 4.7% | 11.6% |
| Heavier period/ cramping | 0% | 2.3% | 27.9% | 0% | 0% |
| Nausea | 0% | 0% | 0% | 0% | 16.3% |
| Not reliable | 11.6% | 0% | 0% | 0% | 2.3% |
| General side effect | 0% | 11.6% | 4.7% | 4.7% | 18.6% |

*Among the interview sample.

are really worried about side effects such as gaining weight, heavy and frequent periods, painful menstruation, and chronic diseases such as kidney problems (associated with oral birth control use). Some stop using birth control because of side effects." Most of the practitioners we interviewed, however, did not believe that side effects were a concern for women users of birth control. This would indicate that these concerns are either not normally expressed to the health care provider or the provider dismisses these concerns. Either scenario is cause for concern in that they both represent a breakdown in communication between patient and doctor that may seriously affect health outcomes.

A review of the data presented in Table 4 suggests that, while there might be near universal knowledge about contraceptives, there are side effects—whether actual or reported misconceptions, misinformation, or exaggerated rumors—that may be hindering usage. The calendar method, when viewed from women's own experiences with birth control, becomes a logical choice. The calendar method also allows women to exercise some control over their own reproductive lives: they do not have to go to a doctor to start using birth control or to receive supplies, and it is easy to stop using the method with fertility returning immediately. When a woman perceives that modern methods of birth control have side effects that are detrimental to their health and are faced with a system of care that is at best confusing and is not conducive to open confidential discussions, it is not surprising that they are opting for the calendar method: "Suffering from unexplained and untreated contraceptive side effects and disillusioned with the quality of service, a high percentage of women drop out of family planning programs" (Hartmann 1995:38). The concern then becomes how to educate women about the calendar method and other natural FP methods so that they become more reliable. While women have been educated about the various methods of birth control, they are often lacking the basic knowledge about how their bodies work and how the methods are able to prevent pregnancy. The use of either modern or traditional methods of birth control without the corresponding biological knowledge keeps women in the dark and serves to increase their misconceptions of and contributes to outright rejection of the various methods. A focus on the practices of women at the local level once again illustrates deficiencies and biases on the part of current family planning programs. Most studies that have been conducted acknowledge the high rates of usage of the calendar method, but the UNFPA, probably due to a bias towards modern, technological methods, has not committed finances to programs designed to educate women about this method or to approve introduction of thermometers and charts that would improve its efficacy.

## Abortion

From the perspective of Mongolians, abortion is clearly an important component of family planning, though there is considerable official ambivalence over its practice. The Population Policy of 1996 "prohibits the promotion of abortion as a method of family planning, but states it should be available, regulated by law, and performed in safe conditions" (UNFPA 2000b:13). It seems to be important for the government to point out that abortion is not a form of birth control. Even though the laws support a woman's access to abortion services, the pro-life sentiments and policies of American foreign policy are felt. In July of 2002, the US government announced that it was withholding the $34 million previously allocated for the United Nations Population Fund (UNFPA). This resulted in a loss of 12% of the UNFPA's total budget. The reason given for withholding the money was the unsubstantiated claim by the Bush administration that the UNFPA was involved with coercive abortion in China (Gillespie 2002). A representative from the UNFPA in Mongolia reported that its position on abortion is thus to "avoid even saying the word." Invoking the "logical" assumption that the introduction of birth control will lower the need for abortions, the UNFPA's explicit aim is to prevent the need for abortion through increased use of contraceptives. The Marie Stopes International Foundation, an international NGO active in Mongolia, does not list abortion as one of its services, despite the fact that it is a well-known abortion provider. When we met with Marie Stopes' staff to try and gather data on their abortion services (how many are done, demographics of the women having them, etc.), we were immediately told that this was "internal" data, and that questions about abortion were "inappropriate." Large, international institutions that can be affected by American funding policies are not willing to take part in dialogue about one of the most important dimensions of reproductive health in Mongolia. Abortion discourses, which carefully elide association with family planning, is an unambiguous example of how those with power, both political and economic, are able to define appropriate dialogues, interventions, and solutions while rendering others unacceptable or invisible. In Mongolia the effect has been to generate new social meanings of abortion, creating stigma and conflict where there had been none.

Women in Mongolia frequently use abortion to terminate pregnancies. As of 2000 there were a reported 230.8 abortions per 1,000 live births in Mongolia (NSO/UNFPA 2001). Historically abortions performed in private clinics were not included in official numbers but as of 1999, the numbers from some, but not all, private clinics are included. Given the rapid growth of a private health care sector and the widespread belief among women that private providers offer superior and confidential services (unlike the public sector, where confidentiality is often compromised), a great many abortions are completed in private settings. The officially reported rates of abortion are likely to be much lower than actual. For example, we interviewed one doctor who claimed that he performs approximately 30 abortions a week and that these abortions are not reported to the state. Given his figure of 30 abortions per week, taking 48 weeks in a year (factoring in a month for vacation that seems to be the norm), this equates to over 1,400 unreported abortions completed per year in just this one clinic. This alone would add 11% to the national totals of 11,837 abortions reported for 2000. In our survey, we found that 37% of women reported having had an abortion. When we look only at women who are not using any form of birth control, we find that 30% have had at least one abortion in the past. This shows that even if a woman is not actively using contraceptives, as defined by Western standards, she is still controlling her fertility. One of the main ways that women in Mongolia do this is through abortion.

The use of abortion to regulate fertility can also be illustrated by the difference in age between never having had a pregnancy and never having given birth. The women who were interviewed were asked how old they were when they had their first child, and the women who completed the survey were asked how old they were when they had their first pregnancy. Almost 19% of the interviewed women had not had a child yet, and 13% of the surveyed women had not had a pregnancy yet. The mean ages for these women were 24 years and 21 years, respectively. The three-year age difference between a woman not having been pregnant and not having had a child may indicate that a first pregnancy ended in abortion and therefore did not result in a first birth. Clinical records for the first half of 2002 from a hospital in the capitol (Ulaanbaatar) indicated that 15% of the abortions performed there were first pregnancies. Another hospital in Ulaanbaatar reported that 23% of the abortions performed there in 2000 were first pregnancies (of these women, 93% had not been using any method of birth control). This is a concern due to higher rates of possible complications for abortions performed for first pregnancies.

In effect, abortion is a form of birth control in Mongolia.[8] Several of the physicians we have interviewed are concerned about the high rates of abortion. One doctor reported that many young people are coming to her to have an abortion. She worries that they don't know about the complications of abortion (here she mentioned that people are having abortions because of money problems). "There are lots of private hospitals doing abortions and it is not restricted, so women think if they get pregnant 'I can just have an abortion'." When asked what she would do to decrease the number of abortions, she said that she would explain "a lot more about birth control. Compared to when she was young, there are many private hospitals, and therefore a woman can go to many places to have an abortion [it is very easy now compared to when she was young]. It is important to give information about birth control and the complications of abortions."

Birth spacing was an issue for 55% of the women who had an abortion, again illustrating how family planning in Mongolia should be reoriented to address the specific needs of women. One in four women reported that they had an abortion because of their economic situation, which leads one to believe that if women were benefiting from "development" or becoming "empowered," they would not be having the abortions. True support for women would result in women being able to achieve their desired family size. With increasing urbanization, the loss of guaranteed educational and employment opportunities, and a break-down in social support, women who find themselves pregnant weigh the immediate situational circumstances of their lives against an uncertain future. For some, the current demands on their time or expectations for their future lead them to a decision to have an abortion. This is less a situation of a woman not wanting to have a baby and thus preventable by contraceptive usage, and more a case of a cost-benefit analysis of a family's situation under circumstances of great political and economic instability. The reasons women gave for having an abortion are given in Table 5.

---

[8] One hospital reported that 75% of abortions in the first half of 2002 were performed for women with their 5th or higher pregnancy.

## Table 5

### Reasons Why Women Have Had an Abortion[*]

| Reason | Number who said | Percent |
|---|---|---|
| Economic | 6 | 27.3% |
| Continuing education | 3 | 13.6% |
| Pregnancy too close to prior birth | 12 | 54.5% |
| No one to watch child/ no support | 1 | 4.5% |
| Physical/drug complications | 3 | 13.6% |
| Too old to have baby | 1 | 4.5% |
| Living with in-laws | 2 | 9.1% |
| Traveling abroad | 3 | 13.6% |
| Unwanted: | 8 | 36.4% |
|   At this time | 6 | 27.3% |
|   Wants no more children | 2 | 9.1% |

[*] Among the interview sample.

One family doctor described her experience of trying to get women to use birth control rather than relying on abortion: "I can't understand why they do not want to use it [birth control] since it is free. When a woman is six months pregnant they will come to me because they do not want the baby but it is too late for an abortion. Before they got pregnant the family doctor offers them birth control, which they did not want, now they come to me when it is too late. I think money is the problem in keeping the baby." That women are not having children because of financial considerations reflects larger social and economic conditions and not the failure of women to use birth control to prevent an unwanted pregnancy. It is important to note here that abortion is not covered by the national insurance system and can be quite expensive in local terms, ranging from approximately US $8 to US$ 20.[9] This serves to restrict access to those women who, in a very real sense, cannot afford to have a child. These women may also feel additional pressure from their OB/GYN to have the abortion (half of the doctors interviewed would recommend a woman to have an abortion based on their assessment that the woman was "poor" or "very poor").

What is urgently needed in Mongolia is a more extensive educational program on the possible complications of abortion. Even taking into account the fact that abortions are mostly performed by dilation and curettage, the rate of post-abortion complications is high in Mongolia at

---

[9] Annual GDP per capita in Mongolia in 1998 was US$ 450 (which had dropped from US$ 1,245 in 1990; UNDP 2000). Among our household sample, the average monthly income was under US$ 15 (Janes 2003).

## Table 6

Complications of Voluntary Abortions, 1998

| Abortions | Total number | Complication number | Complication percent | Uterus perforation | Hemorrhage | Infection | Other |
|---|---|---|---|---|---|---|---|
| UB | 4159 | 453 | 11% | 4 | 399 | 38 | 12 |
| Aimag | 4976 | 200 | 4% | 2 | 54 | 86 | 57 |
| Total | 9135 | 653 | 7% | 6 | 453 | 125 | 69 |

Source: MOHSW (1998).

7% (Report on Requirements and Management of Contraceptives and Essential Reproductive Health Drugs in Mongolia 2000a). Table 6 shows the findings on abortion complications from the 1998 Health Statistical Report. In 2001, the UNFPA developed a pamphlet that discusses the possible complications of abortions and how to prevent unwanted pregnancy. Although these were reported to be widely distributed to health care providers, not one was seen during the entire four-month research period, while various other materials developed by the UNFPA were seen in almost all facilities.

### Conclusions

The picture of Mongolian women's reproductive health needs is very different when viewed from a local versus an internationalized perspective. Global health policy discourse identifies a "Third World" woman who should be liberated from reproductive burdens by the introduction of modern birth control. By relieving women of the burden of fertility, so this argument goes, better health and a higher quality of life will be accessible to all. We do not dispute all of the assumptions that underlie this perspective; rather, we argue that the creation of an undifferentiated group of needy, "underdeveloped" women, who then become the object of a standard, universal set of technological interventions, ignores local realities to such a degree that women become victims rather than beneficiaries. While appropriate intervention, sensitive to local needs and concerns, might allow women to control their fertility in the ways that they wish, the one-size-fits-all approach produced out of the global discourses on family planning is at best inappropriate.

It is deeply ironic that it has taken the transition from a socialist to market economy, led by the intervention of the global financial and health policy institutions of the developed world, to create Mongolia as a Third World country. Although poor, Mongolia is hardly "undeveloped" from the perspective of health and social services. Seventy years of socialist development brought reasonable levels of access to biomedicine, and to contraceptive services, to Mongolian women. Women were encouraged to attain education, and they did so in great numbers; compared to men they have a competitive advantage on the current job market. Mongolian women have largely reduced their fertility, and there are at present no indications that declines in fertility rates achieved over the last two decades will reverse. For Mongolians, fertility is not the problem; rather it is the often desperate economic conditions that many now find themselves in.

For Mongolian women, the concern is not one of having too many children, but rather it is being able to have the number of children they want. This fundamental shift in perspective, from one focused on prevention and proscription to one focused on attainment and possibility, profoundly alters the basis of family planning programs. Policies informed by local women would encompass appropriate birth spacing, encourage culturally acceptable contraceptive methods and, most critically, address the very serious social and financial concerns that lead many women to have abortions. Fertility rates in Mongolia are low relative to most of Asia. Historically, abortion has been a factor contributing to lowered fertility, and the role that it plays now and in the future cannot be ignored just because it is not an acceptable topic for those currently framing the dialogues.

The resistance of Mongolian women to international interference in their reproductive lives and control over their bodies is illustrated by the high rates of usage of the calendar method versus modern methods advocated by the UNFPA (Escobar 1995; Scott 1985). A similar response to family planning programs was noted for Egypt, where "females themselves showed resistance ... the vast majority of Egyptian peasant women prefer indigenous fertility-regulation methods over state-sponsored contraceptives 'even when the latter are free and accessible'" (Morsy 1995:170). Even though women prefer to use the calendar method, there was no indication that any of the aid money was going to be redirected to increasing women's understanding of their bodies so that this method might be more effective for them. All the money is aimed at increasing the usage rates of the "preferred" "modern" (read technological) methods introduced by these aid organizations. It is important to keep in mind that, "improved technology—improved, that is, in terms of increasing its compatibility with the life circumstances and preferences of potential users—seems unlikely, in and of itself, to lead to change from non-use to use, certainly not by people who see substantial advantages in having more children. But increasing the socio-cultural fit of fertility regulating methods is clearly one part of the equation that results in providing couples with real choices in determining their reproductive future" (Polgar and Marshall 1976:205). Currently there is a fundamental disjuncture between what women want and what they are being given. Of further detriment to the women is the seemingly singular focus on family planning and reproductive health (mainly STD treatment) at the expense of a more complete package of health care services for women and their families (Janes 2003).

In this modern age, investigations of the articulation between international programs and policies and local cultures illustrates how power and inequality work to affect health outcomes. Global development programs cannot be viewed independently of the political implications inherent within them. Following Jordanova (1995), "the politics of reproduction is about who gets to shape our sense of ourselves as reproductive beings, about how our reproductive fantasies are fashioned" (p. 382). So while the explicit goals of international family planning programs in Mongolia are vague, the emphasis attached to acceptance is symbolically related to a view of Mongolia as a modernizing nation, following the path of patron (donor) countries. To the global elite, evidence that Mongolia is internalizing imported, Western norms serves as a signal that it is willing to act according to expected behavior and become a participating member of the world economy.

The health needs and concerns of women go far beyond those currently being addressed through family planning and reproductive health programs. Not only is it important for services to address this wider view of women's health beyond reproductive possibilities but it is also important to continually reassess women's needs in view of ever-changing social conditions brought about through increasing incorporation into the world market: occupational hazards through new opportunities in formal and informal employment, increased reliance on food produced outside the home, pollution from increased numbers of cars, importation of tobacco and alcohol products, increased life expectancy resulting in more chronic illnesses, and other conditions. It is also important to investigate how the interplay of political, economic, and social conditions varies from region to region and present a unique epidemiological picture, making it necessary for any program aimed at addressing local health needs to be sensitive to cultural specifics (Paolisso and Leslie 1995).

## References

ADB [ASIAN DEVELOPMENT BANK]
2002        Social Impact Assessment Report: Second Health Sector Development Project. Ulaanbaatar, Mongolia: Asian Development Bank and the Mongolian Ministry of Health and Social Welfare.
CHULUUNDORJ, OYUNA
2001        "Social Inequality and Maternal Mortality in Mongolia." Master's Thesis, Department of Anthropology, University of Colorado, Denver, CO, USA.

DeClerque, J., A.O. Tsui, M.F. Abul-Ata and D. Barcelona
1986 "Rumor, Misinformation and Oral Contraceptive Use in Egypt." *Social Science and Medicine* 1986: 23: 83-92.
Escobar, Arturo
1995 *Encountering Development: The Making and Unmaking of the Third World.* Princeton: Princeton University Press.
Foucault, Michel
1980 *Power/Knowledge.* New York: Pantheon Books.
Gillespie, M.A.
2002 "Tough Times, Tougher Choices: An Interview with Thoraya Obaid, Executive Director of UNFPA." *Conscience* XXIII (4): 17-2.
Ginsburg, Faye D. and Rayna Rapp
1995 "Introduction: Conceiving the New World Order." Pp. 1-17 in *Conceiving the New World Order: The Global Politics of Reproduction*, edited by Faye D. Ginsburg and Rayna Rapp. Berkeley, CA: University of California Press.
Gordon, G.
1996 "Sexual Reality: The Gap Between Family Planning Services and Client's Needs." Pp. 363-379 in *Learning About Sexuality: A Practical Beginning*, edited by S. Zeidenstein and K. Moore. New York: The Population Council.
Griffin, Keith et al., Eds.
2001 *A Strategy for Poverty Reduction in Mongolia.* Ulaanbaatar, Mongolia: United Nations Development Programme.
Hartmann, B.
1995 *Reproductive Rights and Wrongs: The Global Politics of Population Control.* Cambridge, MA: South End Press.
Humphreys, Caroline and David Sneath
1999 *The End of Nomadism? Society, State and the Environment in Inner Asia.* Durham, NC: Duke University Press.
Janes, Craig R.
2003 "Market Fetishism, Post-Socialist Institutional Culture, and Attenuated Primary Care: Producing Poor Medicine for Poor People in Post-Transition Mongolia." *Bulletin of the Royal Institute for Interfaith Studies*, forthcoming.
Janes, Craig R. and Oyuna Chuluundorj
2004 "Free Markets and Dead Mothers: The Social Ecology of Maternal Mortality in Post-Socialist Mongolia." *Medical Anthropology Quarterly* 18(2): 102-129.
Jordanova, L.
1995 "Interrogating the Concept of Reproduction in the Eighteenth Century." Pp. 369-386 in *Conceiving the New World Order: The Global Politics of Reproduction*, edited by Faye D. Ginsburg and Rayna Rapp. Berkeley, CA: University of California Press.
Justice, Judith
1986 *Policies, Plans, and People: Foreign Aid and Health Development.* Berkeley, CA: University of California Press.
Lewin, Ellen
1995 "On the Outside Looking In: The Politics of Lesbian Motherhood." Pp. 103-121 in *Conceiving the New World Order: The Global Politics of Reproduction*, edited by Faye D. Ginsburg and Rayna Rapp. Berkeley, CA: University of California Press.
Morsy, Soheir A.
1995 "Deadly Reproduction among Egyptian Women: Maternal Mortality and the Medicalization of Population Control." Pp. 162-176 in *Conceiving the New World Order: The Global Politics of Reproduction*, edited by Faye D. Ginsburg and Rayna Rapp. Berkeley, CA: University of California Press.
Mueller, A.
1987 "Power and Naming in the Development Institution: The 'Discovery' of 'Women in Peru.'" Paper presented at the Fourteenth Annual Third World Conference, 1987, Chicago, IL.
Mullings, Leith
1995 "Households Headed by Women: The Politics of Race, Class, and Gender." Pp. 122-139 in *Conceiving the New World Order: The Global Politics of Reproduction*,

edited by Faye D. Ginsburg and Rayna Rapp. Berkeley, CA: University of California Press.

NSO [NATIONAL STATISTICS OFFICE OF MONGOLIA GOVERNMENT]
1995     *Living Standards Measurement Survey, 1995.* Ulaanbaatar, Mongolia: National Statistics Office and the UN Development Programme.
1998     *Living Standards Measurement Survey, 1998.* Ulaanbaatar, Mongolia: National Statistics Office and the UN Development Programme.
1999     Mongolian Statistical Yearbook. Ulaanbaatar, Mongolia: National Statistics Office.

NSO/UNFPA [NATIONAL STATISTICAL OFFICE OF MONGOLIA AND THE UNITED NATIONS POPULATION FUND]
1998     *Reproductive Health Survey.* Ulaanbaatar, Mongolia: National Statistics Office and the UNFPA.

NCHD/UNFPA [NATIONAL CENTER FOR HEALTH DEVELOPMENT AND UNITED NATIONS POPULATION FUND]
2001     *Unwanted pregnancies and Abortions in Mongolia.* Ulaanbaatar, Mongolia: UNFPA.

OEY-GARDINER, MAYLING [ASIAN DEVELOPMENT BANK]
2001     "Achievability of the IDG Set Out in the Mongolia Partnership Agreement on Poverty Reduction." Ulaanbaatar, Mongolia: Asian Development Bank.

PAOLISSO, M. AND J. LESLIE
1995     "Meeting the Changing Health Needs of Women in Developing Countries." *Social Science Medicine* 40: 55-66.

PIGG, STACY L.
1992     "Constructing Social Categories through Place: Social Representations and Development in Nepal." *Comparative Studies in Society and History* 34: 491-513.

PLANNED PARENTHOOD FEDERATION OF AMERICA
2003     "Ways to Chart Your Fertility Pattern." Retrieved January 2003. ⟨http://plannedparenthood.org/bc/WaysToChart/html⟩

POLGAR, S. AND J.F. MARSHALL
1976     "The Search for Culturally Acceptable Fertility Regulating Methods." Pp. 204-218 in *Culture, Natality and Family Planning,* edited by S. Polgar and J.F. Marshall. Raleigh, NC: Carolina Population Center.

PRITCHETT, L.H.
1994     "Desired Fertility and the Impact of Population Policies." *Population and Development Review* 20: 17-18.

RABINOW, PAUL
1986     "Representations are Social Facts: Modernity and Post-Modernity in Anthropology." Pp. 234-261 in *Writing Culture: The Poetics and Politics of Ethnography,* edited by James Clifford and George Marcus. Berkeley, CA: University of California Press.

SCOTT, JAMES C.
1985     *Weapons of the Weak: Everyday Forms of Resistance.* New Haven, CT: Yale University Press.

UNDP [UNITED NATIONS DEVELOPMENT PROGRAMME]
2000     *Human Development Report,* Ulaanbaatar, Mongolia: UNDP.

UNFPA [UNITED NATIONS POPULATION FUND]
2000a     "Report on Requirements and Management of Contraceptives and Essential Reproductive Health Drugs in Mongolia." Ulaanbaatar, Mongolia: UNDP.
2000b     "Reproductive Health, Gender and Rights in Mongolia." Ulaanbaatar, Mongolia: UNDP.
2000     "Reproductive Health Needs Assessment in Mongolia." Ulaanbaatar, Mongolia: UNDP.

WARD, M.C.
1995     "Early Childbearing: What is the Problem and Who Owns It?" Pp. 140-158 in *Conceiving the New World Order: The Global Politics of Reproduction,* edited by Faye D. Ginsburg and Rayna Rapp. Berkeley, CA: University of California Press, 1995.

# Access to Healthcare via Telehealth: Experiences from the Pacific

## Roy Smith[*]

### Abstract

Information and communication technologies (ICT) have been fundamental in the evolution of the myriad of processes broadly encapsulated under the rubric of globalization. This article looks at how ICT developments have been applied to the provision of healthcare in remoter parts of the world, especially the Pacific region. This discussion includes a brief overview of how Internet infrastructure and connectivity have spread across the region. This overview, in turn, involves a discussion of the use of, and potential for, elements of telehealth and telemedicine relevant to Pacific island communities. Both the micro and macro aspects of this topic are considered. These aspects relate to the individual level of patient care within these communities, the manner in which broader influences within the global political economy can affect both the type of illness and disease requiring treatment, and also the level of healthcare available.

## An Explanation of Terms

Before the substantive part of this work is commenced, a clarification of the terms to be used is necessary. The relevant literature at times refers specifically to telemedicine or, more broadly, to telehealth. Here, although attention will be paid to telemedicine as the remote consultancy, diagnosis and prescription of healthcare, the broader focus is on the more inclusive area of telehealth. This allows for discussion on aspects of distance learning for health professionals, public health awareness opportunities,

[*] Centre for Asia Pacific Studies, Nottingham Trent University, Nottingham, UK.

and consideration of a range of factors contributing towards good or ill health.

With regard to globalization, this is a word that has become a catch-all term for all manner of phenomena. It can relate to particular perspectives on international relations. These can involve a state-centric analysis, or one geared more towards economic patterns and the implications of increasingly free-flowing capital investments. An alternative view might be more class-based in a neo-Marxist framework, which may encompass greater emphasis on, for example, new social movements. Equally, attention may be drawn towards significant themes such as sustainable development issues or the politics of identity. In short, there is as broad a range of definitions of globalization as there are approaches towards what various commentators see as significant within the realms of human interactions, and those with other species and habitats. When the impact of rapidly evolving technological developments is added to the mix, it is little wonder that globalization has come to mean different things to different people. Even where a commonality of terms and definitions is agreed upon, there can remain stark contrasts when one considers the moral dimensions of who are perceived as the "winners" or "losers" with regard to various aspects of global relations. The subject of telehealth lends itself well to a discussion couched in such terms. When this involves the provision of ICT to areas remote from the core locations of industrialized development, there are also questions to be raised regarding issues of the ownership and usage of such technology. On one hand, this may be viewed as a welcome transfer of technology to enhance healthcare provision. More negatively, it may be seen as highlighting, possibly reinforcing, unequal power relationships in the global economy.

For the purposes of this article, globalization is loosely defined as the increasing interconnectedness of people and places. ICT developments are clearly a key component of this phenomenon. Looking at telehealth, especially as provided to some of the remoter regions of the world, allows for a consideration of how such connections are differentiated both geographically and economically. There can be no doubting the remarkable technological achievement of connecting a remote Pacific island community to, potentially, the finest medical brains and expertise on the planet. Once access to Internet communication has been established, while recognizing that this remains a significant barrier for some communities, it is now possible to access real-time video conferencing, a range of online medical resources and direct consultations on a global basis. Obviously more involved surgical procedures are not possible at a distance, and it is to be expected that there is likely to be a greater margin of error associated with remote diagnoses. Yet, as will be illustrated, there is already a substantial body of evidence that the promotion and take-up of telehealth service provision are expanding at a significant rate. However, the political economy of this process is more complex than simply determining how many remote consultations are taking place and at what cost. Issues such as who is controlling the availability of telehealth infrastructure, what level of local human resource development is taking place with regard to engagement with this technology and, perhaps, even the nature and causes of the illnesses and diseases being treated may be symptomatic of broader international power relationships.

There is an understandable temptation to focus on the wonder of diagnosis at considerable distance from the patient and the undoubted advances this can provide for healthcare provision in remote areas. Financial savings can certainly be made if expensive evacuations to metropolitan hospitals can be avoided. This is even allowing for the initial capital investment of developing telehealth infrastructure and relatively high connectivity charges. Yet there are occasional dissenting voices to be heard which question some aspects of the political economy of such healthcare provision. This can relate to the, largely unavoidable, factor of the development of such technology being driven by actors and forces external to the region. Without local scientific and capital capability to take a lead in such investment, it is difficult to imagine an alternative scenario. Yet, once in place, there is an issue regarding the extent to which both healthcare professionals and ICT specialists are drawn from the local population. Similarly those adopting a structuralist or post-structuralist approach may take the view that, despite the undoubted advantages to be gained from such technology transfer and access to medical training and expertise, it remains the case that a more comprehensive analysis of the relationship between the developed and less-developed parts of the world needs to be maintained. It is with these factors under consideration that the following analysis traces the development and impact of telehealth in the Pacific region.

## Evolution of Internet Infrastructure

The interests of the most developed states and their e-business entrepreneurs have driven the development of a global Internet infrastructure. The classic core-periphery model of development/underdevelopment associated with writers such as Immanuel Wallerstein (1974) and Andre Gunder Frank (1982) is particularly in evidence when technological innovation is discussed. A counter argument to this model could be that ICT can be seen as diminishing the "tyranny of distance" and there is a growing popular perception that geographical factors have less significance within what Castells (2000) has described as a global "network society." From the economic growth-centred view of development, the remoter Pacific island communities have generally been seen as being at some disadvantage within the global economy in terms of their relatively limited resource base and their distance from, and difficulty in engagement with, core metropolitan centers. On a smaller scale, such a model can also be seen as relevant within the domestic jurisdictions of several of these states that are island chains and exhibit patterns of urban drift and uneven development. ICT provision in itself does not necessarily ensure that domestic or international inequalities are overcome. Examples will be cited here of undoubted advantages from connecting previously isolated communities with the medical and other resources now available to them. Yet it is difficult to adequately analyze the impact of telehealth provision in isolation from related socioeconomic and political considerations. The manner in which Internet accessibility has evolved within the region is informative of related patterns of not only healthcare provision but also the level of health among these communities.

Virtually all of the islands of the Pacific region have histories of colonial engagement. The French overseas territories of New Caledonia, French Polynesia and Wallis and Futuna remain under colonial administration, albeit with some elements of self-governance. The independent states, such as Tonga, Samoa, Fiji, Papua New Guinea, and the Solomon Islands, all retain important links with Australia, New Zealand, and, to a lesser extent now, the United Kingdom. In Micronesia, the former Trust Territories of the Pacific Islands maintain what could be described as similar neocolonial links with the United States via their Compact of Free Association agreements. The reason for this reference is that these historical patterns are reflected in the manner in which the subregions of Polynesia, Melanesia, and Micronesia relate to their metropolitan cores, and also inform patterns of ICT development and other aspects of technology transfer. As one would expect for both linguistic and political reasons, the French territories engage most directly with France. The independent Polynesian and Melanesian territories look towards Australia and New Zealand. The Micronesian territories, although increasingly recipients of Japanese aid and trade, remain most closely tied to the United States. One of the possibilities Internet connectivity raises is a less geographically determined set of interactions. However, it is notable that when the focus is on aspects of foreign aid, specifically access to telehealth distance learning and referral opportunities, the patterns that emerge relate closely to historical ties.

During the immediate post-WWII era, colonial administrations relied heavily on over-the-horizon voice and telegraphy services. Many of the outer-lying islands are still reliant on such technology. In December 2002,

Cyclone Zoe passed over the eastern part of the Solomon Islands. The islands of Tikopia and Anuta could not be contacted for a week, other than reports of initial damage assessment from aircraft. This is a particularly dramatic example, but it illustrates the ongoing remoteness of many island communities. Where Internet connectivity has been developed, it has tended to focus on capital cities and relatively limited networking to regional centers. The evolution of telecommunication infrastructure in the region can be seen as developing in relation to two distinct phases of technological innovation. In the 1950s and 1960s, large capacity trans-Pacific submarine cables were laid. The main purpose of these was to improve communications between the United States, Asia, and Australia. A by-product of this endeavour was to enhance the communication capacity of Fiji and, to a lesser extent, Papua New Guinea. Fiji took the greater advantage of this strategic opportunity, which was enhanced when Suva became the location of the Secretariat of the South Pacific Forum and the University of the South Pacific (USP). USP continues to be a major player in the delivery of distance learning opportunities across the region, using the same networks shared by telehealth providers. The initial impetus for telecommunication enhancement reflected the interests of powers external to the region. In part this can be seen within the context of alliance politics and the enhancement of trading and investment opportunities in the region. It is important to note that this is the underlying dynamic of the international system and that utilizing ICT for more altruistic development goals has come to the fore only more recently.

The second significant technological leap forward has been in the field of satellite-based communication systems. As a result of their proliferation in recent years, these systems have extended the range of communication infrastructure beyond the reliance on the cabling referred to above. This development has two important impacts on the extent and usage of ICT in the Pacific region. First, it has brought many more of the previously remote island communities into an emerging globally networked society, although it must be remembered that there remain significant cost restrictions on usage even when the ICT infrastructure is in place. In conjunction with this technological development, there have also been advances in the political will to make use of such facilities to engage in development strategies that are not solely focused on economic growth as an apparent end in itself. Debates on taking a top-down or bottom-up approach to development have a history far longer than that of the electronic means to achieve this end. What is more novel is the opportunity for aid agencies and non-governmental organisations to engage more directly in the delivery of primary healthcare. This is an enabling process that has been significantly facilitated by the introduction of electronic portals that can transmit vast amounts of knowledge and expertise that would otherwise have required the physical transportation of trained staff and the necessary support equipment. Not only are the practicalities of transport often imprecise and expensive in the region the location of highly skilled medical staff serving small, remote communities is not generally cost-efficient. Even if the economic growth-centred developmental approach is availed it is clear that such management of human and related resources will not bring the greatest benefit to the greatest number.

Despite a variety of opinions regarding the most appropriate approach towards development priorities, there is a broad consensus that an unhealthy population is a drain on a national economy. Telehealth has become recognized as a priority area by both the governments of the region and external donors. This is reflected in the number of regional government meetings that have identified health provision as one of the key principles of their development goals. Several factors have contributed towards this situation. First, there is a clear demand from Pacific Islanders themselves. Access to healthcare is a universal human need and, as greater information becomes available on the nature of various illnesses and possible alleviations, there is an understandable desire to pursue the best diagnosis and treatment. Second, regional governments are concerned not only for the health of their population on humanitarian grounds but also in a more instrumental sense, as the depletion of a state's human capital has clear implications for both social cohesion and economic performance. Similarly, donor governments and health-related NGOs recognize the need to stabilize and positively enhance community health. Perhaps most importantly, technological advances have provided the opportunity to put in place major health programs based on the delivery of distance learning programs for island-based health officials and practitioners. These programs, added to the remote diagnosis and database accessing made possible where ICT is now available, have led to a sea-change in attitudes towards what is possible in the field of healthcare provision in even the remotest of communities.

The following section looks at specific examples of how regional governments and their donor partners have targeted ICT development in various sectors, particularly healthcare.

## Regional Strategies for Telehealth Delivery

The first Conference of the Ministers of Health of the Pacific Island Countries was held in Fiji in March 1995. This meeting resulted in the *Yanuca Island Declaration of Health in the Pacific in the 21st Century*. This conference as well as subsequent meetings, has led to what has become known as the Healthy Islands Program. Simultaneously, there has been regional cooperation in broader ICT capacity building. "Information and Communication Technologies for every Pacific Islander" is the theme for the *Pacific Islands Information and Communication Technologies Policy and Strategic Plan*. This plan was published in 2002 by the ICT Working Group of the Council of Regional Organisations of the Pacific (CROP). It feeds into the United Nations sponsored World Summit on the Information Society. There is a clear intention to raise the profile of ICT provision within the Pacific region. It appears to now be regarded as one of the fundamental pillars for the formulation and delivery of regional development goals. A recent survey for UNESCO reviewed the development and use of the Internet among the island states. Although most states reported a relatively low take-up of household connectivity, with the majority being less than 25%, there was a significantly higher return of 50-75% in the categories of public access via libraries and Internet cafes. Higher still was the connectivity of government ministries and departments. Although it was noted that there remains a significant barrier in terms of training for wider-spread computer literacy and maintenance, there is evidence that Internet connectivity is increasing across the region. The survey also noted a marked tendency for clustering of connectivity in capital cities and a few larger urban areas. This tendency is unsurprising as these areas are where government offices and any major businesses are most likely to be centered. This factor highlights the core-periphery patterns of development associated with the introduction of new technologies.

In line with the Yanuca Island Declaration, and with the backing of the major external donors, CROP's ICT strategic plan has four guiding principles. These focus on human resources; infrastructure development; cooperation between stakeholders; and appropriate policy and regulation. Somewhat surprisingly, healthcare is not explicitly highlighted. However, one could argue that this is an integral dimension of human resource development. The general tone of this document is to emphasize the need to extend Internet connectivity and computer literacy across the region. The manner in which this process is to take place is also hinted at with repeated references to the region's wish to attract private investment in developing this sector and to reduce connection charges by encouraging market competition. In general, this desire is in line with the dominant developmental thinking as promulgated by the World Bank, IMF, and WTO. Deregulation and the opening of markets are perceived as the most efficient manner to promote economic growth and enhance service delivery in a range of sectors. Such a view reflects the top-down approach to development referred to above. With regard to healthcare, there is an inherent tension between the political responsibility and duty of care that governments have towards their citizens and the market mechanisms by which such care is provided. It is virtually impossible for governments to produce an economic formula for cost of providing healthcare for individual citizens; plus, this is a politically sensitive and emotive issue. Calculations can be undertaken with regard to the costs of hospitals, the training of medical staff, health education programs and so on. Yet the overall costs to a government exchequer with regard to the costs and benefits of maintaining a healthy population are both complex and, very often, subsumed by other governmental priorities.

The above point on the costs of healthcare is pertinent to the earlier distinction made between telemedicine and telehealth. Telemedicine is most closely related to the concept of a curative approach, where an existing illness or disease is identified and treated. In contrast, telehealth is a broader conceptualization of well-being that also encompasses a more proactive approach, thereby emphasising health education and the prevention of illness and disease. Clearly, in the longer-term a proactive approach is more cost-effective. Initial capital investment is required to provide health education, but such an investment more than offsets the costs of dealing with the implications of failing to address preventable healthcare problems. A significant dimension of telehealth is the distance learning opportunities it opens up for developing a preventative, rather than curative, emphasis towards healthcare. To date, the emphasis on the healthcare applications of distance learning has been predominantly on the training of healthcare professionals. CROPS's ICT guiding principle of human resource development could utilize the opportunity of increased Internet connectivity to spread a message of self-reliant preventative health education programmes. Of course, the assumption is that health education is the guiding light by which the majority of healthcare issues could be solved. Such a view is particularly pertinent in relation to the growing incidence of noncommunicable or lifestyle-related illnesses, such as heart disease and diabetes. The prevalence of illnesses associated with more sedentary lifestyles and changing dietary patterns is a notable dimension of healthcare provision in the region. Yet it is not simply health education that is required. Pacific Islanders, and other groups, can be well informed about the implications of a poor diet or excessive consumption of alcohol and tobacco, yet continue to adopt unhealthy lifestyles. Other factors, such as cost and availability of a well-balanced diet or a healthy environment, are also significant factors with regard to Pacific Islanders' lifestyle options and choices.

In considering the Pacific island governments' strategies for ICT provision and related healthcare services, there are two distinct, but related, ways of looking at this situation. First, there is the initial impression that the governments appear to have a good grasp on what healthcare issues they confront and what ICT opportunities are available to help tackle them. Certainly, investing in the basic infrastructure for ICT provision across the region is a fundamental starting point for healthcare and a range of other sectors, both public and private. There would appear to be little scope for disagreement with the argument that it is a net gain to have access to better medical expertise and guidance than that which is available locally. Yet, when the overall dynamic of the nature of the illness or disease being treated is looked at more closely, a more complex scenario may be recognized than first appeared. If the case in question is, for example, seeking advice on the correct positioning for a traction device for a patient suffering from a fracture, then the advantages of direct contact from remote areas to core facilities are clear. Such cases are relatively straightforward technically, with the transmission of digital images of x-rays and photographs of the position of a patient. More complicated is the treatment or prevention of the increasingly common lifestyle-related illness and diseases. While the importance of maintaining health education programs must not be downplayed, it would appear that lack of education is one of the lesser factors in determining the incidence of noncommunicable illness and disease. Far more significant are the lifestyle changes commonly associated with the dominant processes of modernization and globalization.

As noted elsewhere in this collection, the health transition associated with many Pacific island communities involves a shift in prevalence from communicable to non-communicable lifestyle-related illness and disease. This is a result of moving away from predominantly subsistence-based economies to ones that are more cash-based. Simultaneously, this shift has also coincided with patterns of urban drift, often to areas lacking the basic infrastructure to support growing populations. This shift, therefore, has health implications in relation to overcrowded living conditions and the management of waste disposal. Perhaps of most significance is the reliance on waged labor for the income to purchase goods, including food. Despite a widespread assumption outside of the region that the Pacific islands are bountiful destinations with easy access to the fruits of land and sea, this assumption is often far from the truth. Dietary patterns are influenced by the range and cost of available foodstuffs. Many urban Pacific communities are increasingly reliant on imported food. This is often of low nutritional value with high fat and sugar content. Moreover, given the increasing range of goods available to buy, it is quite likely that consumers may prioritise "luxury" consumer items, at the detriment of paying for more nutritious food. Added to this, aspects of stress may also contribute to unhealthy levels of alcohol and tobacco consumption. Such patterns are far from unique to the Pacific islands and are readily identifiable in most "developed" states. With the advantages of modernization, as represented by the possibilities opened up with Internet connectivity, comes a range of potential disadvantages, as the greater connectivity with core economies appears to transmit some of the more negative aspects of modern life.

Telehealth strategies in the region need to recognize the health transition briefly outlined above. Technology is often referred to as a two-edged sword. For every potential benefit there can be potential costs in relation to how particular technologies are applied. Internet connectivity is a central feature of the processes of globalization. Although there are clear benefits involved in allowing greater access to medical expertise, such channels of communication are also responsible for drawing remote communities ever closer to the core values and practices of modern industrialized economies. This is not intended to be a polemic argument for idealizing or romanticizing subsistence communities. Far from it, as there are undoubted advantages to be had in the transfer of technological expertise in not only healthcare but also in all manner of human endeavor. Rather, there is a wish to draw attention to the broader processes that are influencing the type of healthcare that is becoming increasingly required among Pacific island communities. The following section looks at some specific examples drawn from Micronesia. This discussion will consider not only the type of consultations that are being undertaken but also their socio-economic and political context.

## Telehealth in Micronesia

Micronesia presents a good example of how telehealth and telemedicine are evolving in the Pacific region. In part this is due to the particular relationship the Micronesian territories have with the United States. Arguably, the health transition experienced by Micronesians is directly related to socioeconomic changes that took place under the US administration of the former Trust Territories. Although the agency of Micronesians in determining their own future cannot be denied, it is the case that US policies towards the region during the Trusteeship period did foster a certain economic dependency on the United States. Patterns of employment, urban drift, and consumerist lifestyles all contributed to the present situation. Yet the Compacts of Free Association signed with the United States by Palau, the Federated States of Micronesia (FSM) and the Marshall Islands do also allow access to some of the most advanced telehealth and telemedicine facilities available.

Most of the remote consultancies are referred to the Tripler Army Medical Center (TAMC) in Hawaii. Typically, prior to Internet connectivity, referring patients off-island accounted for a disproportionate amount of Micronesian health ministries' budgets. This cost could be between 10-

30% of the overall budget, with the benefit accruing to only 1-2% of the total population. Significant savings have been made possible by reducing this expenditure. Also, for example, Pohnpei State in FSM used to spend approximately $1,500 per month on telephone bills for overseas consultations. This amount has now been reduced to less than $500 per month in Internet connection charges. Added to this financial saving, the quality of service is also improved as Internet facilities allow transmission of attachments with visual data, plus the option of real-time patient/consultant video interaction. The largest proportion of FSM's referral cases, 46% according to figures published in 2000, is surgical. In the Marshall Islands, this figure is 54%. Of these, the majority are diabetes-related amputations. It would be wrong to attribute all cases of diabetes to lifestyle changes brought about by the impacts of modernization on these communities. Yet this is far and away the most notable incidence of requiring surgery in the islands. Apart from the personal tragedy involved, such surgeries are a significant drain on medical resources, even allowing for remote consultations. There are also social implications for longer-term care for such patients. In addition to requiring such surgery, diabetic patients may also suffer night, or complete, blindness. Such examples have a high profile, but those suffering from obesity, often with heart disease complications, are also a significant drain on health budgets. Within this context, there is a strong argument for recognizing the financial, and human, benefits in tackling the initial causes of such illnesses and diseases in a proactive, preventative manner.

Although it has been noted that educational programs may not be enough to alter people's lifestyle options and choices, there remains a significant role to be played in terms of distance education programmes. In 1994, the University of Guam's College of Nursing and Health Sciences began teaching courses via the Pan Pacific Education and Communications Experiment by Satellite (PEACESAT). This endeavor had two main aims. The first was to enhance the personal development of health professionals in the region. The second was to emphasis the need to address the problem of lifestyle-related illness and disease. Two core courses were taught: Leadership/Management for Nurses and Nutrition for Health Professionals. An expressed aim of this program has been to take a primary healthcare approach focusing on health education, particularly targeting certain groups such as women and younger people. In the Marshall Islands, the group Youth to Youth in Health provides a good example of a community group that is dealing with aspects of unhealthy lifestyles among teenagers. It is recognized that lifestyle preferences and habits are better tackled at an early age. This group not only educates young people about the nutritional content of their diets, it also encourages practical solutions in the form of growing local produce, rather than relying on less healthy, and often expensive, imported goods. Greater self-awareness and self-help is a policy identifiable in both local government policies towards healthcare, and also the input of several nongovernmental organizations. In an irony indicative of many aspects of globalization, much of this self-awareness is being generated and facilitated by information now becoming available via the Internet.

Internet usage may be thought of as an indicator of the level of engagement communities have with the wider world. This is not to say that other forms of engagement had not taken place prior to Internet connectivity. As mentioned above, the majority of the Pacific islands have, or continue to have, colonial or neocolonial ties of one form or another. Even those with formal political independence have economies that are, to a greater or lesser degree, tied into trading and other relationships with other states and their multinational corporations. What is qualitatively different about the Internet revolution is the manner in which individual citizens are personally affected by it. Aspects of ill or good health are but one aspect of this revolution, although there is an argument in suggesting that one's level of health could be significantly determined by how successfully one is interacting with this wider environment. Internet connectivity allows individuals to become better informed about, and treated for, a variety of symptoms of ill health. To some extent, this information does increase personal agency to act. If one is better educated one can, in theory, make more informed choices. However, such choices may be restricted by the available options. There have been claims that the Internet will reduce the significance of geographical factors and act as a great leveller or equalizer of social and other disparities. There is certainly the potential for this to happen, or at least for events to move in that direction. However, for now, Pacific island communities such as those in FSM and the Marshall Islands remain fundamentally affected by aspects of their post-WWII history, the nature of their dependency economy, the limitations of their physical and human resources and the socioeconomic and cultural pressures of adapting to processes of modernization and globalization.

The above discussion has highlighted some of the difficulties and opportunities presented to these communities in the realm of healthcare. Telehealth technology allows for a remarkable expansion of the medical expertise available to act in a curative manner. Distance education for both health professionals and their patients also presents a wealth of opportunities to advance a programme of preventative healthcare.

## The Political Economy of Telehealth

The provision of telehealth and telemedicine services to Pacific island communities draws attention to several of the contradictions inherent in the complex processes of globalization. On the one hand there is an unquestionable advantage in being able to remotely access the combined resources of overseas consultants and related databases. Yet the type of illnesses and diseases that are most commonly being consulted on are noncommunicable lifestyle-related ones. The rise in their incidence appears to be directly related to the position of the Pacific islands within the global political economy. Some acceptance of personal choice certainly has to be taken into account, as not all Pacific islanders suffer the same type and level of illness. Also, the incidences of diabetes, cancers, obesity, and heart disease are high in the most developed states as well. This fact leads to the conclusion that there are aspects of modern consumerist lifestyles that can result in a rise in non-communicable illness and disease. As the Pacific islands, and other areas of the world formerly remote from interaction with the core states and their economies, become more closely interconnected they also suffer a greater incidence of these illnesses and diseases.

Regional governments, external donors, health professionals, and health-related nongovernmental organizations have certainly made inroads in providing improved healthcare by way of extending telehealth and telemedicine provision. It is important to reiterate the potential of health-related interconnectivity to develop and share good practice in healthcare delivery. However, one of the aims of this piece has been to draw attention to the broader political economy within which such provision operates. The technological opportunities afforded to remote areas by improved telecommunication systems cannot easily be separated from other, less positive, aspects of modernization and globalization. The rising incidence of lifestyle-related illness and disease is reflected in the nature of the cases referred for remote consultation. Health education programmes can only go so far in addressing this problem. As suggested above, people's lifestyle choices must be considered within the context of what options are afforded to them — "Afforded" being the operative word in increasingly market-driven communities. Even the regional governments' ICT strategy follows the line of further deregulation and the opening of markets. The underlying ethos of economic liberalization has direct implications on the purchasing power of Pacific islanders, other aspects of their lifestyles, and the manner in which this impacts on their health.

Telehealth and telemedicine undoubtedly have a role to play in the provision of healthcare in remote communities. The difficulty facing Pacific island governments and communities is to take advantage of the technological opportunities available to them via greater interaction with the core economies, while at the same time avoiding the more negative aspects of such interaction. To date, the health transition identifiable among Pacific islanders suggests that it is some of the more negative aspects that are taking hold. Improved access to healthcare resources and expertise may go some way to dealing with these issues. However, improving the health of Pacific islanders will be most effective if a holistic approach is adopted that recognizes the underlying factors that give rise to many of the health problems these communities are facing.

# References

CASTELLS, MANUEL
2000        *The Rise of the Network Society.* Oxford, Blackwell.
THE COUNCIL OF REGIONAL ORGANISATIONS OF THE PACIFIC ICT WORKING GROUP
2002        *Pacific Islands Information and Communication Technologies Policy and Strategic Plan.* Suva, Pacific Islands Forum Secretariat.
DAVY, GRAHAM
1984        "Telecommunications Development in the South Pacific Region." Pp. 15-24 in *Transport and Communications for Pacific Microstates: Issues of Organisation and Management,* edited by Christopher Kissling. Suva, Institute of Pacific Studies.
FOCHTMAN, MAUREEN
2000        "Distance Nursing Education in Micronesia." *Pacific Health Dialog* 7(2): 81-83.
FRANK, ANDRE GUNDER
1982        *Dependent Accumulation and Underdevelopment.* London, Macmillan.
GREENIDGE, CARL
2002        "The Challenge of Information and Communication in Rural Areas." *The Courier* 195: 34-35.
GUNAWARDINE, KAMAL
2000        "Telemedicine in Majuro Hospital, Marshall Islands." *Pacific Health Dialog* 7(2): 51-53.
HEDSON, JOHNNY
2000        "Teleconsultations in Pohnpei State, Federated States of Micronesia." *Pacific Health Dialog* 7(2): 46-50.
MCMURRAY, CHRISTINE AND ROY SMITH
2001        *Diseases of Globalization: Socio-Economic Transition and Health.* London, Earthscan.
OMI, SHIGERU
2002        *The Work of the World Health Organization in the Western Pacific Region: Report of the Regional Director, 1 July 2001 - 30 June 2002.* Manila, Regional Office for the Western Pacific, WHO.
PACIFIC ISLANDS FORUM SECRETARIAT
2003        *Pacific Islands Regional Input Paper.* Asian Regional Conference for the World Summit on the Information Society, Tokyo, 13-15 January 2003.
PERSON, DONALD
2000        "Pacific Island Health Care Project: Early Experiences with a Web-Based Consultation and Referral Network." *Pacific Health Dialog* 7(2): 29-35.
PRYOR, JAN, ET AL.
2000        "Telehealth in the Pacific Islands: A Perspective and Update from the Fiji School of Medicine." *Pacific Health Dialog* 7(2): 6-10.
RUTSTEIN, DAVID
2000        "Telemedicine in the Federated States of Micronesia." *Pacific Health Dialog* 7(2): 40-45.
SECRETARIAT OF THE PACIFIC COMMUNITY
1999        *Pacific Telehealth Conference, Noumea, New Caledonia, 30 November - 3 December 1998: Report of Meeting.* Noumea, SPC.

WALLERSTEIN, IMMANUEL
1974        *The Modern World System.* New York: Academic Press.
WHO
1999        *Workshop on Healthy Islands, Suva, Fiji. 22-25 February 1999: Report.* Manila,
            Regional Office for the Western Pacific, WHO.
ZWIMPFER COMMUNICATIONS LTD.
2002        *Internet Infrastructure and e-Governance in Pacific Island Countries: A Survey on the
            Development and Use of the Internet.* UNESCO, Apia.

# Globalization of Risks for Chronic Diseases Demands Global Solutions

DEREK YACH[*] AND ROBERT BEAGLEHOLE[**]

## ABSTRACT

Debates about globalization and health focus almost exclusively on communicable diseases. However, chronic diseases—especially cardiovascular diseases, cancer, chronic respiratory diseases and diabetes—now constitute the bulk of the global burden of disease. This chapter provides updated information on trends in the major macro-determinants of chronic diseases such as urbanization, globalization, and aging. Further, it summarizes evidence of the impact of known risk factors for chronic diseases such as tobacco, diet/nutrition, physical activity, and alcohol. Reasons for failure to invest in prevention are outlined and the importance of implementing available knowledge about preventive and therapeutic strategies is stressed.

## Summary

For many years, the major debates about globalization and health focused almost exclusively on communicable diseases. New global alliances and funds have been developed to address some of these diseases, particularly HIV/Aids, malaria, tuberculosis and vaccine-preventable conditions.

In contrast, chronic diseases, especially cardiovascular diseases, cancer, chronic respiratory diseases and diabetes, have been neglected in reality

---

[*] Professor of Public Health, Yale University, New Haven, Connecticut, USA. Formerly Executive Director of Noncommunicable Diseases and Mental Health, World Health Organization, Geneva, Switzerland.

[**] Director of Chronic Diseases and Health Promotion, World Health Organization, Geneva, Switzerland.

and now constitute the major component of the global burden of disease and do so in all regions, with the exception of Africa.

This chapter provides updated information on trends in the major macro-determinants of chronic diseases, such as urbanisation, globalisation, and ageing, which are contributing to rapid increases in chronic diseases in developing countries. Further, this chapter highlights new evidence of the impact of known risk factors for chronic diseases on the incidence of deaths and disability. Major risks to health such as tobacco, diet/nutrition, physical inactivity, and alcohol are discussed. Reasons for failure to invest in prevention and health promotion are outlined. Finally, the importance of implementing already available knowledge about preventive and therapeutic strategies to tackle these risks from a national and international perspective is stressed.

## Introduction

The impact of the modern phase of globalization on the health of populations has been extensively debated (Yach and Bettcher 1998; Commission on Macroeconomics and Health 2001; Woodward et al. 2001). Attention has been almost exclusively on the major infectious diseases epidemics, access to affordable therapies and to a lesser extent on the effect of health on trade and finance agreements. The changing role of the state and governance for health has also been discussed (Zwi and Yach 2002).

Policymakers and the donor community have neglected the rapidly growing burden of chronic diseases (Beaglehole and Yach forthcoming). The magnitude of this burden is well documented as are the causes and the preventive strategies. The response to these epidemics, despite the threat they pose to health systems, has been grossly inadequate. This chapter provides updated information on trends in the major macro-determinants of chronic diseases and highlights new evidence on the impact of known risk factors for chronic diseases on the incidence of deaths and disability. Major risks to health, such as tobacco, diet/nutrition, physical inactivity, and alcohol are discussed. Reasons for failure to invest in prevention and health promotion are outlined. Finally, the importance of implementing already available knowledge about preventive and therapeutic strategies to tackle these risks from a national and international perspective is stressed.

## The Global Burden of Noncommunicable Diseases (NCD)

In 2000 there were an estimated 56 million deaths globally, with chronic diseases accounting for 60% of these deaths (WHO 2002a). The leading chronic diseases are cardiovascular disease (CVD), especially coronary heart disease (CHD) and stroke (16 million deaths); cancer (7 million deaths); chronic respiratory disease (3.5 million deaths); and diabetes (almost 1 million deaths). Mental health problems are important contributors to the burden of disease in many countries (WHO 2001c).

Table 1 indicates that chronic diseases are leading causes of death in developing and developed countries. Only in the African region are communicable diseases more frequent as causes of death than chronic diseases. The importance of chronic diseases in China and India is often underestimated. In the year 2000, 2.8 million CVD deaths occurred in China and 2.6 million in India. Chronic diseases are major causes of premature adult mortality (between the ages of 15 and 59 years) with the highest levels being in central and eastern European countries (WHO 2001c). Chronic diseases are an important contributor to health inequalities within and between countries and are predominate among poor populations, largely because of inequalities in the distribution of major chronic disease risk factors (Evans, Whitehead, and Diderichsen 2001; Kunst, Groenhof, and Mackenback 1998; Leon and Watt 2001). In turn, these inequalities in risk factors are driven by more fundamental causes of ill-health in the socioeconomic environment. The global pattern of death and disability will continue to be dominated by chronic diseases; CHD and stroke are expected to be the leading causes of death and of disability adjusted life years lost (DALYs) by the year 2020 (WHO 2002a).

## The Causes of Chronic Diseases

The current burden of chronic diseases reflects the cumulative exposure to past risks to health. The future burden of disease will be determined by current population exposures to the major risk factors. Although the causes of the chronic disease epidemics are more complex than infectious disease epidemics, they are well known. The major risk factors explain the occurrence of almost all new events within populations (Magnus and Beaglehole 2001; Stamler et al. 1999). Most of these risk factors are common to the main categories of chronic diseases and all are modifiable, albeit with some difficulty. The relationship between the major risk factors and the chronic diseases is very similar in all regions of the world, although there are some quantitative differences; in some situations the relationships are stronger in developing countries (Rodgers, Lawes, and MacMahon 2000).

Population aging is due mainly to a decline in fertility rates and an increase in child survival; it is an important underlying determinant of the chronic disease epidemics because of the strong association between disease incidence and age. In addition, global forces in trade and marketing are encouraging the entrenchment of the causes of the chronic disease in all

## Table 1

Ten Leading Causes of Death, Globally and in Developing and Developed Countries, Estimates for 2000

| | World | % of total deaths | | Developed Countries* | % of total deaths | | Developing Countries | % of total deaths |
|---|---|---|---|---|---|---|---|---|
| 1 | Ischaemic heart disease | 12.4 | 1 | Ischaemic heart disease | 22.6 | 1 | Ischaemic heart disease | 9.1 |
| 2 | Cerebrovascular disease | 9.2 | 2 | Cerebrovascular disease | 13.7 | 2 | Cerebrovascular disease | 8.0 |
| 3 | Lower respiratory infections | 6.9 | 3 | Trachea, bronchus, lung cancers | 4.5 | 3 | Lower respiratory infections | 7.7 |
| 4 | HIV/AIDS | 5.3 | 4 | Lower respiratory infections | 3.7 | 4 | HIV/AIDS | 6.9 |
| 5 | Chronic obstructive pulmonary disease | 4.5 | 5 | Chronic obstructive pulmonary disease | 3.1 | 5 | Perinatal conditions | 5.6 |
| 6 | Perinatal conditions | 4.4 | 6 | Colon and rectum cancers | 2.6 | 6 | Chronic obstructive pulmonary disease | 5.0 |
| 7 | Diarrhoeal diseases | 3.8 | 7 | Stomach cancer | 1.9 | 7 | Diarrhoeal diseases | 4.9 |
| 8 | Tuberculosis | 3.0 | 8 | Self-inflicted injuries | 1.9 | 8 | Tuberculosis | 3.7 |
| 9 | Road traffic accidents | 2.3 | 9 | Diabetes | 1.7 | 9 | Malaria | 2.6 |
| 10 | Trachea, bronchus, lung cancers | 2.2 | 10 | Breast cancer | 1.6 | 10 | Road traffic accidents | 2.5 |

*Developed countries include European countries, former Soviet countries, Canada, USA, Japan, Australia, New Zealand.

regions. The nutrition transition towards diets with a high proportion of saturated fat and sugars is well underway in all but the poorest populations (Popkin 2002). This diet, when combined with a low level of physical activity and regular tobacco consumption, sets the scene for population-wide atherosclerosis and the global distribution of chronic diseases.

The contribution of the major chronic disease risk factors to the burden of disease is summarized in Table 2. In developed countries these risk factors constitute seven of the ten leading risk factors contributing to the burden of disease, compared to six of ten among low mortality developing countries, and three of ten in high mortality developing countries. In most developing countries, the secular trend for chronic disease risk factor levels has been negative over the last decade, portending a massive increase in the occurrence of chronic diseases over the next two decades in these countries.

## Table 2

Contribution (%) of 10 Selected Risk Factors to Burden of Disease by Level of Development and Mortality

| Developed countries[*] (population: 1.4 billion) | | Developing countries[*] | | | |
|---|---|---|---|---|---|
| | | High mortality (population: 2.3 billion) | | Low mortality (population: 2.4 billion) | |
| Tobacco | 12.4% | Underweight | 14% | Alcohol | 6.3% |
| Blood pressure | 11.0% | Unsafe sex | 11.7% | Underweight | 5.8% |
| Alcohol | 9.3% | Unsafe water, sanitation & hygiene | 5.6% | Blood pressure | 5.0% |
| Cholesterol | 7.6% | Indoor smoke from solid fuels | 3.8% | Tobacco | 4.2% |
| Body mass index | 7.5% | Zinc deficiency | 3.3% | Body mass index | 2.7% |
| Low fruit & vegetable intake | 3.9% | Iron deficiency | 3.2% | Cholesterol | 2.1% |
| Physical inactivity | 3.3% | Vitamin A deficiency | 2.9% | Iron deficiency | 2.0% |
| Illicit drugs | 1.9% | Blood pressure | 2.5% | Low fruit & vegetable intake | 1.9% |
| Underweight | 1.3% | Tobacco | 1.9% | Indoor smoke from solid fuels | 1.9% |
| Iron deficiency | 0.8% | Cholesterol | 1.9% | Unsafe water, sanitation & hygiene | 1.8% |

[*] See World Health Report 2002 for full list. Developed countries include the USA, Japan, and Australia; low mortality developing countries include China, Brazil, and Thailand; and high mortality developing countries include India, Mali, and Nigeria.

Tobacco, alcohol, and high blood pressure are major contributors to the burden of disease in all categories of countries. Further, widespread emergence of the diet and physical activity-related complex of risks (overweight or a high body mass index, lack of physical activity, low fruit and vegetable consumption, high blood pressure and cholesterol levels, and excessive alcohol consumption) indicates the extent of neglect by policymakers and leads to widespread adult and child obesity, type II diabetes, cardiovascular disease and certain cancers.

The relationship between risk levels and social class is dynamic and closely related to levels of disposable income, exposure to health education programs, corporate marketing and access to potentially harmful products. Generally, consumption of tobacco and "obesogenic" food is low in the poorest countries and communities but rises rapidly with urbanization and increased incomes when marketing becomes more evident and accessibility to these products almost ubiquitous. In the absence of government education programs and legislation that supports making healthy choices the easy choices, consumption of these products increases fast. With further economic development, and when governments start to take action, reductions in consumption are often seen, especially in the more privileged groups. The policy challenge is to ensure that governments act more decisively at a point when risk levels are still low. However, for many countries this point has long passed and risk factor levels are now often highest among the poorest communities. More affluent communities have been protected to a certain extent by their ability to respond more easily to messages about the harm caused by such products.

Panel 1 provides updated information on chronic disease risks and the current impact in the world's most populous country, China. The impact of chronic diseases is not confined to urban areas. Among the over 800 million people who live in rural areas, chronic diseases in 1998 already accounted for 83% of all deaths.

## Globalization and the Emergence of Adverse Risks to Population Health

Globalization can be summarized as the increasing interconnectedness of countries and the openness of borders to ideas, people, commerce, and financial capital (Woodward et al. 2001). It has beneficial and harmful effects on the health of populations (Yach and Bettcher 1998). Financial and economic globalization and the World Trade Organization (WTO) rules which regulate trade have the potential to improve population health status by increasing national incomes. However, this benefit has not reached most poor populations (UNCTAD 2002). In fact, in many circumstances, the global trade rules and power imbalances limit the ability of national health services to respond adequately to health problems. Although governments have the power to shape the international trade rules, their influence has been curtailed by the lack of resources, expertise and technical support. Although some rhetorical advances were made at the WTO Ministerial Meeting in Doha in 2001 (Doha Declaration), these have not yet been translated into practical gains for poor countries.

---

**Panel 1: Chronic Disease Risks and Impact in China**

The leading causes of death have undergone significant changes in China. Chronic diseases, including cerebrovascular disease, cancers, heart disease, respiratory diseases, and injuries, and poisoning, have become the top five causes of deaths. The proportion of all deaths from chronic diseases, including noncommunicable diseases and injuries, has increased from approximately 46% in 1954 to 83% in 2000, with cardiovascular disease accounting for 40% of all NCD deaths, chronic obstructive respiratory disease for 24%, and cancers for 23% (Shao 2001).

Risk factors for chronic diseases have reached worrying levels in China. Currently, 320 million people smoke—67% of men and 4% of women (Niu et al. 1998; Hou 2001): approximately 90 to 100 million adults are estimated to be hypertensive; rapid nutrition transition (with an 11% decline in cereal consumption and a 323% increase in dairy consumption from 1982 to 1998) and reduction in physical activity levels (with a doubling of annual motor vehicle sales to 1 million from 1997 to 2002) are all driving a rise in CVD death rates, childhood obesity and type II diabetes.

At the request of the Chinese government, the World Bank cooperated with several sections of the Chinese government to develop a long-term health strategy in 1988. Since then, China has initiated new policies and regulations related to NCD control, supported many programmes for NCD researchers, surveillance, prevention and management, and capacity building. For instance, community-based demonstration projects for integrated NCD prevention and control were initiated in 1994, and a total 28 projects have been established in 28 provinces between 1994 to 2002.

---

Globalization drives chronic diseases risks in many complex ways, both directly and indirectly (Woodward et al. 2001). The indirect effects act through national economic performance and changes in household incomes, government expenditure, the exchange rate, and prices. National income is especially important because of its effects on public sector resources available for health and on household health-related behaviours, especially low-income households. The cost of health care and especially out-of-pocket direct costs are closely related to national income and the priority given to national coverage for health interventions. The direct negative effects of globalization are illustrated by the increasingly globalized production, promotion, and marketing of tobacco, alcohol, and other products with adverse effects on population health status.

The continuing protection of domestic producers by most developed countries and their regional organizations has a direct impact on the risks for the chronic disease epidemics. For example, the USA and the European Union agricultural subsidies limit competition from primary producers of fresh produce in developing countries and seriously reduce the incomes of the poor countries. The subsidization of tobacco production by the European Union reflects the continued power of tobacco interests and is a major policy anomaly hindering progress on tobacco control; the EU spends approximately Euro 1 billion on tobacco production subsidies and only Euro 10-20 million on tobacco control programs. The importance and urgency of removing such agricultural subsidies was endorsed in Doha and again during the Johannesburg World Summit on Sustainable Development in 2002. Although a timetable for revisions to the European Common Agricultural Policy (CAP) has been proposed, several countries that stand to lose much from the revisions to the CAP have protested vigorously.

Modern information and communication technologies influence health status both positively and negatively. On the positive side these technologies can be used in innovative ways to disseminate health promoting measures. However, the greatest effects on health are negative. For example, the marketing of tobacco, alcohol, and salty, sugary and fatty foods now reaches most parts of most countries. A significant proportion of global marketing is now targeted at children under the age of 14 (Hawkes 2002). Globally, 600 million urban-based 5 to14-year-olds spend over $200 billion per year on themselves and influence parental spending of over 10 times that amount (McNeal 2000), with fast food products, soft drinks, cigarettes and alcohol being common purchases. Marketers increasingly use sophisticated means to ensure that their messages "slip below the radar of critical thinking" (Walsh 2002), take advantage of weak regulatory environments, and use false, misleading, or deceptive advertising to reach their targets (see panel).

## Globalization of the Tobacco Pandemic

Tobacco companies aggressively exploit the potential for growth in tobacco sales in developing countries. This is of course not surprising since they are motivated only by their obligations to shareholders. The main targets of the industry and the associated marketing campaigns are now young people and women, most of whom do not smoke (Brands and Yach 2002). In many developing countries, marketing strategies are used that have long been banned in many developed countries, for example, the promotion of sporting events that appeal to youth and the use of glamorous images. Tobacco companies have long undermined scientists and their research documenting the adverse effects of tobacco—especially of passive smoking (Ong and Glantz 2001; Yach and Bialous 2001). Over 30 years ago, Philip Morris scientists were concerned that "the public have not yet arrived at the consensus that smoking causes heart disease, so cardiovascular developments must be watched extremely carefully" (WHO Tobacco Control Report 1999). The response then, as it has been recently in relation to passive smoking, was to publicly deny the evidence and pay scientists to carry out spurious research aimed at confusing the public and delaying action. For many years tobacco companies have operated to deliberately subvert the tobacco control efforts of the WHO (Zeltner et al. 2000).

---

**Panel 2: Marketing to Children**

Globally, billions of dollars are spent annually on marketing, through direct and indirect advertising, strategic product design, and calculated promotions, thus associating products and potentially unhealthy behaviours with powerfully attractive images. Aware that consumption habits developed in childhood persist for decades, companies vie for the "early adoption age" target market to foster brand loyalty among pre-teens as young as six years and among teenagers.

Food and beverage marketing appeals to young people's preference for high fat, sugar, and salt content, often supplanting water and traditional nutrient-rich diets. Similarly, tobacco and alcoholic beverages mask unappealing tastes with sweeteners and are aimed at teen subcultures, fostering appeal through low prices, and promotions.

Food, alcohol, and tobacco companies sponsor facilities, events, and promotions popular with children. Marketers use popular characters— human and cartoon—to capture children's attention: Celebrities are chosen "who are suitable for the image of youth and modernity." These efforts result in significant sales growth.

Such marketing is increasingly global in scope and exploits children's inability to meaningfully distinguish between sources and quality of information, between advertising and reality. The resultant earlier initiation, increased consumption of unhealthy products, and adoption of risky behaviors can undermine young people's later health.

In 1999 a review commissioned by a tobacco company of WHO's progress with respect to developing the Framework Convention on Tobacco Control (FCTC), indicated that WHO staff were under close and constant surveillance. Details of internal meetings, speeches, and future FCTC plans are analyzed in the report (WHO Tobacco Control Report 1999). A few months earlier, in another tobacco company's internal report (WHO Executive Board Report 1998), concern is expressed by tobacco companies about the use of Article 19 in WHO's Constitution to develop its first treaty (FCTC) and about possible expanded use of Article 21 to develop regulations, initially in relation to infectious disease control, but later in other areas, including tobacco. The article is illustrative of how tobacco companies continue to privately oppose any effective international regulatory regime while publicly maintaining that they support "responsible" public health measures.

There is a strong link between increased tobacco consumption and free trade and tobacco-related foreign direct investment (Bettcher et al. 2001). The bilateral agreements negotiated between the USA and several Asian countries under threat of sanctions in the 1980s resulted in an overall increase in demand for tobacco, with a greater effect in poorer countries (Taylor et al. 2000). New cross-border challenges such as Internet commerce and the illicit trade in tobacco products, often sanctioned by the major tobacco companies, pose additional challenges. On-line marketing by major tobacco manufacturers has increased dramatically over the last three years, and one company, R.J. Reynolds, began marketing its new brand, Eclipse, only through the Internet. Some sites offer toll-free numbers for off-line orders of tobacco products (McNeal 2000). WTO member governments retain the ability to implement the legal and regulatory tools that constitute a comprehensive tobacco control policy, provided they apply equally to all tobacco products regardless of country of origin. However, countries vary greatly in their political willingness and capacity to implement these policy measures; in large part, the response of countries is determined by the power of anti-tobacco nongovernmental organizations (McNeal 2000).

### The Nutrition Transition and the Global Promotion of Alcohol Consumption

The nutrition transition is the replacement of the traditional diet rich in fruit and vegetables by a diet rich in calories provided by animal fats and lower in complex carbohydrates (Popkin 2002). This transition is well underway in all but the poorest countries. It is part of the more general health transition and will lead to increased chronic disease rates in countries that have been protected by balanced and healthy diets. Asia is experiencing a particularly marked shift in consumption patterns. The rapidity of the transition and the reductions in the energy expended on physical activity in all but the poorest countries, and especially in urban areas (DiGuiseppi et al. 1998), are reflected in the rapid rise of urban obesity (Popkin 2002); in China the prevalence of obesity in urban children aged 2-6 years increased from 1.5% in 1989 to 12.6% in 1997 (Luo and Hu 2002). In many countries, especially in the poorer countries of Asia and Africa, there is an increasing coexistence of undernutrition with overnutrition, often in the same family, and this may predispose developing countries to a more rapid increase in chronic diseases than occurred in developed countries because of the influence of early nutritional status on adult obesity and other chronic disease patterns.

There has been a major transformation in farming practices and technologies (Goodman and Watt 1997), distribution (Brown 1997), transportation (Paxton 1994), shopping practices (Raven and Lang 1995; Marsden, Flynn, and Harrison 2000), and the consumption of food outside of the home (Ebbeling, Pawalk, and Ludwig 2002). Cooking has been altered by the development of microwave ovens and the availability of relatively cheap prepared meals with high fat and caloric content (Mintz 1996). The changes in patterns of production and consumption are fundamental to the emergence of the chronic disease epidemics; of even more significance, these changes threaten attainment of sustainable development goals. The combination of overgrazing by growing beef herds and overploughing has led to massive soil erosion and the generation of major dust storms in central China; excessive fishing for short-term commercial gains has seriously depleted many species; and the irresponsible use of water for irrigation and industrial uses has depleted major aquifers in many parts of the world (von Schirnding and Yach forthcoming). Changes in the food supply chain have relied on non-renewable energy use with adverse effects on the local and global environment.

The alcohol industry is becoming as globally integrated and pervasive as the tobacco industry (Jernigan 1997). The effect of alcohol consumption on chronic disease is more complex than the effect of tobacco consumption. There is a direct relationship between alcohol consumption and some cancers and liver cirrhosis, and most causes of injuries—especially road injuries— and violence. At very low levels of consumption, alcohol reduces the risks of CVD, but this effect is only important for people who are at relatively high risk, for example, middle-aged and older people in developed countries. Binge drinking is an important cause of CVD and contributed to the dramatic and devastating decline in middle-aged life expectancy in Russian men following the collapse of the Soviet Union (McKee, Shkolnikov, and Leon 2001). The promotion of alcohol to young people, especially through its association with sporting events and with gender-specific roles, indicates the pressing need for global action.

## Global Solutions to the Globalization of Chronic Diseases Risks

There have been major reductions in chronic disease rates in many wealthy countries, notably for lung cancer in men and CVD in both men and women. The reduction in lung cancer mortality is due to the substantial decline in tobacco consumption by men as a result of comprehensive tobacco control policies from taxation policies to advertising restrictions. The lung cancer epidemic is still increasing in women, following their later widespread adoption of smoking and the inability of most health promotion programs to counter the power of the tobacco marketing campaigns directed towards young women. The reasons for the declines in CVD mortality are more complex and are due to both improved management of high risk people, particularly in the USA, and prevention programs directed towards the reduction of population risk levels (Beaglehole and Dobson 2003). The early declines in CHD mortality rates in the 1970s could only have been due to preventive messages because effective therapeutic interventions were not widely available. These early declines are notable because comprehensive programs were not generally in place, illustrating the importance of the relatively informal uptake of the results of public health research by at least some sections of the community (Powles and Cumio 2003). There is no doubt that an important component of the later declines in CHD mortality have come from the effects of the wide range of effective and relatively cheap interventions that are now widely available in most developed countries.

The application of existing knowledge has the potential to make an even greater contribution to the prevention and control of the chronic disease epidemics (Beaglehole 2001). However, constraints on the implementation of effective policies need to be more widely recognized and overcome. The global health agenda is dominated by the notion that communicable diseases need to be prevented and treated before chronic diseases receive attention. The report of The Commission on Macroeconomics and Health paid little attention to the growing burden of chronic diseases (WHO 2001b), with the exception of cost-effectiveness of tobacco cessation, perhaps because of the misconception that chronic diseases are still the preserve of wealthy countries and populations. Although the epidemiological and health transitions are well advanced in all but the poorest countries, the institutional response to disease prevention and control is still based on the infectious disease paradigm. As a consequence, the global and national capacity to respond to chronic disease epidemics is woefully inadequate, and few countries have implemented comprehensive prevention and control policies. This weak capacity is also a feature of the public health workforce in almost all countries. The USA has only just developed its first comprehensive prevention and control policy (CDCP 2003).

Many powerful and persuasive commercial entities involved in the production and promotion of unhealthy products exert an adverse influence on health policy developments. This has been well documented in the case of tobacco (Hawkes 2002), and more recently the influence of some major food companies on the development of USA dietary guidelines and food policy has been described (Nestle 2002). Appropriate environmental and policy interventions are available to promote physical activity in urban environments. However, the implementation of these policies is still at an early stage, their effects are not well documented, and they face powerful countervailing forces (Kalm et al. 2002). A comprehensive response to all these challenges is required to reduce the global chronic disease burden.

### Lessons from Progress in Global Tobacco Control

The progress made in developing a global response to the tobacco threat is shown in Table 3 and provides a useful model for a comprehensive response to the global chronic disease epidemics. For the first time and under WHO leadership, an international treaty directed towards the control of tobacco use is being negotiated. The Framework Convention on Tobacco Control (FCTC) links the science of tobacco control with the political process of negotiating an international treaty and associated protocols on tobacco control priorities such as advertising restrictions, illicit trade in tobacco products, and product regulation (Correa 2002; Taylor and Bettcher 2000). The process of developing the FCTC has led to a coherent UN-wide approach to tobacco control with demand reduction as the primary goal. This experience is now being translated into intersectoral plans and actions within many countries (UN Economic and Social Council 2002).

A simple and standardized approach to surveillance of all the major risk factors is an essential activity for monitoring progress, providing data for policymakers, and strengthening preventive programs (Bonita et al. 2001). A good example of this process is a school-based surveillance system, the Global Youth Tobacco Survey (GYTS), which ensures that standardized means of monitoring progress are being established (Global Youth Tobacco Survey Collaborative Group 2002). Initial results, based upon surveys in 43 countries and involving 230,000 children aged 13-15 years, indicate that 18% currently smoke, about half are exposed to second-hand smoke at home, and nearly 80% are confronted daily by tobacco advertising. Already one million children from almost 100 countries have been enrolled

## Table 3

Progress in Global Tobacco Control

| | |
|---|---|
| **Advocacy** | World No Tobacco Day (frequent high-level media coverage) |
| **Norms / International Legal Instruments** | Framework Convention on Tobacco Control |
| **Surveillance** | Global Youth Tobacco Survey (now in 80 countries) |
| **Intersectoral Action** | UN Task Force on Tobacco Control |
| **Research and Training** | Canadian (RITC) and USA (NIH-FIC) Support for Global Research and Training |
| **Partnerships** | Tobacco-Free Sports: Smoking Cessation |

in GYTS, and this will become a critical means of assessing whether the FCTC and national commitments to tobacco control are being met. An important set of questions included in GYTS asks smokers about the usual brand they consume. This information will be useful as a means of countering the claims of tobacco companies that they do not market to children.

New partnerships have been established between WHO and pharmaceutical industries to expand access to tobacco cessation and with NGOs in developing and developed countries to enhance global advocacy. Until recently, only a few NGOs, mainly based in the USA and Europe, focused on tobacco control. Now there are well over 150 NGOs, mostly from developing countries, actively promoting effective tobacco control policies. Major sports federations, including the International Olympic Committee, the FIFA (the international football association), the FIA (the international automobile association), and the international volleyball association, have joined forces with WHO to make tobacco-free sport the future norm.

### Global Advocacy for Chronic Disease Prevention: A Weak Link

There is only limited advocacy at the global level for the chronic disease prevention and control agenda, and what there is tends to be fragmented and risk-factor or disease-specific. The lack of connection between evidence and action reported in the USA (McGinnis 2001) also applies globally. Many of the potential advocacy groups have their origins in specialist health professional organizations and have not yet coalesced to become strong promoters of broad prevention and control policies (Beaglehole 2001). This lack of strong voices for disease prevention and health promotion programs is in contrast to the growing dominance of commercial and consumer groups who have placed treatment at the center of health policy debates and funding priorities. Because of their origins, the most effective advocates for prevention have concentrated on single risk factors or specific diseases, often with great success, for example, national tobacco control advocacy groups. Stronger and broader alliances of major health professional bodies, consumer groups, enlightened industries and academics are now needed to effectively prioritize the prevention of major risk factors for chronic diseases. Slowly this is happening with the World Heart Federation, the World Medical Association and its associated health professional's alliance (which includes nurses, pharmacists and dentists), and International Cancer Control Union, all of whom are increasingly working together on chronic disease promotion issues. Full activation of their national associations would bring a powerful global voice to a neglected area of public health.

## Innovative Interactions with the Private Sector Are Possible

WHO and governments cannot address the challenges of chronic disease prevention and control alone. As with tobacco control, partnerships are critical. In addition to interaction with international consumer groups, new forms of interaction with global commercial food multinationals, retailers, sporting goods companies, and insurance companies are essential if progress is to be made in improving the quality and access of people to healthy foods and increased physical activity. Until recently, the relationship between multinationals and the public sector were mainly adversarial, and multinational companies were not well organized for effective interaction with governments and WHO. WHO has embarked upon a global consultative process aimed at developing a strategy to address diet and physical activity in relation to chronic diseases. The process has led to the development of a new set of dietary guidelines, and extensive consultations have produced a Global Strategy for Diet, Physical Activity and Health which was adopted as policy by all 192 WHO member states on May 22 2004.

Progress has been made in the development of a multistakeholder approach to the promotion of fruit and vegetables; and over the next year it is expected that continued interaction with food and related companies will lead to other joint initiatives. The dangers and difficulties of these partnerships are recognized by all concerned. WHO has been clear that there are complex areas where companies and the public health community have different perspectives, for example, in the way in which some companies market their products to children.

The public health community has yet to develop clear guidelines for interaction with food companies. In the absence of such clarity, there remains a confused and often ambiguous debate about the best way to promote healthy diets and physical activity. The media has exploited this confusion, and this can lead to public scepticism about any pronouncements in this field. The alcohol field presents especial challenges. WHO has begun to interact with elements of the alcohol industry in order to assess whether the industry's self-regulatory approaches will be effective in reducing marketing to young people and can lead to a reduction in drunk driving.

## Capacity and Resources for Prevention Remain Weak

The capacity at the national level for chronic disease prevention and control is weak in terms of personnel, infrastructure and resources (Alwan, Maclean, and Mandil 2001). There is a need for a significant investment in the capacity of countries to plan and manage health projects for infectious diseases and even more for chronic diseases (Morrow 2002; Berwick 2002). Unfortunately, donors and governments have been reluctant to invest in national institutions and infrastructure for chronic disease prevention. A global commitment is needed if sustainable progress in policy development and implementation for chronic diseases, as well as other aspects of public health, is to be assured. WHO's Tropical Disease Research Program funded by a consortium of donors, has developed over the last two decades an impressive network of communicable disease researchers (Nchinda 2002) and provides many useful lessons for chronic disease control efforts. The USA National Institutes for Health, through their Fogarty International Center, and Canada's IDRC have begun to invest modestly in tobacco control research in developing countries, and this needs to be expanded to other aspects of chronic diseases.

## Global Norms and Standards for Preventive Actions

There is an increasing need to establish global norms in a wide range of spheres to balance the otherwise unrestrained influences of powerful actors. To do so, public health capacities in trade and political science must be strengthened so as to effectively participate in the WTO where health issues are increasingly considered (Zwi and Yach 2002) and to develop stronger WHO-led norms that could be used as the basis for resolving trade disputes in relation to products with health impacts (WHO/WTO 2002). The FCTC is one example of a global norm; others that are important for chronic disease control include the International Code of Marketing of Breast-milk Substitutes, the Codex Alimentarius Commission (with its likely increased focus on food labelling and health claims); but more will be needed.

Treaties are probably not the solution to the complex issues related to nutrition transition or physical inactivity. A combination of multistake-holder and intergovernmental codes are better options to pursue, especially in relation to better labelling of products and restricting marketing of alcohol and foods to young children. A number of options in this regard were recently summarized (Chopra, Galbraith, and Darnton-Hill 2002). These approaches are already being used in a wide variety of areas related to improving labor conditions, environmental quality, and human rights (UN NGLS 2002).

## Health Services Delivery: Missed Opportunities for Chronic Disease Control

Untold lives are lost prematurely because of inadequate acute and long-term management of chronic diseases. Simple and cheap treatments exist for the treatment and long-term management of many chronic diseases; there is, for example, excellent evidence on the effectiveness of relatively cheap interventions for CVD (Yusuf 2002). Even in wealthy countries the potential of these interventions for secondary prevention is far from fully utilized (Campbell et al. 1998). The situation in poorer countries is probably even less satisfactory although the data are limited. Effective means of preventing, treating, and providing palliative care for cancer exist (WHO 2002b), but are not implemented in most countries. There are many opportunities for coordinated chronic disease risk reduction as well as care and long-term management; for example, smoking cessation is a priority for all patients irrespective of the reasons for consulting a health service provider (WHO 2001a).

## Conclusion

The global distribution of the major risks for chronic diseases is now almost complete and their prevalence is increasing in most populations. However, the prospects for chronic disease prevention and control are improving only slowly and have not kept pace with the growing burden of NCD. Sustained progress will only occur when governments and influential international bodies involved in health policy and funding acknowledge that the scope of global public health action must be rapidly broadened to include chronic diseases and their risk factors. The challenges are enormous and the ongoing tobacco wars in both developed and developing countries indicate that progress will continue to be slow unless the response to the epidemics is scaled up in a manner commensurate with their burden on both families and societies.

# References

ALWAN, ALA, DAVID MACLEAN AND A. MANDIL
2001    *Assessment of National Capacity for Noncommunicable Disease Prevention and Control.*
        Geneva, Switzerland: World Health Organization.

BEAGLEHOLE, ROBERT
2001    "Global Cardiovascular Disease Prevention: Time to Get Serious." *Lancet* 358:
        661-3.

BEAGLEHOLE, ROBERT AND ANNETTE DOBSON
2003    "The Contributions to Change: Risk Factors and the Potential for Prevention."
        In *Coronary Heart Disease Epidemiology*, edited by M. Marmot and P. Elliot.
        Oxford, United Kingdom: Oxford University Press.

BEAGLEHOLE, ROBERT AND DEREK YACH
2003    "Globalization and the Prevention and Control of Noncommunicable Disease:
        The Neglected Chronic Diseases of Adults." *Lancet* 362: 903-908.

BERWICK, DAN
2002    "A Learning World for the Global Fund." *British Medical Journal* 325: 55-6.

BETTCHER, DOUGLAS, CHITRA SUBRAMANIAM, EMMANUEL GUINDON ET AL.
2001    *Confronting the Tobacco Epidemic in an Era of Trade Liberalization.* Geneva,
        Switzerland: World Health Organization.

BONITA, RUTH, MAX DE COURTEN, TERRY DWYER, KONRAD JAMROZIK, AND
        REGINA WINKELMANN
2001    *Surveillance of Risk Factors for Noncommunicable Diseases: The WHO STEPwise
        Approach.* Geneva, Switzerland: World Health Organization.

BRANDS, ANNEMIEKE AND DEREK YACH
2002    *Women and the Rapid Rise of Noncommunicable Diseases.* Geneva, Switzerland: World
        Health Organization.

BROWN, S.A.
1997    *Revolution at the Checkout Counter.* Cambridge, MA: Harvard University Press.

CAMPBELL, C.N., J. THAIN, G.H. DEANS, ET AL.
1998    "Secondary Prevention in Coronary Heart Disease: Baseline Survey of
        Provision in General Practice." *British Medical Journal* 316: 1430-4.

CENTER FOR DISEASE CONTROL AND PREVENTION
2003    *A Public Health Action Plan to Prevent Heart Disease and Stroke.* Atlanta, GA: CDCP.

CHOPRA, MICKEY, SARAH GALBRAITH, AND IAN DARNTON-HILL
2002    "A Global Response to a Global Problem: The Epidemic of Overnutrition."
        *Bulletin of the World Health Organization* 80: 952-8.

DIGUISEPPI C., I. ROBERTS, L. LI, AND D. ALLEN
        "Determinants of Car Travel on Daily Journeys to School: Cross Sectional
        Survey of Primary School Children." *British Medical Journal* 316: 1426-8.

DOHA DECLARATION
        http://www.wto.org

EBBELING, C.D., D.B. PAWALK, AND DAVID LUDWIG
2002    "Childhood Obesity: A Public Health Crisis, Common Sense Cure." *Lancet*
        360: 473-82.

EVANS, TIM, MARGARET WHITEHEAD, FINN DIDERICHSEN ET AL., EDS.
2001    *Challenging Inequities in Health: From Ethics to Action.* New York, NY: Oxford
        University Press.

GLOBAL YOUTH TOBACCO SURVEY COLLABORATIVE GROUP
2002    "Tobacco Use Among Youth: A Cross Country Comparison." *Tobacco Control*
        11: 252-270.

GOODMAN, DAVID AND MICHAEL WATTS
1997    *Globalising Food.* London, United Kingdom: Routledge.

HAWKES, CORRINA
2002    "Marketing Activities of Global Soft Drink and Fast Food Companies in
        Emerging Markets: A Review." In *WHO Globalization, Diets and Noncommunicable
        Diseases.* Geneva, Switzerland: World Health Organization.

HOU, PEISEN
2001    "Progress and Challenges of Tobacco Control in China." Paper Presented at

the National Conference on Policy Development of Tobacco Control in China in the 21st Century. May 29-31, Beijing, China.

JERNIGAN, DAVID
1997 *Thirsting for Markets: The Global Impact of Corporate Alcohol.* Marin County, CA: Marin Institute for the Prevention of Alcohol and Other Drug Problems.

KALM E.B., L. RAMSEY, R.C. BROWNSON ET AL.
2002 "The Effectiveness of Interventions to Increase Physical Activity: A Systematic Review." *American Journal of Preventive Medicine* 22: 73-107.

KUNST, ANTON, F. GROENHOF, AND JOHAN MACKENBACK
1998 "Mortality by Occupational Class Among Men 30-64 Years in 11 European Countries." *Social Science and Medicine* 46: 459-76.

LEON, DAVID AND GILLIAN WATT
2001 *Poverty, Inequality and Health: An International Perspective.* Oxford, United Kingdom: Oxford University Press.

LUO J. AND F.B. HU
2002 "Time Trends of Obesity in Pre-School Children in China From 1989 to 1997." *International Journal on Obesity and Related Metabolic Disorders* 26: 553-6.

MAGNUS, PAUL AND ROBERT BEAGLEHOLE
2001 "The Real Contribution of the Major Risk Factors to the Coronary Epidemics: Time to End the 'Only 50%' Claim." *Annals of Internal Medicine* 161: 2657-60.

MARSDEN R., A. FLYNN, AND M. HARRISON
2000 *Consuming Interests: The Social Provision of Foods.* London, United Kingdom: University College Press.

MCGINNIS, JAMES M.
2001 "Does Proof Matter? Why Strong Evidence Sometimes Yields Weak Action." *American Journal of Health Promotion* 15: 391-6.

MCKEE, MARTIN, VICTOR SHKOLNIKOV, AND DAVID LEON
2001 "Alcohol Is Implicated in the Fluctuations in Cardiovascular Disease in Russia Since the 1980s." *Annals of Epidemiology* 11: 1-6.

MCNEAL, JIM
2002 *Children as Consumers of Commercial and Social Products.* Washington, D.C.: Pan American Health Organization.

MINTZ, SIDNEY
1996 *Tasting Food, Tasting Freedom: Excursions in Eating, Culture, and the Past.* Boston, MA: Beacon Press.

MORROW, RICHARD
2002 "Macroeconomics and Health." *British Medical Journal* 352: 53-4.

NCHINDA, THOMAS
2002 "Research Capacity Strengthening in the South." *Social Science and Medicine* 54: 1699-1711.

NESTLE, MARIAN
2002 *Food Politics: How the Food Industry Influences Nutrition and Health.* Berkeley, CA: University of California Press.

NIU, SHIU ET AL.
1998 "Emerging Tobacco Hazards in China: Early Mortality Results From a Prospective Study." *British Medical Journal* 317: 1423-1424.

ONG, ELIZE AND STAN GLANTZ
2001 "Constructing Sound Science and Good Epidemiology: Tobacco Lawyers and Pubic Relations Firms." *American Journal of Public Health* 91: 1749-1757.

PAXTON, A.
1994 *The Food Miles Report.* London, United Kingdom: SAFE Alliance.
2002 "An Overview on the Nutrition Transition and Its Health Implications: The Bellagio Meeting." *Public Health Nutrition* 5: 93-103.

POPKIN, BARRY
2002 "The Bellagio Conference on the Nutrition Transition and its Implications for Health in the Developing World." *Public Health Nutrition* 5: 93-280.

POWLES, JOHN AND FLAVIO CUMIO
2003 "Public Health Infrastructure and Knowledge." In *Global Public Goods for Health,* edited by R. Smith, Robert Beaglehole, David Woodward, and Nick Drager. Oxford, United Kingdom: Oxford University Press.

RAVEN, H. AND TIM LANG
1995        *Off Our Trolleys?Retailing and the Hypermarket Economy.* London, England: Institute of Public Policy Research.
RODGERS, ANTHONY, CARLENE LAWES, AND STEPHAN MACMAHON
2000        "Reducing the Global Burden of Blood Pressure-Related Cardiovascular Disease." *Journal of Hypertension Supplement* 18: S3-6.
SEIXAS CORREA AND LUIZ FELIPE
2002        "The Framework Convention on Tobacco Control." *Bulletin of the World Health Organization* 80: 924.
SHAO, RUITAI
2001        "Meet Challenges in Disease Patterns Change." *Chinese Journal of Preventive Medicine* 35: 5-6.
STAMLER, JEREMIAH, ROSE STAMLER, J.D. NEATON ET AL.
1999        "Low Risk-Factor Profile and Long-Term Cardiovascular and Non-Cardiovascular Mortality and Life Expectancy. Findings for 5 Cohorts of Young Adult and Middle-Aged Men and Women." *Journal of American Medical Association* 282: 2012-18.
TAYLOR, ALLYN AND DOUGLAS BETTCHER
2000        "A WHO Framework Convention on Tobacco Control: A Global Public Good for Health." *Bulletin of the World Health Organization* 78: 920-9.
TAYLOR, ALLYN, FRANK CHALOUPKA, EMMANUEL GUINDON, AND M. CORBETT
2000        "Trade Policy and Tobacco Control." In *Tobacco Control in Developing Countries*, edited by P. Jha and F. Chaloupka. Oxford, United Kingdom: Oxford University Press.
UNITED NATIONS CONFERENCE ON TRADE AND DEVELOPMENT (UNCTAD)
2002        *Escaping the Poverty Trap: The Least Developed Countries Report 2002.* New York, NY: United Nations.
UNITED NATIONS NONGOVERNMENTAL LIAISON SERVICE (NGLS)
2002        *Voluntary Approaches to Corporate Responsibility. Readings and a Resource Guide.* Geneva: Switzerland: United Nations NGLS.
UNITED NATIONS ECONOMIC AND SOCIAL COUNCIL
2002        "Report of the Secretary-General. Ad Hoc Inter-Agency Task Force on Tobacco Control." July 1-24, New York, NY.
VON SCHIRNDING, YASMIN AND DEREK YACH
2002        "Unhealthy Consumption Threatens Sustainable Development." *Revista de Saúde Pública* 36(4): 1-5.
WALSH, DAVID
2002        "Slipping Under the Radar: Advertising and the Mind." Paper Presented at the World Health Organization Symposium: "Marketing to Young People," April 2002, Treviso, Italy.
WOODWARD, DAVID, NICK DRAGER, ROBERT BEAGLEHOLE, AND DEBORAH LIPSON
2001        "Globalization and Health: A Framework for Analysis and Action." *Bulletin of the World Health Organization* 8: 875-81.
WORLD HEALTH ORGANIZATION INTER-OFFICE CORRESPONDENCE
1971        Review of Directory of Ongoing Research in Smoking and Health. Philip Morris Incorporated. August 30, 1971. Bates Number: 1000211682.
WORLD HEALTH ORGANIZATION
1998        "New Developments at WHO of Significance to Tobacco." A Report on the 101st Session of the Executive Board, January 19-28, Geneva, Switzerland.
1999        Monthly Report on Tobacco Control. January 1999. Bates Number 2081298822-40.
2001a        "Innovative Care for Chronic Conditions: Building Blocks for Action." Geneva, Switzerland: WHO.
2001b        Commission on Macroeconomics and Health (CMH). *Macroeconomics and Health: Investing in Health for Development.* Geneva, Switzerland: WHO.
2001c        *World Health Report 2001.* Geneva, Switzerland: WHO.
2002a        *World Health Report 2002.* Geneva, Switzerland: WHO.
2002b        *National Cancer Control Programmes: Policies and Managerial Guidelines.* Geneva, Switzerland: WHO.

WORLD HEALTH ORGANIZATION/WORLD TRADE ORGANIZATION
2002      *Multilateral Trade Agreements and Public Health.* Geneva, Switzerland: WHO/WTO.
YACH, DEREK AND DOUGLAS BETTCHER
1998      "The Globalization of Public Health, I: Threats and Opportunities." *American Journal of Public Health* 88: 735-8.
YACH, DEREK AND STELLA BIALOUS
2001      "Junking Science to Promote Tobacco." *American Journal of Public Health* 91: 1745-8.
YUSUF, SALIM
2002      "Two Decades of Progress in Preventing Vascular Disease." *Lancet* 360: 2-3.
ZELTNER, THOMAS, DAVID KESSLER, ANKE MARTINY, AND FARZAL RANDERA
2000      *Tobacco Industry Strategies to Undermine Tobacco Control Activities at the World Health Organization.* Report of the Committee of Experts on Tobacco Industry Documents. Geneva, Switzerland: World Health Organization.
ZWI, ANTHONY B. AND DEREK YACH
2002      "International Health in the 21st Century: Trends and Challenges." *Social Science and Medicine* 54: 1615-20.

# The People's Health Movement:
# A People's Campaign for
# "HEALTH FOR ALL—NOW!"

RAVI NARAYAN* AND CLAUDIO SCHUFTAN**

ABSTRACT

The People's Health Assembly and the People's Health Movement have been a civil society effort to counter the ill effects of globalization on health and health care. The Assembly, through an interactive dialogue, developed the People's Charter for Health as a tool for advocacy and a call for radical action. Consisting of a wide range of action initiatives, the People's Charter for Health, now translated into over forty languages, is helping to promote a movement that involves geographical circles of health professionals and activists that organize street-level rallies, policy debates and dialogues, and public education. The movement's advocacy efforts with the WHO and other major international health players and health campaigns are all focused on the goal of "Health for All—Now!"

## Background

In 1978, an International Health Assembly at Alma-Ata in USSR, co-sponsored by the World Health Organization (WHO), United Nations' Children's Fund (UNICEF); and others, gave the World a slogan "Health for All by 2000" and endorsed the famous Alma-Ata Declaration, which brought people and communities to the center of health planning and health care strategies, and emphasized the role of community participation,

---

* People's Health Movement Global Secretariat, Bangalore, India.
** People's Health Movement, Hanoi, Vietnam.

appropriate technology, and intersectoral coordination. The declaration was endorsed by most of the governments of the world and symbolized a significant paradigm shift in the global understanding of health and health care (WHO—UNICEF 1978).

Twenty-two years later, after much policy rhetoric, some concerted but mostly ad hoc action, misplaced euphoria, assault and distortions by the growing market economy of medicine, and a lot of governmental and international health agency amnesia, this declaration remains unfulfilled and mostly forgotten. As the world comes to terms with the new economic forces of globalization, liberalization, and privatization, the dream of providing health for all is receding. The People's Health Assembly in Savar, Bangladesh, on December 4-8, 2000, and the People's Health Movement that evolved from it represent a civil society effort to counter this global amnesia and challenge health policymakers around the world with a people's health campaign for "Health for All—Now!"

## The People's Health Assembly

The global People's Health Assembly held at Savar, Dhaka, from December 4-8, 2000, brought together 1453 people from 92 countries, in an unusual five-day event, sharing people's concerns about the unfulfilled Health for All initiative launched in Alma-Ata two decades earlier (Narayan 2000). The assembly included a variety of interactive dialogue opportunities for all the health professionals and activists who gathered for this significant event. These activities included the following:

- A march for health.
- Meetings at which testimonies on the health situation from many parts of the world and struggles of people were shared and commented upon by multidisciplinary resource persons (People's Health Movement 2002).
- Parallel workshops to discuss a range of health and health-related challenges.
- Cultural programs to symbolize the multiregional, multicultural, and multiethnic diversity of the peoples of the world; also exhibitions and video/film shows.
- Dialogue, in small and big groups, using formal and informal opportunities.

The assembly in Savar was preceded by a series of preassembly events all over the world. The most exceptional of these was the mobilization in India. For nearly nine months preceding the assembly, there were grassroots, local, and regional initiatives of people's health enquiries and audits; health songs and popular theater; subdistrict and district level seminars; policy dialogues and the translation of national consensus documents on health into regional languages; and campaigns to challenge medical professionals and the health system to become more Health for All-oriented.

Finally, over 2000 delegates arrived in Kolkata, mostly by five people's health trains, bringing ideas and perspectives from 17 state conventions and 250 district conventions. At Kolkata, the assembly endorsed the Indian People's Health Charter, after two days of conferences, parallel workshops, exhibitions, a march for health, a public rally, and cultural programs. About 300 delegates from this assembly then traveled to Bangladesh, mostly by bus, to attend the global People's Health Assembly. Similar activities, though less intense, took place in Bangladesh, Nepal, Sri Lanka, Cambodia, the Philippines, Japan, and other parts of the world, including Latin America, Europe, Africa, and Australia.

## The People's Charter for Health

Finally, at the end of a whole year of mobilization and five days of a very intense and interactive assembly at Savar, Bangladesh, a global people's health charter emerged, which was endorsed by all the participants (People's Health Assembly 2000a). This charter provides:

- an expression of common concerns;
- a vision of a better and healthier world;
- a call for radical action;
- a tool for advocating people's health; and
- a rallying point for global health movements, networks, and coalition building.

The global people's health charter is a significant development for many reasons. First, it endorses health as a social, economic, and political issue and a fundamental human right. Second, it identifies inequality, poverty, exploitation, violence, and injustice as the roots of ill health. Third, it underlines the imperative that Health for All means challenging powerful economic interests, opposing globalization in its existing iniquitous model, and drastically changing political and economic priorities. Fourth, it includes perspectives and voices of the poor and marginalized (rarely heard) people, and encourages them to develop their own local solutions. Finally, it encourages people to hold accountable their own local authorities, national governments, international organizations and corporations.

The vision and the principles of the charter, more than any other document preceding it, extricate health from the myopic biomedical-techno-managerialism of the last two decades, with its vertical, selective magic bullets approach to health, and centers squarely in the context of today's global social, economical, political, cultural, and environmental realities. However, the most significant gain of the People's Health

Assembly and the Charter is that, for the first time since the Alma-Ata Declaration (1978), a Health For All action plan unambiguously endorses a call for action that tackles the broader determinants of health. These include health as human right; economic challenges for health; social and political challenges for health; environmental challenges for health; tackling war, violence, conflict, and natural disasters; evolving a people-centered health sector; and encouraging people's participation in creating a healthy world.

In a nutshell, the People's Health Movement promotes a wide range of approaches and initiatives to combat the ill-effects on health, health systems, and health care initiatives of the triple assault by the forces of globalization, liberalization, and privatization. These approaches include the following:

- Combating the negative impacts of globalization as a worldwide economic and political ideology and process.
- Significantly reforming the international financial institutions and the WTO to make them more responsive to poverty alleviation and the Health for All Now movement.
- Forgiveness of the foreign debt of the least developed countries and the use of its equivalent for poverty reduction, health, and education activities.
- Greater checks, restraints, and mechanisms to ensure their compliance on the freewheeling powers of the transitional corporations, especially pharmaceutical firms.

In addition to these initiatives aimed at the existing institutional framework of the global economic system, the movement promotes a large number of more specific initiatives aimed at the following:

- Greater and more equitable household food security.
- Some type of a Tobin tax that will tax runaway international financial transfers.
- Unconditionally supporting the emancipation of women and respecting their full rights.
- Putting health higher in the development agenda of governments.
- Promoting the health (and other) rights of displaced people.
- Halting the privatization of public health facilities and working towards greater controls on the already installed private health sector.
- More equitable, just, and empowered people's participation in health and development matters.
- A greater focus on poverty alleviation in national and international development plans.
- Greater and unconditional access of the poor to health services and treatment regardless of their ability to pay.

- Strengthening public institutions, political parties, and trade unions involved in the struggles of the poor.
- Opposing restricted and dogmatic fundamentalist views of the development process.
- Greater vigilance and activism in matters of water and air pollution, the dumping of toxics, the disposal of waste, climate changes and $CO_2$ emissions, soil erosion, and other attacks on the environment.
- Militant opposition to the unsustainable exploitation of natural resources and the destruction of forests.
- Protecting biodiversity and opposing biopiracy and the indiscriminate use of genetically modified seeds.
- Holding violators of environmental crimes accountable.
- Systematically applying environmental assessments of development projects and people-centered environmental audits.

Moreover, the movement has taken a position on a number of critical global political issues such as the following:

- Opposing war and the current USA-led, blind "anti-terrorist" campaigns.
- Categorically opposing the Israeli invasion of Palestinian towns, having, among others, a sizeable negative impact on the health of the Palestinian people.
- The democratization of the UN bodies and especially the Security Council.

Finally, the movement promotes a large number of initiatives aimed at transforming health in the most comprehensive manner possible. These include the following:

- Making a renewed call for a comprehensive, a more democratic people's health care that is given the resources needed and that holds governments accountable in this task.
- Independent national drug policies focused on essential, generic drugs.
- The transformation of WHO, supporting and actively working with its new Civil Society Initiative (CSI) and making sure it remains accountable to civil society.
- Assuring WHO stays staunchly independent from corporate interests.
- Sustaining and promoting the defense of effective patient's rights.
- Expanding and incorporating traditional medicine.
- Changing the training of health personnel to assure that it covers the great issues of our time as depicted in the People's Charter for Health.
- Public health-oriented (and not for-profit) health research worldwide.
- Strong people's organizations and a global movement working on health issues.

- More proactive countering of the media that are at the service of the globalization process.
- Promoting people's empowerment leading to their greater control of the health services they need and get.
- Creating the bases for more effective analysis and concerted actions by the PHM's members through their greater involvement in the PHM's website and listserve.
- Fostering a global solidarity network that can support and mobilize fellow members when facing disasters, emergencies, or acute repressive situations.
- Getting more actively involved in actions addressing the silent epidemic of violence against women.
- Assuring more prompt responses and preventive/rehabilitative measures in cases of natural disasters.

The decision to pursue this comprehensive combination of health initiatives, as we enter the new millennium, is probably the most significant achievement of the People's Health Assembly and the evolving People's Health Movement (Schuftan 2002).

## Significant Gains of the People's Health Assembly and the PHM

The mobilization process at the global level, the assembly, and the development of the movement have already made many significant gains. For the first time in decades, health and non-health networks have come together to mobilize global solidarity and act collectivity for health. The main organizations that have taken the lead in this effort include the International People's Health Council (IPHC), Health Action International (HAI), Consumer International (CI), Asian Community Health Action Network (ACHAN), Third World Network (TWN), Women's Global Network for Reproductive Rights (WGNRR), Gonoshasthya Kendra (GK), and the Dag Hammaeskjold Foundation (DHF). More recently, new networks such as the Global Equity Gauge Alliance (GEGA) and the Social Forum Networks have joined the effort.

At the country level similar developments are beginning to happen. In India, for instance, the movement has gained the support of various scientific groups, women's movements, the alliance of people's movements, health networks and associations, research and policy networks, and some trade unions. Another significant development has been the development of solidarity between national movements. This solidarity has found symbolic expression in various collective documents at the global level (People's Health Assembly 2000b, 2000c). These documents have included themes such as Health in the Era of Globalization: From Victims to Protagonists;

the Political Economy of the Assault on Health; Equity and Inequity Today; the Medicalization of Health Care and the Challenge of Health for All; the Environmental Crisis: Threats to Health and Ways Forward; Communication as if People Mattered: and Adapting Health Promotion and Social Action to the Global Imbalances of the Twenty-First Century. Taken together, these documents represent an unprecedented, emerging, global consensus on a wide range of critical issues.

These kinds of "consensus documents" to support public education and policy advocacy have also been evolving at the country level. In India, for instance, five small booklets, now translated into most Indian languages are now being widely distributed on the following five issues: (1) what globalization means for people's health; (2) whatever happened to health for all by 2000 AD; (3) making life worth living by meeting basic needs of all; (4) a world where we all matter by focusing on the health care issues of women, children, street kids, the differently abled and the aged; and (5) confronting the commercialization of health care. These booklets have been published by 18 national networks that together form the national coordination committee in India and represent an unprecedented consensus on these issues, the first of its kind in five decades.

The People's Health Assembly itself was an unprecedented achievement. This international health gathering expresses and symbolizes an alternative health and development culture based on dialogue and the celebration of people's health. Another significant gain has been the translation of the People's Charter for Health into nearly 40 languages. These include Arabic, Bangla, Chinese, Danish, English, Farsi, Finnish, Flemish, French, German, Greek, Hindi, Indonesian, Italian, Japanese, Kannada, Malayalam, Ndebele, Nepalese, Philippine, Portuguese, Russian, Shona, Sinhala, Spanish, Swahili, Swedish, Tamil, Urdu, Ukrainian, and in the process are Tonga, Lithuanian, Norwegian, Welsh, Thai, Cambodian, Vietnamese, Pastun, Dhari, and Creole. An audio tape in English with Braille titles is also available. All these translations have been translated by volunteers who are committed to the People's Health Movement.

Audio visual aids, including videos for public education, exhibitions, slides, and other forms of communication, are being developed and distributed. There is a new BBC Life Series video on the Health Protesters, which focuses on the PHM movement. The movement itself has evolved a communication strategy, which includes a website (www.phmovement.org); an e-group exchange/discussion group (PHA-Exchange@kabissa.org); news briefs (nine since January 2001) and a host of press releases on a wide variety of themes, special events, and crises.

Presentations of the People's Health Charter have taken place at national, regional, and international fora. They have included the World

Health Organization, the Global Forum for Health Research (GFHR— Forum 5 & 6), and the World Health Assembly. The relationship that has developed between the PHM and WHO is particularly interesting. In April 2001, a very effective and assertive lobbying effort by a visiting PHM consultant to a WHO research seminar resulted in the formation of the WHO Civil Society Initiative (WHO CSI) announced at the World Health Assembly in May 2001. Six PHM leaders were subsequently invited to meet and dialogue with the WHO Director General. In May 2002, WHO CSI invited PHM to present the People's Charter for Health as a Technical Briefing to the World Heath Assembly. Thirty-five PHM members participated in this event. In May 2003, over 80 PHM delegates from 30 countries attended the 2003 World Health Assembly and made statements on primary health care, TRIPS and other issues and were invited to meet the new Director General designate, who welcomed greater dialogue with PHM members at all levels of the WHO so that the organization can be in touch with the realities of the lives of the poor and the marginalized. The 2003 World Health Assembly was preceded by a PHM Geneva meeting on the Alma-Ata Anniversary, which was attended by some WHO staff, including the Pan-American Health Organization Regional Director. These developments represent small but incremental movements towards a critical collaboration between PHM and the WHO.

In many countries of the world, country-level PHM circles are beginning to organize public meetings and local campaigns that include taking health to the streets as a human rights issue. Discussions on the charter held with professional associations and public health schools, articles and editorials in medical/health journals are also beginning to increase. Policy dialogues and action research circles are also being developed on the WHO/WHA, Poverty and AIDS, Women's Access to Heath, Health Research, Access to Essential Drugs, Macroeconomics and Health, Public Private Partnerships, and Food and Nutrition Security issues. Everyday the list of actions increases.

## Conclusion

The People's Health Assembly and the People's Health Movement that have emerged from it have been an unprecedented development in the journey towards the goal of Health for All. The PHM movement:

- is a multiregional, multicultural, and multidisciplinary mobilization effort;
- brings together the largest collection of activists and professionals, civil society representatives, and people's representatives themselves;
- develops global instruments of concern and action; and

- expresses solidarity with the health struggles of people around the world, especially the poor and the marginalized who are affected by the current global economic order.

Recognizing that we need a continous, sustained, collective effort, the People's Health Movement process reminds us, through the People's Health Charter, that a long road lies ahead in the campaign for Health for All.

# References

NARAYAN, RAVI
2000        "The People's Health Assembly—A People's Campaign for Health for All Now." *Asian Exchange* 16: 6-17.
PEOPLE'S HEALTH ASSEMBLY
2000a       "People's Charter for Health." People's Health Assembly. December 8, GK Savar, Bangladesh.
2000b       Discussion Papers Prepared by PHA Drafting Group, PHA Secretariat. GK Savar, Dhaka, Bangladesh.
2000c       "Health in the Era of Globalization: From Victims to Protagonists." Discussion Paper by PGA Drafting Group, PHA Secretariat. GK Savar, Dhaka—Bangladesh.
PEOPLE'S HEALTH MOVEMENT
2002        "Voices of the Unheard—Testimonies from the People's Health Assembly." December 2000, GK Savar, Bangladesh.
SCHUFTAN, CLAUDIO
2002        "The People's Health Movement (PHM) in 2002: Still at the Fore Front of the Struggle for Health for All Now." Issue Paper 2 for World Health Assembly. May 2002, People's Health Movement.
WHO/UNICEF
1978        "Primary Health Care." Report of the International Conference on Primary Health Care, September 6-12, Alma Ata, USSR.

# The Globalization of Health: Risks, Responses, and Alternatives

DR. RICHARD L. HARRIS[*] AND
DR. MELINDA J. SEID[**]

ABSTRACT

This essay provides a summary and synthesis of the wealth of information, analysis, and conclusions provided by the other contributors to this collection of essays on globalization and health. The major themes addressed are the health risks and health effects of globalization, the responses to these risks and effects at the national and global levels, and the alternatives to the present patterns of globalization in which the health of billions of people around the world and the planet's ecological sustainability are threatened.

## Introduction

In the introduction to this collection of essays on globalization and health, we pointed out that, according to the existing literature on globalization and health, it is generally accepted that certain aspects of globalization have "enhanced health and life expectancy in many populations," while other aspects of globalization "jeopardize population health via the erosion of social and environmental conditions, the global division of labor, the exacerbation of the rich-poor gap between and within countries, and the accelerating spread of consumerism" (McMichael and Beaglehole 2000). These threatening aspects of globalization present major challenges for

[*] Global Studies Program, California State University, Monterey Bay, Seaside, California, USA.

[**] Health Science Program, California State University, Sacramento, Sacramento, California, USA.

health researchers, practitioners, and policymakers today, and they are the major focus of this collection of essays.

The contributors to this collection of essays on globalization and health provide a wealth of information, analyses and conclusions on many of the health risks and health effects of globalization, on the responses to these risks and effects, and on the search for alternatives to how the contemporary forces of globalization affect health around the world today. In the pages that follow, we provide a summary and synthesis of the major findings on these themes that the contributors to this collection of essays have reported in the preceding pages.

## The Health Benefits and Risks Associated with Globalization

Most of the contributors to this collection of essays agree that there have been some significant health benefits from globalization. For example, Badawi, Labonte, McMurray, Smith, and Yach and Beaglehole acknowledge in their essays that the global diffusion of new health-related knowledge and technologies as a result of international trade and investments has contributed to disease surveillance, treatment and prevention around the world as well as the spread of sanitation and vaccines that have greatly reduced the threat of many deadly diseases.

McMurray states in her essay that "there is no doubt the spread of Western medicine through out the world and the implementation of global health programs has brought numerous benefits"; however, she also points out that "at the same time, globalization has promoted patterns of dependency, development, settlement and lifestyles that have been detrimental to health." Smith's essay reveals how new information and communication technologies (ICT) are being applied to healthcare in some of the more remote areas of the Pacific islands, and he argues that these technologies have the potential to provide "a remarkable expansion of the medical expertise available to act in a curative manner" and to advance preventative healthcare in these remote areas of the world. However, Smith's essay also reveals how these technologies, which are a central feature of globalization, are a "two-edged sword."

On the one side of the sword, the new information technologies and Internet connectivity enhance the provision of healthcare to people in remote and marginalized areas, but on the other side, they reinforce the neocolonial ties and unequal power relationship that exist between these areas and the developed core economies. They also transmit the more negative aspects of the consumerist life-styles associated with these economies.

The essay by Finau, Wainiqolo, and Cuboni focuses on how the "changes in health of Pacificans are about the power imbalances brought about by globalization, imperialism and colonialism." They see "the continuance of colonialism and imperialism in different forms" in the present context of globalization. They also argue that many contemporary "technologies and ideologies contribute to the reproduction and the strengthening of the pattern of power relations that feed imperialism." In their essay on women's reproductive health in post-transition Mongolia, Rak and Janes provide an example of how this works. Their research shows how the global discourse on family planning and reproductive health as well as global reproductive health policies are based on assumptions that "fail to consider the local cultural context of reproductive decision-making, do not meet women's needs, and are therefore seriously flawed." Nevertheless, external donors and consultants who are in a very real sense the agents of globalization in this case are imposing these global norms and policies on women in Mongolia.

Most of the contributors to this collection of essays reveal either explicitly or implicitly that, in fact, what is generally referred to as "globalization" is none other than the global expansion and integration of contemporary forms of capitalist production, distribution, and consumption. Their essays reveal that the global expansion and integration of twenty-first century capitalism involves not only the global diffusion of certain technologies, products, and practices, it also involves the global dissemination of certain ideologies and cultural norms.

Together, these forces of capitalist globalization have inadvertently or purposively promoted the following types of global health risks:

- The global spread of various communicable and noncommunicable diseases.
- The global promotion of unhealthy products and practices.
- The global diffusion of a wide range of technologies and production processes that are hazardous both to human health and to the health of the natural environment.
- The global promotion of inequitable forms of private health care and the commercialization of health services and medicines that place them beyond the reach of large sectors of the world's population.
- The global diffusion of Western norms, practices, and ideological models/paradigms of health care that often conflict with local values and needs and that create/reinforce inequitable power relationships and social inequities.

As we learn more about these and other adverse health effects of the global expansion and integration of modern capitalism, it is clear that many of the contemporary effects of the globalization of twenty-first century capitalism are a serious threat to not only the health of billions of people around the world but also to the sustainability of the planet's entire biosphere.

As Labonte points out in his essay, we have now lived through more than twenty years in which the global diffusion of knowledge and technology has taken place under a neoliberal capitalist regime of trade liberalization and global economic integration; yet the health impacts of this process of liberalization and globalization have been largely negative, especially the effects of this process on what Labonte refers to as the two fundamental health-determining pathways of globalization: poverty/inequality and environmental sustainability.

The liberalization and globalization of the economies of many developing countries have been accompanied by a corresponding increase in the poverty, environmental degradation, and poor health of a large proportion of the population. Loewenson notes in her essay that the incomes of a quarter of the world's population declined at the end of the last millennium when globalization was going at top speed. Even many of the positive effects of the global expansion and integration of capitalism have adverse consequences. Labonte's essay gives the example of how the opening of the economies of many developing countries to international trade and investment has increased the access of women to wage-earning employment and contributed to their empowerment in gender relations. However, he points out that more often than not they are employed in low-paid, unhealthy and insecure jobs, frequently in so-called free trade export zones where labor organizations are prohibited and only single young women are employed under hazardous working conditions (and often exploited and sexually harassed). Loewenson reports in her essay that these young women have been documented to experience high levels of job stress and reproductive health problems, including miscarriages, problems with pregnancies, and poor fetal health.

McMurray's essay illustrates how the globalization of capitalism intensifies disparities in health between and within nations and also how it can create paradoxical health outcomes in the most peripheral areas of the global capitalist economy. Her essay reveals that in the smallest and most remote countries within the global system, such as the Pacific island countries, the negative health effects of capitalist globalization impact the population more in the globalized (Westernized) and urbanized core areas than in the thinly populated and more peripheral rural areas that have less access to modern health services but relatively better environmental health conditions. McMurray focuses on how globalization affects these societies through, "first, its impact on environmental quality, second, its impact on the quality and accessibility of health services, and third, its promotion of unhealthy lifestyles."

As Labonte's essay and our own introductory essay in this collection indicate, the extent to which the forces of globalization affect the health of the population in individual countries depends upon the prevailing economic, social, and political conditions in these countries; their level of technological and economic development; and their natural endowments (Cornia 2001; Drager, Labonte, and Torgerson 2002; Woodward et al. 2001). These indigenous factors mediate most of the direct effects of globalization on the national/domestic level as well as many of the indirect effects of globalization on the community and household levels.

Labonte's essay reveals that the forces of capitalist globalization affect population health at the national level through various channels or pathways, such as externally imposed macroeconomic policies (e.g., IMF structural adjustment programs and monetary policies), the enforcement of trade agreements, the flows of trade associated with these agreements, official development assistance (from the United States and other major "donor" countries), the international transfer of health-related knowledge and information, and the influence of the global communications and entertainment media. There are also "environmental pathways" through which capitalist globalization affects health. These pathways include cross-border pollution, the depletion/contamination of natural resources (water, the soil, fish stocks, and forests), and the destruction of the biodiversity in local ecosystems. Many of the essays in this collection touch upon the health effects of these environmental pathways of globalization.

## Globalization and Life Style Changes

Most of the essays in this collection support the thesis that certain contemporary patterns of death and disability are caused by the lifestyle changes promoted by globalization, particularly the increased consumption of unhealthy processed foods and products. These lifestyle changes and particularly the unhealthy consumption patterns they entail are, as Yach and Beaglehole demonstrate in their essay, contributing to an alarming global increase in chronic and noncommunicable diseases (NCDs)—the so-called diseases of affluence (although they are increasingly suffered by the poor). McMurray, Smith, and Finau and his colleagues all address the negative health impact of these lifestyle changes and the increased consumption of unhealthy foods, especially in the island nations of the Pacific.

All three essays on the Pacific call attention to the health effects of both the disruptive changes and the uneven pattern of economic and social development that have been promoted in the developing countries by contemporary forms of capitalist investment, trade and production. Finau, Wainiqolo and Cuboni emphasize the disruptive and destructive nature of many of these changes and attribute them to the Western capitalist model of development that has been imposed on the Pacific peoples by colonialism, imperialism, and globalization.

According to Yach and Beaglehole, an unprecedented epidemiological or "health transition" is taking place in the world, and this transition is responsible for the global increase in NCDs and the "double burden of disease" (both communicable and noncommunicable diseases) suffered by the populations of most of the developing countries. They cite data, which indicate that NCDs have become the main cause of death and disability throughout the world. They attribute this development to both the positive aspects of globalization, which have contributed to the aging of the world's population through the diffusion of modern medicine and sanitation, and to the negative aspects of globalization, which have promoted the adoption of unhealthy lifestyles.

They also note that the uneven development and social inequalities associated with globalization are largely responsible for the fact that many communicable diseases continue to be a major cause of death and disability in the least developed areas (e.g., in sub-Saharan Africa and South Asia) and in the poorer sectors of the population throughout the developing countries. Thus, the poor in these areas suffer the so-called double burden of disease (both communicable and NCDs) caused by the uneven patterns of development and "poverty gaps" associated with the global expansion of capitalism.

However, Finau, Wainiqolo, and Cuboni question the validity of the "health transition" paradigm that Yach and Beaglehole and other global health researchers use in their work. They question how much of the so-called heath transition or what they call the "mortality transition" in the Pacific countries is really due to the spread of NCDs as opposed to underlying infectious risk factors, such as the emerging evidence that certain NCDs may be caused by *Heliocobacter pylori, Chlamydia pneumoniae,* and oral bacterial diseases. They also note that, for many Pacificans, the quality of life they are now living "due to various transitions, may as well mean that they are dead long before the certification of the expiry of life."

Finau and his colleagues argue that it is in fact a cluster of various types of transitions (religious, economic, environmental, political, social, etc.) and particularly inequitable power relationships established by colonialism and imperialism that are responsible for the poor health, dependency, and lack of control over their own socio-economic development suffered by the Pacific peoples. They blame the contemporary forces of globalization for reinforcing and masking these determinants of health in the Pacific.

McMurray's contribution to this collection of essays calls our attention to the fact that one of the effects of capitalist globalization in the developing countries is the migration of large numbers of people to the urban areas in these countries, where they hope to find wage-earning employment and access to modern consumer goods. However, most urban migrants are exposed to poor nutrition, substandard housing, and unsanitary environments in these urban areas. As McMurray indicates in her essay, the limited employment and the low incomes that these migrants generally earn leave them "no choice but to purchase the cheapest food, which tends to be the least nutritious." Moreover, their consumption of unhealthy foods is generally combined with their exposure to unsanitary environmental conditions.

The problem is that there are very few employment opportunities in the urban areas and most jobs do not provide an adequate income. As a result, there is widespread unemployment, and most people who are employed do not earn enough income to maintain a nutritious dietary intake or healthy lifestyle. McMurray also reveals that under these circumstances of urbanization without adequate employment, young people generally have little incentive to maintain a healthy lifestyle and often engage in various types of substance abuse and other unhealthy forms of behavior. Based on her research in the Pacific, McMurray has found that "the negative impact of urban lifestyles on health is clearly evident in that the incidence of early onset NCDs" in the Pacific "is lower in the outer islands and remote areas ... where traditional foods are consumed and people are engaged in subsistence agriculture and food gathering." She contends that similar conditions "can be observed in peripheral areas everywhere, including remote and economically depressed areas within most industrialized countries."

According to McMurray, the rising incidence of early onset NCDs among the urban population in the Pacific is "a direct consequence of global forces that have led to urbanization without industrialization, idealization of Western lifestyles and imports of cheap food, alcohol and cigarettes." She argues that no real improvements in the population health of the Pacific island nations and other developing countries can be achieved under these conditions "until their people are empowered and have the means to choose healthy lifestyles."

As indicated, Yach and Beaglehole also hold globalization responsible for the lifestyle changes that have produced the rapid increases in chronic diseases (especially cardiovascular disease, coronary heart disease, stroke, cancer, chronic respiratory disease and diabetes) in the developing countries and the fact that these diseases are now the major components of the global burden of disease in all regions of the world. Moreover, they argue that "policy makers and the donor community have neglected the rapidly growing burden of chronic diseases" even though they are the major cause of death and ill-health in most of the developing as well as the developed countries of the world.

Yach and Beaglehole contend that these diseases "predominate among poor populations largely because of inequalities in the distribution of major chronic disease risk factors." They claim these risk factors are "driven by the more fundamental causes of ill health in the socio-economic environment." They blame "global forces in trade and marketing" for promoting "the entrenchment of the causes of these chronic diseases in all regions." The health risks they identify are tobacco consumption, unhealthy diet/nutrition, physical inactivity and alcohol use, as well as the failure to invest in appropriate prevention and health promotion measures. They indicate that "most of these risk factors are common to the main categories of chronic diseases and all are modifiable, albeit with some difficulty."

According to Yach and Beaglehole, the aging of most populations due to declining fertility rates and increasing child survival rates (one of the health benefits of globalization), and the "nutrition transition" to diets that are high in saturated fats and sugars but low in fruits and vegetables, as well as smoking and alcohol usage, are being promoted by the forces of globalization. They also note that the nutrition transition to unhealthy diets is generally combined with lower levels of physical activity and regular tobacco and alcohol consumption. In fact, they cite WHO data that indicate tobacco and alcohol consumption, high blood pressure, and high cholesterol levels are the major contributors to the global burden of chronic diseases.

Yach and Beaglehole say that globalization has contributed to the rise in chronic diseases through a complex array of both direct and indirect factors. They focus on "the direct negative effects of globalization," which they claim are best "illustrated by the increasingly globalized production, promotion and marketing of tobacco, alcohol and other products with adverse effects on population health status." They blame major transnational corporations and the global communications media for "the marketing of tobacco, alcohol, sugary and fatty foods" in nearly all parts of the world. They indicate that "a significant portion of all global marketing is now targeted at children under the age of 14," since the companies that market high sugar and high fat fast foods, cigarettes and alcoholic beverages seek "to foster brand-loyalty among pre-teens, as young as six years, and teenagers."

They give particular emphasis to what they call the "globalization of the tobacco pandemic," and the "strong link between increased tobacco consumption and free trade and tobacco-related foreign direct investment." Based on their research for the WHO, they have found that "tobacco companies aggressively exploit the potential for growth in tobacco sales in developing countries." They claim this practice is "not surprising since they are motivated only by their obligations to shareholders." According to Yach and Beaglehole, "the main targets of the industry and the associated marketing campaigns are now young people and women, most of whom do not smoke."

Having been closely associated with the WHO's tobacco control efforts and the international campaign on behalf of the Framework Convention on Tobacco Control, Yach and Beaglehole know a great deal about the tactics that have been used by the transnational tobacco corporations to subvert and oppose "any effective international regulatory regime" dealing with the marketing, sale, and consumption of tobacco products. Included among these tactics are the companies' frequent public refutation or denial of the evidence about the harmful effects of smoking and their practice of "paying scientists to carry out spurious research aimed at confusing the public and delaying action" to control tobacco marketing and consumption.

Yach and Beaglehole's research also leads them to conclude that the "alcohol industry is becoming as globally integrated and pervasive as the tobacco industry." They claim that there is a direct link between the consumption of alcohol and certain cancers, cirrhosis of the liver, and most injuries, especially motor vehicle-related injuries and injuries resulting from violence. For this reason, they argue that there is a pressing need for global action to control the marketing of alcohol to young people, "especially through its association with sporting events and with gender specific roles."

## Trade Liberalization and the Privatization of Health Care

The essays by Labonte, Badawi and McIntyre, Thomas and Cleary as well as the contribution by Yach and Beaglehole reveal the adverse effects on health of multilateral agreements such as the General Agreement on Tariffs and Trade (GATT), the Technical Barriers to Trade (TBT) Agreement, the Agreement on the Application of Sanitary and Phytosanitary Measures (SPS), the Agreement on Trade-Related Intellectual Property Rights (TRIPS), and the General Agreement on Trade in Services (GATS). The essay by McIntyre, Thomas, and Cleary reveals how the GATS contributes to the already existing problem of the migration of skilled health professionals from South Africa (and other developing countries) to the developed countries. Their essay also reveals the difficulties TRIPS imposes on poorer countries that try to import or produce affordable medicines to fight the disastrous effects of global diseases such as HIV/AIDS.

Badawi states that "access to low-cost, safe and effective essential drugs is largely threatened by the agreement on TRIPS." He argues that "technology transfer, production and global movement of health commodities are also threatened by the monopoly TRIPS gives to the companies who hold patents protected by the TRIPS agreement." In fact, as Labonte indicates, agreements such as TRIPS do not promote "free trade"; rather they promote the protection and entrenchment of the so-called intellectual property rights and lucrative profits of companies and individuals in the wealthier developed countries.

Labonte points out that the global "brain drain" of trained health professionals from the developing to the developed countries has so far cost the developing countries at least an estimated 500 million US dollars in training costs. The GATS agreement is likely to accelerate this transfer of skilled health practitioners from the developing to the developed countries. Labonte notes that some 54 members of the WTO (including many developing countries) have so far agreed to liberalize/privatize their health care systems under the terms of the GATS agreement. The implementation of the GATS provisions on the "progressive liberalization" of services will contribute to the regressive privatization of health care systems, promote the brain drain of health practitioners, and benefit the health of the wealthier at the expense of the poorer sectors of the population.

The essays by Labonte, Yach and Beaglehole, Loewenson, and Badawi indicate that the trade liberalization measures and the neoliberal economic reforms associated with capitalist globalization have shifted a greater burden of the costs of health care to those who can least afford to assume these costs: low-paid workers in the export zones and industrialized urban areas within the developing countries; self-employed and casual workers in the growing "informal sector" of the economies of these countries; landless peasants and agricultural workers; and the large numbers of unemployed, disabled and indigenous/tribal peoples around the world. They generally do not have access to adequate health care and other forms of social protection.

The IMF, World Bank, WTO and the main donors of official development assistance have promoted the downsizing of the public sector and the privatization of health care and other social services around the world. Largely as a result of their influence, the governments of the developing countries and the former socialist countries ("emerging economies") have privatized their health services and/or imposed so-called user fees and/or other types of "cost recovery" measures that have raised the cost of such services above the capacity of large sectors of the population to pay for them.

Badawi, Loewenson, and McIntyre and her associates call attention to the fact that the poorer sectors of the population are not covered by health insurance in most of the developing countries where health care is being privatized. Moreover, the governments of these countries generally do not have sufficient funds to provide adequate social protection to the population, especially under the "state shrinking" and fiscal restraints imposed on them by the IMF, the World Bank, and the other guardians and promoters of globalization. As Loewenson notes, under these circumstances job-related injuries and ill health generally lead to not only the loss of employment and household income, but to impoverishment and the breakdown of the overburdened informal mechanisms of social protection provided by the extended family and local community.

The privatization of health care has been particularly unkind to the poor and to low-income households. As Badawi notes in his essay, many people in the developing countries have been caught between the inability of their governments to continue providing free public health services and their own inability to pay the rising costs of basic health care. The forces of globalization have led governments to reduce their spending on health and other forms of social protection, to sell off many of their public health facilities, and to encourage the privatization and commercialization of health services and products. As a result, there has been a marked deterioration in the health services of many of these countries and restricted access to these services—both of which threaten the health of large sectors of the population.

In the present context of increasing privatization and the promotion of neoliberal policies at both global and the national levels by the IMF, World Bank, and the WTO, national government responsibility for providing basic health care for all members of the population has been replaced by so-called selective primary health care, public-private partnerships, and the privatization of health services and health care facilities. As the essay by Narayan and Schuftan indicates, this shift in responsibility for providing health care is considered by many critics of globalization and the current trends in health to be a betrayal of the international commitment made in the late seventies to provide primary health care for all by the year 2000. This was the official commitment made by most of the governments represented at the 1978 International Health Assembly held at Alma-Ata in the central Asian republic of what was then the Union of Soviet Socialist Republics (PHA 2000:1).

The Alma-Ata declaration set forth the goal of achieving "Health for All by the Year 2000" and charged the health ministries and health workers around the world with the responsibility for providing comprehensive primary health care to all the members of their societies by the beginning of the new millennium. As Narayan and Schuftan indicate in their essay, the global network of health activists and health advocacy organizations involved in the People's Health Movement (PHM) seek to halt the privatization and commercialization of health care. The PHM holds that health is a fundamental human right and that national governments have an obligation to ensure universal access to quality health care, education, and other social services in accordance with people's needs, not their ability to pay. They are mobilizing broad-based popular movements around the world in a global campaign to achieve the goal of "Health for All—Now!" by pressuring governments to provide comprehensive primary health care to their populations and incorporate health and other human rights into their national constitutions and legal systems.

## The Health Effects of Dependency, Neocolonialism, and Western Ideological Paradigms

The essays by McMurray, Narayan and Schuftan, Rak and Janes, and Finau and his colleagues reveal that Western medicine has been imposed as the universal standard around the world, and that the health systems of most developing countries are generally dependent upon the development assistance they receive from the governments and NGOs of the developed Western countries as well as international organizations such as the World Bank and the World Health Organization (WHO). McMurray contends that the health programs in the Pacific countries "are determined by global health policies, set by the World Health Organization and other health sector donors." Moreover, she argues that much of the assistance these programs receive "fosters dependency and imposes conditions" on the recipients that force them to accept donor policies, practices and medicines as well as consultants from the donor countries.

Narayan and Schuftan indicate that the People's Health Movement believes that it has extricated health and health systems around the world from the "myopic biomedical-techno-managerialism of the last two decades, with its selective magic bullets approach to health." The PHM's analysis of the political economy of health in the world today (PHA 2001) lead its advocates to conclude that the most significant determinants of health in the world today are economic and political factors that have colonial roots. Moreover, the movement's analysis indicates that people's health around the world is under a triple assault from globalization, liberalization, and privatization, which Narayan and Schuftan claim "have ensured that health for all is a receding dream." The PHM argues that "health services today are inaccessible, unaffordable, inequitably distributed and inappropriate in their emphasis and approach" (PHA 2001:3). The movement also claims that "health care is increasingly used as a subtle and widespread instrument of social control," and that the Western model or "ideology of medicine ... mystifies the real causes of illness, often attributing disease to faulty individual behavior or natural misfortune, rather than to social injustice, economic inequality and oppressive political systems" (PHA 2001:18).

The essay by Finau, Wainiqolo, and Cuboni as well as the essay by McMurray trace the current dependency and Western orientation of the health care systems in the developing countries to the imposition of the Western curative model of health care on these societies by their former Western colonial rulers. They attribute the continued dominance of Western health policies, standards and practices in these societies to the development assistance they receive from the developed countries, the globalizing influence of Western education and training, and the economic dependency of these countries on the developed Western countries (as well as "Westernized" Japan). In fact, as Finau and his colleagues assert in the case of the Pacific island societies, many developing countries "are still practically colonies," and as such they are still subjected to the racism, imperialist domination and exploitation they suffered under colonialism— in the health field as well as in other fields.

Finau, Wainiqolo, and Cuboni argue that "imperialists control all phases and determinants of the health transition" in the Pacific countries, and "the socialization of Pacificans, through foreign education, is another imperialist tool to enhance control" over the Pacific peoples. In fact, Finau and his colleagues take the position that "globalization is the latest label for capitalism, colonialism and imperialist expansion combined," and they regard the ideology of globalization as nothing more than an updated version of the classic imperialist justification for the Western domination of non-Western peoples formerly known as the "white man's burden." According to Finau, Wainiqolo, and Cuboni most Western-trained health personnel practice, reflect, and promote the Western emphasis on fighting disease at the individual level rather than promoting community health in a holistic manner. They argue most doctors and nurses are trained as disease fighters to save individuals rather than as health promoters to save communities. Imperialist ideologies and logics perpetuate and reproduce the power imbalance and inequities of the past as well as strengthen the pattern of inequitable power relations associated with contemporary forms of imperialism under the guise of globalization.

Rak and Janes' essay on reproductive health in Mongolia reveals how global reproductive health policies, promoted by international NGOs and the governments of developed countries such as the United States, impose family planning methods on women in countries such as Mongolia that often run counter to the beliefs, experiences, and needs of the local population. These imposed paternalistic and ethnocentric family planning methods have ignored local cultural values and devalued the alternatives that exist at the local level. Rak and Janes reveal the contradictions in this approach within the context of Mongolia's rapidly deteriorating health services caused by the adoption of market-based reforms, the reduction of the public budget for health care and the privatization of the health sector.

## The Health Effects of the Inequities Promoted by Globalization

At the outset of the new millennium, the WHO noted that "the greatest burden of health risks is borne by the poor countries, and by the disadvantaged in all societies" (WHO 2002:13). These sectors of the world's population have the misfortune of suffering the health effects of poverty as well as well as the other social and economic inequities that characterize the present era of capitalist global expansion and integration. Most of the essays in this collection reveal that globalization is associated with economic policies that create, reinforce, and intensify the inequities in health found throughout the world. Thus, Loewenson states in her essay that "within the current processes of globalization, inequality is not simply happening but is being constructed by powerful economic and political interests and public policies" that keep the benefits of globalization from reaching those who need them the most. Finau, Wainiqolo, and Cuboni contend that the economic and social inequities (including the health inequities) that the Pacific peoples have inherited from colonial rule are reinforced today by the contemporary forces of globalization, which they hold responsible for the continuation of Western imperialism.

McIntyre, Thomas, and Cleary reveal in their essay how the struggle to overcome the "legacy of massive inequalities in income, health status and access to health and other social services" resulting from South Africa's colonial, racist, and repressive past has been hindered by the contemporary forces of globalization. Moreover, they reveal that it is not just the obvious forms of global intervention such as IMF loan conditions, externally enforced compliance with the TRIPS Agreement on patented HIV/AIDS medicines, and the World Bank's privatization of health care programs that exacerbate the existing inequities in South Africa. It is also the more subtle and indirect influences of globalization that have led the post-apartheid government in South Africa to adopt "self-imposed" structural adjustments in order not to run afoul of the major forces in the global economy. These self-imposed policies and practices tend to reinforce the health inequities created by centuries of colonialism, racism, and European domination on the African continent.

The essay by McIntyre and her colleagues reveals the extent to which the global trend towards the privatization of health care and the indirect impact of global health actors on the health sector in South Africa have contributed to the "rapid and uncontrolled growth of the private sector," which in turn "has contributed to disparities in health service access and the health of South Africans." Today, less than 20 percent of the population has access to more than 60 percent of the financial resources for health care, while the remaining 80 percent of the population have access to less than 40 percent of the financial resources devoted to health care in the country. Moreover, only one-fourth of the doctors in the country work in the public health sector, which serves the historically disadvantaged majority of the population.

Rak and Janes premise their analysis of the global discourse on reproductive health and its application to Mongolia on the assertion that poverty in its modern sense was created in the developing countries by the spread of the market economy and years of colonial rule, and they argue that the current policies to "develop" these countries "have exacerbated the divide between the rich and the poor." Since the country adopted market reforms, privatization, and the integration of its economy into the global capitalist economic system, Mongolia has experienced a rapid deterioration in its health services, increasing social inequality, and a high level of male unemployment. Rak and Janes conclude that "it has taken the transition from a socialist to a market economy, led by the intervention of the global financial and policy institutions of the developed world, to create Mongolia as a Third World country."

The PHM, as Narayan and Schuftan's essay explains, sees a direct relationship between existing health inequities and globalization. The members of this global movement consider inequality, poverty, exploitation, violence and injustice as the root causes of ill health in the world today. As Narayan and Schuftan make clear in their discussion of the People's Charter for Health, achievement of the PHM's goal of "Health for All—Now!" requires "challenging the powerful economic interests that dominant the existing global order, opposing globalization in its existing iniquitous form, and drastically changing the political and economic priorities at all levels of the global system."

## The Environmental Health Effects of Globalization

The wide variety and scope of globalization's environmental effects make it difficult to provide a sufficiently comprehensive analysis of these effects in any single book or collection of essays. This collection of essays does little more than scratch the surface of the health impact of some of the more complex and far-reaching environmental effects of globalization, such as global climate change, the depletion of the ozone layer, and the contamination of oceans, lakes, and rivers around the world.

As we indicated in our introductory essay to this collection, there is mounting evidence that the global diffusion of capitalist patterns of production and consumption developed in the Western industrial societies has created a multitude of environmental problems. In a research study undertaken by Diaz-Bonilla and his colleagues on the health risks of the poor in developing countries, they claim that "poor environmental quality has been calculated to be directly responsible for around 25 percent of all preventable ill-health in the world today" (Diaz-Bonilla et al. 2002:38). They attribute much of this "poor environmental quality" to the environmental "spill-over" effects of economic globalization.

Many of the essays in this collection recognize the threats to health posed by the environmental effects of globalization. For example, Badawi notes that environmental threats to health have resulted from the increasing international trade in technology, capital, goods, services and labor. He notes that many "environmentally unfriendly" industries have moved from the developed to the developing countries, where there is generally less concern about the health hazards caused by their technology and often a lack of environmental health safeguards. Badawi also states that the over exploitation of fishing licenses, deforestation, industrial waste, and the dumping of health-hazardous materials are part of a long list of environmental health threats confronting the populations of the developing countries. Moreover, he warns that the indigenous germ pool and medicinal plants in the developing countries are threatened by the "commercial exploitation" of giant transnational corporations and warns that "genetically modified organisms, microbiological pathogens and hazards in animal production represent a real health risk for the developing countries."

Finau, Wainiqolo, and Cuboni contend that the cultivation of cash crops, mining, and industrialization threaten the fragile environment of the Pacific islands, and they say the "green house effect and rising sea levels caused by metropolitan modern societies' efforts to maintain their consumption level are threatening the Pacificans' habitat." They also claim that the environments in these societies "have become obesogenic, toxic and insecure, due to crime and violence." As a result, the Pacific countries are undergoing what they refer to as an "environmental transition" that has brought about "not only physical and social changes, but also developed uncertainty and stress in the Pacific psyche."

McMurray's essay analyzes the effects of globalization on environmental health in the Pacific and other developing countries. She notes that "modernization" and globalization are responsible for the development of urban areas and the increasing concentration of the population in these areas. She cites United Nations data that indicate most developed countries now have 70 percent or more of their population concentrated in urban areas and that the number of these areas is increasing in most countries. One of the environmental health problems created by this increasing urbanization of the population and the globalization of these societies is that they have adopted the costly portable water and sanitation systems of the most developed countries in most of their urban areas, as a result of their colonial legacy and/or the development assistance they have received in recent decades. McMurray indicates that they now have difficulty maintaining and extending these systems because they lack the resources and technology needed to do this. She gives various examples of the rising problems of pollution and contamination in the urban areas of the Pacific resulting from the breakdown of their sewage and piped water systems.

Loewenson's essay on the health and safety aspects of working conditions in Southern Africa reveals that most workers in this region of the world "continue to experience work related hazards that have long been controlled or even eliminated in high income countries." According to Loewenson, "the expansion of chemical, electronic and bio-technology industries and of the service and transport sectors ... widened the spread of work-related risks and their interaction with non work factors of ill health, including environmental pollution." Employment in the large informal economy exposes workers in this sector to the health risks associated with "poor access to clean water and sanitation, ergonomic hazards, hazardous hand-tools and exposure to dusts and chemicals." Loewenson also points out that work in the agriculture, mining, and manufacturing sectors within the southern African economies is associated with high rates of injury from the mechanical, electrical, and physical hazards in their work environment.

The essays by Badawi, Labonte, Loewenson, McMurray, and Finau and his colleagues acknowledge the fact that globalization and trade liberalization have promoted the deregulation of production, health, and the environment. These forces have seriously weakened the capacity of the public sector to respond to the environmental and occupational health risks posed by industry, mining, transportation/shipping, and commercialized agriculture; they also have undermined the already inadequate forms of worker protection and social protection (including health) in existence in these countries.

Labonte's essay argues that environmental issues are becoming "inherently global" and are no longer purely national or domestic issues. He notes that the "environmental impacts of human activities are planetary in scale and scope" and that "almost one-sixth of humanity is on the move to escape environmental or economic degradation and conflict." Labonte sees this situation as evidence of the need for global solutions to these problems.

## Community Health Care, Grassroots Action, and Globalization from below

As Finau, Wainiqolo and Cuboni contend in their essay, community-based, grassroots, and ethnic-specific health care has improved the access, acceptability, availability, and affordability of the health care provided to the communities it serves. This model of health care has also improved the effectiveness, efficiency, efficacy, and equity of the health services provided to these populations through changing the power relationships between the health care providers and receivers. They argue that this model of health care addresses the oppression and assimilation implanted by Western colonialism and "borne by imperialism through globalization." According to Finau and his colleagues, community-based health care releases the participants from the oppression of the Western health care model imposed first by Western colonialism, and more recently by contemporary forms of imperialism under the guise of globalization (e.g., the globalization of Western medical education and training, the transfer of Western medical knowledge and technology, the bureaucratization and privatization of health care along Western lines).

Narayan and Schuftan's essay on the People's Health Movement (PHM) reveals the emphasis this new movement gives to community control of health care, grassroots action, and global action based on the use of international health advocacy networks. These are important elements in the movement's global campaign to combat the health inequities associated with globalization and to make sure that universal access to comprehensive primary health care is provided everywhere in the world. This movement is engaged in what amounts to "globalization from below" as it builds support for its global Health for All—Now strategy, lobbies at the global level, and mobilizes a grassroots-based campaign to realize the vision and achieve the goals of the People's Charter for Health.

The Charter, which is the PHM's visionary statement of goals and its main tool for advocacy, calls for "a people-centered health sector that is democratic and accountable" (PHA 2000:9). The Charter calls on the people of the world to: (1) build and strengthen people's organizations as a basis for analysis and action; (2) promote, support, and engage in actions that encourage people's involvement in decision-making in public services at all levels; (3) demand that people's organizations be represented in local, national and international fora that are relevant to health; and (4) support local initiatives towards participatory democracy through the establishment of people-centered solidarity networks across the world (PHA 2000:10). One of the primary principles of the Charter is the proposition that "the participation of people and people's organizations is essential to the formulation, implementation and evaluation of all health and social policies and programs" (PHA 2000:4).

McIntyre, Thomas, and Cleary conclude in their essay that "the growth in number, size and power of civil society organizations combined with the increased networking of these organizations across national boundaries" is having a "countervailing effect" on the negative health impacts of globalization. They give the example of how civil society organizations in South Africa gained the support of civil society groups in the Untied States to pressure the US government into dropping its efforts to convince the South African government to change its policy relating to the importation of medicines so that it would not contravene the TRIPS agreement. They show how these groups in South Africa also teamed up with international groups such as Médecins sans Frontières and Health Action International to oppose the efforts of the transnational pharmaceutical corporations (with the support of their host governments) to pressure the South Africa government and the governments of other developing countries (such as Thailand) into restricting their use of certain provisions in the TRIPS agreement that permit governments to obtain urgently needed patented medicines at reduced prices.

The adverse effects of existing international trade agreements on health, human rights, and the environment have been subjected to increasing public criticism in recent years. As Labonte notes in his essay these agreements have "become the focus for progressive social movements." The global networking and collaboration that have developed among these social movements, such as the PHM, represent a form of "globalization from below" that is rising up to challenge the "globalization from above" imposed by the transnational corporations and their allies in the IMF, World Bank, WTO, the Group of 8 governments (led by the US government), and certain large international non-governmental organizations that are closely associated with these forces.

Labonte notes in his essay that the WTO has been besieged by a broad coalition of forces that are opposed to its global trade liberalization agenda. He argues that there are several reforms in the global trade regime that health activists in league with other progressive forces are promoting in their efforts to change the current effects of the WTO's trade liberalization efforts. These reforms would:

- Extend "special and differential" trade agreement exemptions for developing countries;
- Ban the patenting of life forms, exempt patent protection legislation for poor countries indefinitely, decrease the patent protection period and permit parallel importing under the TRIPS agreement;

- Impose a Tobin Tax (named after the Nobel economist who first proposed this idea) on international currency exchange transactions to raise about US $150 billion annually for an international development fund;
- Negotiate an overarching and enforceable rule in trade agreements that would require, when there is any conflict, for environmental and human rights agreements (including the right to health) to override the trade agreements; and
- Exclude health, education and other essential services (such as water and sanitation) from privatization since they are essential to human life and health.

In addition, Labonte argues that the WTO needs to be overhauled by making its decision-making more democratic and transparent. However, he disagrees with those activists and social movements who are calling for its abolition. He contends that this would be a mistake since "there is no other vehicle where the unequal balance of economic power globally might be subject to enforceable change." Labonte believes that the struggles of civil society organizations and the developing countries "to wrest reforms from the WTO are giving rise to a new system of global governance for the common good."

## The Current State of Global Health Governance

As Labonte points out in his essay, social, economic, environmental and health issues are becoming "inherently global" rather than purely national or domestic. He argues that the evidence in favor of the need for global solutions to these issues is irrefutable, including the evidence about the rapid spread of infectious diseases, the increased adoption of unhealthy lifestyles, and the increasing international promotion of unhealthy foods and products such as tobacco and alcohol. Labonte concludes that "we live in the most important historical moment of our species, [since] the planet is dying, there is excessive affluence and poverty, [and] once far-away conflicts and diseases are imperiling global health and security." Faced with this unprecedented situation, he optimistically contends that "we are struggling forward to some system of global governance for our common good."

Yach and Beaglehole take a similar position. They conclude that the global diffusion of the major risks of chronic diseases is now almost complete and the prevalence of these diseases is increasing in most regions of the world. They contend, however, that the prevention and control of these diseases have not been able to keep pace with their globalization and growth. Therefore, they conclude that sustained progress against these diseases "will only occur when governments and influential international bodies involved in health policy and funding acknowledge that the scope of global public health must be rapidly broadened to include chronic diseases and their risk factors."

Based on their experience in the ongoing struggle over the international control of tobacco, Yach and Beaglehole predict that "progress will continue to be slow unless the response to the epidemics [of chronic diseases] is scaled up in a manner commensurate with their burden on both families and societies" around the world. They believe that global solutions are needed to address the global health risks responsible for the epidemics of chronic disease that are taking place around the world.

However, Yach and Beaglehole argue that the global health agenda is currently dominated by what they call "the infectious disease paradigm." The main global health organizations and funding sources believe priority should be given to the prevention and treatment of infectious or communicable diseases before addressing chronic diseases. Because most institutional responses to disease prevention and control are based on this infectious disease paradigm, Yach and Beaglehole argue that the global and national responses to the spread of chronic diseases are "woefully inadequate and few countries have implemented comprehensive prevention and control policies."

They contend that a comprehensive response that combats all the health risks responsible for the global spread of chronic diseases is necessary, and they argue this response must overcome the "powerful countervailing forces" that presently stand in the way of changing the status quo. According to Yach and Beaglehole, a successful global response to the existing configuration of major health risks has to overcome the "many powerful and persuasive commercial entities involved in the production and promotion of unhealthy products." They claim these entities "exert an adverse influence on health policy developments" as well as on the development and implementation of environmental policies.

Yach and Beaglehole conclude that "stronger and broader alliances of major health professional bodies, consumer groups, enlightened industries and academics are now needed to effectively prioritize the prevention of the major risk factors" responsible for the global spread of chronic diseases. They suggest that the global campaign for tobacco control provides a successful model for how to organize a comprehensive response to the global spread of chronic diseases.

Yach and Beaglehole ultimately conclude that there is an increasing need to establish global norms on a wide range of global issues "to balance the otherwise unrestrained influences of powerful actors." They argue that, if the WHO is strengthened it can be used to establish these norms in the health sphere and then use the norms to resolve trade disputes and other health-related global issues in a manner that promotes positive health outcomes. However, they do not think the WHO and national governments alone can address the challenges of chronic disease prevention and control. As in the case of tobacco control, they believe collaborative partnerships and interaction are needed with international consumer advocacy groups, international and national sports federations, sporting goods companies, transnational food corporations, retail food businesses, and insurance companies to improve the quality and access of people to healthy foods and increased physical activity. They advocate a consultative and "multi-stakeholder approach" with all interested parties as well as joint initiatives with the transnational food companies rather than an adversarial relationship. However, they recognize the dangers and difficulties that are involved in this approach.

Badawi's essay urges the developing countries to make more effective use of the provisions in the WTO agreements (the GATT, GATS, TBT, and Anti-Dumping agreement) that allow for "special and transitional arrangements." He contends that they can take the "compensatory actions" allowed under these agreements to limit the negative effects of globalization on their economies, environments, and protective social services. Badawi says that, unfortunately, these agreements are not well studied by policymakers and specialists in the developing countries. He recommends that they develop their national capacity and expertise for "expert reading" of the provisions of these agreements so that they can use their special exemptions to protect what he and the International Labor Organization refer to as the "social dimension" (social protection and social services such as health) as well as the environmental health of their populations.

Badawi also argues that the developing countries need to "cooperate and consult with other developing and developed countries to influence decision-making" at the WTO, the WHO, and other global institutions as well as to negotiate multilateral and bilateral agreements that confront the health hazards posed by globalization. Moreover, he argues that the governments of the developing countries, contrary to the prevailing feeling that [they] have lost control of their mandates, must, "adopt the measures necessary to protect the public interests in the environment, public health and nutrition."

Loewenson argues in her essay that "there is a growing understanding that global security and equity cannot be built on the significant burdens of deprivation borne by communities in the south," and that "globalization has produced powerful tools, new communications technologies, more widely connected social movements and an increasingly global recognition of universal rights as fundamental to policy." She contends that the full potential of these tools can be used to create concerted global action to protect workers' health. The democratization and extension of the enforcement powers of international agencies such as the ILO and WHO would certainly help to improve the social protection of workers and the many other sectors of the world's population that are being harmed and disadvantaged by the global expansion and integration of twenty-first century capitalism.

Most global health advocates argue that a genuinely health-centered (and people-centered) process of globalization can be achieved only by ensuring that the interests of the developing countries and vulnerable populations are fully represented in all international decision-making on global health issues (Woodward et al. 2001:880). According to Badawi, Labonte, and Yach and Beaglehole, the democratization of decision-making in the existing international regulatory and financial organizations such as the WTO, IMF, and World Bank is needed to transform these institutions into global governance institutions that will advance the interests of the great majority of the world's population rather than the interests of the powerful economic elites they now represent.

## Alternatives to the Globalization of Health from above

The People's Health Movement (PHM) is clear evidence that the existing linkages between globalization and health are contestable. In fact, most of the essays in this collection indicate that the adverse health effects of globalization are being challenged at the global, national, and local levels. The People's Health Movement and the People's Charter for Health provide a significant expression of alternatives "from below" to the present globalization, privatization and commercialization of health coming "from above." As Narayan and Schuftan state in their essay, this People's Charter for Health provides a vision of a better and healthier world, a call for radical action, a tool for advocacy for people's health, and a rallying point for building a global health movement based on international networks and coalition building.

The People's Charter for Health lays out a blue print for the transformation of the existing global order through democratization at all levels of the existing system and through what some people in the global social justice movement call "globalization from below" (Brecher, Costello, and Smith 2000). It is based on the fundamental, but radical, assumption that "to ensure health, people's basic needs for food, water, sanitation, housing, health services, education, employment and security must be met" in the present time frame (PHA 2001:1). In addition, it is based on the assumptions that global decisions must be democratized and that people's organizations and organized grassroots action can bring about an "alternative vision of development—one that promotes human and environmental well-being" (PHA 2001:3). To achieve this vision, the PHM is pursing the democratization of health decisions and outcomes at all levels.

According to Narayan and Schuftan, the Charter for People's Health calls upon national governments and global institutions to recognize health as a fundamental human right and as a social, economic, and political issue deserving the highest priority. It also identifies inequality, poverty, exploitation, violence, and injustice as the roots of ill-health, and it makes clear that the achievement of universal access to primary health care requires challenging powerful economic interests; opposing privatization and globalization (in its present inequitable form); and drastically changing the prevailing political and economic priorities at all levels in the global order.

The Charter also makes it clear that the PHM wants the poor and marginalized (rarely heard) peoples throughout the world to participate in health decision-making and develop their own local solutions to their health problems. The movement encourages people to hold local authorities, national governments, and international organizations and corporations accountable for ensuring that the goal of Health for All is achieved now, not at some distant point in the future. However, even though the PHM firmly believes national governments have the primary responsibility for promoting an equitable approach to health and human rights, the movement knows that it will take pressure from people's organizations to force their governments to meet this responsibility. This statement reflects one of the most important strategic assumptions held by the PHM: that it will take organized grassroots action as well as concerted action at the global level to bring about the profound social changes that are needed to achieve the sweeping vision and radical goals of the movement.

All the essays in this collection provide suggestions and/or proposals for creating alternatives to the present conditions, in which the adverse effects of globalization threaten the health of people around the world and the planet's ecological sustainability. In their essay Finau, Wainiqolo, and Cuboni provide a series of models or strategies for thinking about the management of change in the field of health. They are all based on the assumption that change is inevitable and that the present power imbalances in the world must be changed in order for substantial progress to be achieved in the domain of health as well as in the other major domains of human existence.

These models/strategies provide useful conceptual tools for thinking about alternatives to the present global patterns and direction of change in health. We hope that this entire collection of essays serves the same purpose as the models presented by Finau, Wainiqolo, and Cuboni—that it contributes not only to the ongoing discourse on globalization and health but also to the efforts that are being made around the world to find alternatives to the adverse effects of globalization on the health of the planet's human population as well as the sustainability of its biosphere.

## References

BRECHER, JEREMY, TIM COSTELLO AND BRENDAN SMITH
2000        *Globalization from Below*. Boston: South End Press.
CORNIA, GIOVANNI
2001        "Globalization and Health: Results and Options." *Bulletin of the World Health Organization* 79: 834-841.
DIAZ-BONILLA, EUGENIO, JULIE BABINARD AND PER PINSTRUP-ANDERSEN
2002        "Opportunities and Risks for the Poor in Developing Countries" (Working Paper 83). Indian Council for Research on International Economic Relations, New Delhi, India. Retrieved December 9, 2002 (http://www.icrier.res.in/pdf/risk.pdf).
DRAGER, NICK, RONALD LABONTE AND RENEE TORGERSON
2002        "Frameworks for Analyzing the Links Between Globalization and Health" (Draft Document). Retrieved March 30, 2002 (http://dev.www.uregina.ca/spheru/PDF%20Files/Labonte-Frameworks-Links.PDF).
PEOPLE'S HEALTH ASSEMBLY (PHA)
2000        *People's Charter for Health*. Bangalore, India: PHM Secretariat.
2001        "Health in the Era of Globalization: From Victims to Protagonists." A Discussion Paper prepared by the PHA drafting group. Savar, Bangladesh. PHA Secretariat, Gonoshasthaya Kendra.
WOODWARD, DAVID, NICK DRAGER, ROBERT BEAGLEHOLE AND DEBRA LIPSON
2001        "Globalization and Health: A Framework for Analysis and Action." *Bulletin of the World Health Organization* 79: 875-880.

# General Index

burden of disease (includes double burden of disease and global burden of disease): 12, 17-20, 22, 45, 170, 213-218, 232, 250-252

capitalism (see globalization of capitalism): 16, 22-23, 31, 45, 48, 69, 113-114, 120, 175, 247-248, 250, 257, 267

chronic diseases (see also non-communicable diseases): 15-16, 18-21, 93, 105-106, 111, 121-124, 187, 213-230, 249-253, 264-265

colonialism (see also imperialism): 28, 109, 112-114, 117, 120, 174, 247, 250, 256-258, 262

communicable diseases (includes infectious diseases): 5, 7, 12-22, 27, 29, 40-42, 50, 53, 93, 106, 108, 213-214, 215, 224, 228, 250, 264-265

community-based health: 123, 249, 237, 240, 262

consumption patterns (of unhealthy foods and products, consumerism, etc; see also life styles): 2, 4, 21, 35, 44, 56, 83, 88, 105-106, 120, 124-125, 204-205, 217-219, 221-224, 232, 247, 249, 251-253, 259-260

developed countries: 13, 16, 18-10, 22-23, 28-30, 35, 39-40, 58-63, 65-66, 75, 77-87, 92-98, 100-101, 113, 122, 174, 192, 215-217, 220-221, 223-226, 228-229, 246, 252-254, 256-257, 259-261, 263, 266

developing countries (includes less developed countries, Third World and Global South): 9, 11, 14, 16-23, 25, 27-35, 37-41, 43-44, 49, 51, 55-56, 58-63, 65-68, 73-87, 97, 101, 114-115, 122, 126, 168, 172, 175-177, 180, 192, 195, 214-217, 220-229, 231-232, 248-257, 259-261, 263-267, 269

development (includes models and types of development, modernization, and industrialization): 8, 11, 13-17, 19, 21, 23-27, 31-32, 36-39, 42-44, 47, 51, 53-54, 56, 58, 63-64, 71-72, 74-76, 78, 82, 84, 87, 91, 95, 103, 106-107, 108, 114, 118-119, 124, 144, 156, 160, 165, 168-169, 174-179, 190-196, 198-204, 210-211, 217-218, 223, 238-239, 241, 251, 260, 268

diseases of globalization (includes global diseases and diseases of affluence; see also non-communicable diseases – NCDs): 15-18, 20-21, 42, 44-45, 108, 210, 214-215, 217-219, 224, 229, 247, 249, 251-253, 264-265

environmental health threats, risks and problems: 4-5, 7, 35-36, 59, 94-96, 106, 121, 154, 157, 168, 239, 248-249, 251, 259-261, 264, 266

epidemiological transition (see health transitions)

family planning (see reproductive health)

gender health issues (includes male and women's health issues; see also reproductive health): 27-30, 38, 40, 46, 51, 53-54, 66, 102-103, 105, 113, 116-117, 119-120, 127-129, 140, 154, 159-160, 166-167, 171-196, 207, 219, 221, 224, 230, 232, 247-248, 253, 257, 259

General Agreement on Tariffs and Trade (GATT): 7, 17, 57-59, 63, 76-77, 84, 88, 144, 152, 253, 266

General Agreement on Trade in Services (GATS): 7, 61-62, 69, 71, 76-77, 84, 133, 142-143, 152, 161, 253-254, 266

global health (includes global health issues, risks, and/or threats): 1-2, 4-5, 7, 13, 20, 33, 49, 54, 66-67, 70, 91, 96, 171, 173, 192, 224, 237, 246-247, 256, 258, 262, 264-267

global governance and regulation (includes global health governance and regulation): 45, 66-67, 70, 224-226, 228-229, 264-267

global warming (includes health effects of global climate change): 2, 10, 14, 15, 35-37, 42, 44, 45, 46, 56-57, 119, 239, 259-260

globalization, analysis, conceptualization and definition of: 2-12, 47-48, 52-54, 73-75, 91-92, 109-114, 126, 132, 148, 198, 218, 257

globalization from below (and from above): 34, 42, 43, 262-263, 267, 269

globalization of disease: 12-15, 49, 50, 53n, 94, 100, 205, 209, 219-230, 247

health, definition of: 9, 11, 110-113, 237

health inequities: 22-28, 148-149, 157, 163, 167, 230, 258-259, 262

health policy (includes global health policies): 8, 28, 30, 34, 43, 70, 97, 131-149, 162, 163, 164-165, 171-172, 174-176, 180, 182, 188-189, 192-194, 195, 208, 214, 218-219, 220, 222, 224-229, 235-236, 239-241, 247, 256-257, 263, 265

health-related technologies (includes telehealth and telemedicine): 1, 4, 15, 39-41, 49, 91, 96, 114, 120, 122-124, 125, 144, 145-149, 156, 161, 171, 176, 180, 188, 192, 193, 197-211, 220, 235-236, 246-248, 253, 261, 262, 266

health transitions (includes epidemiological transition and nutrition transition): 16, 18-21, 25, 41, 92-94, 97, 107-108, 109-129, 178-179, 192, 205-206, 210, 217, 219, 222-223, 224, 228, 231, 250, 252, 257, 260

HIV/AIDS: 10, 13, 14, 18, 27-28, 29, 42, 53n, 60, 70, 100, 121, 132, 141, 145-148, 150, 159-160, 167, 213, 216, 242, 253, 258

imperialism (see also colonialism): 2, 109, 111-114, 120, 123-126, 128, 247, 250, 257-258, 262

inequality (includes gap between rich and poor): 4, 8, 9, 14, 22-25, 27-28, 32, 51, 54-55, 67, 69, 120, 131, 153-154, 157, 161, 169, 177, 194, 215, 231, 237, 245, 248, 250, 252, 256, 258-259, 268

infectious diseases (see communicable diseases)

International Monetary Fund (IMF): 7, 9, 25, 26, 28, 29, 31, 32, 33, 34, 49, 51, 64n, 67, 114, 115, 116-117, 133, 136, 148, 203, 249, 254-255, 258, 263, 267

lifestyle/s (includes health effects of lifestyle changes): 15-16, 17, 20-21, 30, 41, 46, 91-92, 93, 94, 99, 100-102, 103, 105, 106-107, 108, 110, 118, 119, 124, 127, 204-205, 206, 207, 209, 246, 248, 249-251, 264

neoliberalism and neoliberal reforms (see Structural Adjustment Programs)

noncommunicable diseases (NCDs): 15-16, 18-19, 20, 21, 41, 46, 93, 105-106, 111, 121, 122, 124, 213n, 214, 219, 229, 230, 247, 249, 250

Pacific Islands and Pacificans: 17, 36, 39, 41, 45, 91, 92, 94-108, 109-129, 197-211, 246, 248, 249-251, 256-258, 260-261

People's Health Movement (PHM; includes People's Health Assembly and People's Charter for Health): 34-35, 42, 43, 235-243, 255-256, 259, 262-263, 267-269

Privatization (includes privatization of health care and private sector health care): 9, 28, 30, 31-35, 38, 42, 44, 50, 55, 56-62, 64, 69, 77-78, 81, 131-132, 135-142, 148-149, 150, 152, 161, 173-174, 177, 178n, 179, 189, 190, 203, 227, 236, 238, 247, 253-255, 256, 258-259, 262, 264, 267-268

reproductive health (includes birth control and family planning): 29, 30, 38, 97, 107, 121, 123, 155, 171-196, 240, 247, 248, 257, 259

Structural Adjustment Programs or SAPS (and other neoliberal reforms): 23-27, 31-34, 42, 44, 49-50, 55, 63, 76, 115-117, 134, 138, 141, 148, 150, 158-159, 166, 167-169, 177, 248-249, 254-255, 258

telehealth and telemedicine (see health-related technologies): 1, 15, 39-41, 43, 46, 77-81, 85, 120, 122, 123, 124, 144-150, 154, 161, 171, 176, 180, 188, 192-193.197-211, 220, 236, 246-247, 253, 261, 262

tobacco (includes consumption of, tobacco companies, and tobacco control): 4, 7, 9, 16, 20-21, 30, 53, 73, 83, 88, 194, 204, 205, 213-214, 217-218, 220-233, 252-253, 264, 265, 266

trade (includes trade liberalization, trade policies and health effects of trade): 2, 4, 7-9, 12, 13, 14, 17, 21, 23, 24, 27, 28, 31, 32, 38, 42, 47-72, 74-80, 83-89, 91, 95, 116, 118, 119, 120, 132, 133-136, 142-152, 155-156, 159, 160-162, 163, 165, 177, 214, 215, 218-219, 222, 225, 228, 230-232, 246, 248, 249, 252, 253-254, 260, 261, 263-264, 265

Trade-Related Intellectual Property Rights (TRIPS) Agreement: 7, 28, 53n, 60, 63, 68, 72, 77, 79-80, 133, 144-149, 152, 242, 253-254, 258, 263

urbanization (includes health effects/risks associated with urbanization): 9, 14-16, 38, 54, 91, 95, 96, 100-107, 143, 154, 159, 166, 169, 185, 190, 200, 203, 205, 206, 213, 214, 218, 220, 223, 225, 248, 250-251, 254, 260-261

Western influence on health (including Western medicine, healthcare, standards and medical education): 8, 21, 35, 48, 50, 67, 91, 96-97, 103, 107, 114, 119, 120, 123, 124, 125, 176, 179, 181, 189, 194, 246, 247, 248, 249, 251, 256-258, 259, 262

women's health issues (see gender health issues and reproductive health)

World Bank (WB): 7, 9, 18, 22, 24, 25, 28, 29, 30-34, 40, 43, 44, 49, 50, 54n, 55, 63, 64n, 67, 69, 71, 86, 110, 112, 114-115, 116-117, 129, 133, 134, 148, 150, 151, 161, 167, 178n, 182, 203, 219, 254, 255, 256, 258, 263, 267

World Health Organization (WHO): 3, 4, 6, 11, 13, 18, 20-21, 22, 33, 34, 36, 40, 41, 43, 45, 46, 47n, 50, 65, 69, 70, 71, 72, 77, 87, 88, 93, 96-97, 107, 108, 110, 127, 167, 170, 202, 213n, 214, 215, 217n, 221, 222, 224, 225-229, 230-233, 235, 236, 239, 242, 243, 252-253, 256, 258, 265-266, 267, 269

World Trade Organization (WTO): 7, 9, 17, 25, 29, 31, 32, 34, 42, 57-60, 62, 63-66, 68, 69-72, 75, 79-80, 83-84, 86, 88, 116, 133, 135, 136, 142, 144, 145, 147, 148, 152, 165, 203, 218-219, 222, 228, 233, 238, 254-255, 263-264, 266, 267

# INTERNATIONAL STUDIES
# IN
# SOCIOLOGY AND SOCIAL ANTHROPOLOGY

21. FUSÉ, T. (ed.). *Modernization and Stress in Japan.* 1975. ISBN 90 04 04344 6
22. SMITH, B.L. (ed.). *Religion and Social Conflict in South Asia.* 1976.
    ISBN 90 04 04510 4
23. MAZRUI, A.A. (ed.). *The Warrior Tradition in Modern Africa.* 1977.
    ISBN 90 04 05646 7
25. SMITH, B.L. (ed.). *Religion and the Legitimation of Power in South Asia.* 1978.
    ISBN 90 04 05674 2
31. LELE, J. (ed.). *Tradition and Modernity in* Bhakti *Movements.* 1981.
    ISBN 90 04 06370 6
32. ARMER, J.M. *Comparative Sociological Research in the 1960s and 1970s.* 1982.
    ISBN 90 04 06487 7
33. GALATY, J.G. & P.C. SALZMAN (eds.). *Change and Development in Nomadic and Pastoral Societies.* 1981. ISBN 90 04 06587 3
34. LUPRI, E. (ed.). *The Changing Position of Women in Family and Society. A Cross-National Comparison.* 1983. ISBN 90 04 06845 7
35. IVERSON, N. (ed.). *Urbanism and Urbanization. Views, Aspects and Dimensions.* 1984.
    ISBN 90 04 06920 8
36. MALIK, Y.K. *Politics, Technology, and Bureaucracy in South Asia.* 1983.
    ISBN 90 04 07027 3
37. LENSKI, G. (ed.). *Current Issues and Research in Macrosociology.* 1984.
    ISBN 90 04 07052 4
39. TIRYAKIAN, E.A. (ed.). *The Global Crisis. Sociological Analyses and Responses.* 1984.
    ISBN 90 04 07284 5
40. LAWRENCE, B. (ed.). *Ibn Khaldun and Islamic Ideology.* 1984. ISBN 90 04 07567 4
41. HAJJAR, S.G. (ed.). *The Middle East: from Transition to Development.* 1985.
    ISBN 90 04 07694 8
43. CARMAN, J.B. & F.A. MARGLIN (eds.). *Purity and Auspiciousness in Indian Society.* 1985. ISBN 90 04 07789 8
46. SMITH, B.L. & H.B. REYNOLDS (eds.). *The City as a Sacred Center. Essays on Six Asian Contexts.* 1987. ISBN 90 04 08471 1
47. MALIK, Y.K. & D.K. VAJPEYI (eds.). *India. The Years of Indira Ghandi.* 1988.
    ISBN 90 04 08681 1
48. CLARK, C. & J. LEMCO (eds.). *State and Development.* 1988. ISBN 90 04 08833 4
49. GUTKIND, P.C.W. (ed.). *Third World Workers. Comparative International Labour Studies.* 1988. ISBN 90 04 08788 5
50. SELIGMAN, A.B. *Order and Transcendence. The Role of Utopias and the Dynamics of Civilization.* 1989. ISBN 90 04 08975 6
51. JABBRA, J.G. *Bureaucracy and Development in the Arab World.* 1989.
    ISBN 90 04 09194 7

52. KAUTSKY, J.H. (ed.). *Karl Kautsky and the Social Science of Classical Marxism.* 1989.
    ISBN 90 04 09193 9
53. KAPUR, A. (ed.). *The Diplomatic Ideas and Practices of Asian States.* 1990.
    ISBN 90 04 09289 7
54. KIM, Q.-Y. (ed.). *Revolutions in the Third World.* 1991. ISBN 90 04 09355 9
55. KENNEDY, C.H. & D.J. LOUSCHER (eds.). *Civil Military Interaction in Asia and Africa.* 1991. ISBN 90 04 09359 1
56. RAGIN, C.C. (ed.). *Issues and Alternatives in Comparative Social Research.* 1991.
    ISBN 90 04 09360 5
57. CHOUDHRY, N.K. (ed.). *Canada and South Asian Development. Trade and Aid.* 1991.
    ISBN 90 04 09416 4
58. RAZIA AKTER BANU, U.A.B. (ed.). *Islam in Bangladesh.* 1992.
    ISBN 90 04 09497 0
61. AHMAD, A. (ed.). *Science and Technology Policy for Economic Development in Africa.* 1993.
    ISBN 90 04 09659 0
62. VAJPEYI, D.K. (ed.). *Modernizing China.* 1994. ISBN 90 04 10046 6
63. BRADSHAW, Y.W. (ed.). *Education in Comparative Perspective.* New Lessons from around the World. 1997. ISBN 90 04 10734 7
64. UDOGU, E.I. (ed.). *Democracy and Democratization in Africa.* Toward the 21st Century. 1997. ISBN 90 04 10733 9
65. BEHAR, J.E. & A.G. CUZÁN (eds.). *At the Crossroads of Development.* Trans-national Challenges to Developed and Developing Societies. 1997.
    ISBN 90 04 10732 0
66. LAUDERDALE, P. & R. AMSTER (eds.). *Lives in the Balance.* Perspectives on Global Injustice and Inequality. 1997. ISBN 90 04 10875 0
67. LOVEJOY, P.E. & P.A.T. WILLIAMS (eds.). *Displacement and the Politics of Violence in Nigeria.* 1997. ISBN 90 04 10876 9
68. JABBRA, J.G. & N.W. JABBRA (eds.). *Challenging Environmental Issues.* Middle Eastern Perspectives. 1997. ISBN 90 04 10877 7
69. SASAKI, M. (ed.). *Values and Attitudes Across Nations and Time.* 1998.
    ISBN 90 04 11219 7
70. SPERLING, J., Y. MALIK & D. LOUSCHER (eds.). *Zones of Amity, Zones of Enmity.* The Prospects for Economic and Military Security in Asia. 1998.
    ISBN 90 04 11218 9
71. NANDI, P.K. & S.M. SHAHIDULLAH (eds.). *Globalization and the Evolving World Society.* 1998. ISBN 90 04 11247 2
72. ARTS, W. & L. HALMAN (eds.). *New Directions in Quantitative Comparative Sociology.* 1999. ISBN 90 04 11411 4
73. ISHWARAN, K. (ed.). *Ascetic Culture: Renunciation and Worldly Engagement.* 1999.
    ISBN 90 04 11412 2
74. PATTERSON, R. (ed.). *Science and Technology in Southern Africa and East and South Asia,* 1999. ISBN 90 04 11413 0
75. ARTS, W. (ed.). *Through a Glass, Darkly.* Blurred images of cultural tradition and modernity over distance and time. 2000. ISBN 90 04 11597 8
76. GERRITSEN, J.W. *The Control of Fuddle and Flash,* A Sociological History of the Regulation of Alcohol and Opiates. 2000. ISBN 90 04 11640 0
77. LEE, W.C. (ed.). *Taiwan in Perspective.* 2000. ISBN 90 04 11849 7
78. LUMUMBA-KASONGO, T. (ed.). *Dynamics and Policy Implications of the Global Reforms at the End of the Second Millennium.* 2000. ISBN 90 04 11847 0

79. HARRIS, R. & M. SEID (eds.). *Critical Perspectives on Globalization and Neoliberalism in the Developing Countries*. 2000. ISBN 90 04 11850 0

80. HOWARD, G.J. & G. NEWMAN (eds.), *Varieties of Comparative Criminology*. 2001. ISBN 90 04 12245 1

81. NDEGWA, S.N. (ed.), *A Decade of Democracy in Africa*. 2001. ISBN 90 04 12244 3

82. JREISAT, J.E. (ed.), *Governance and Developing Countries*. 2002. ISBN 90 04 12247 8

83. KEITA, M. (ed.), *Conceptualizing/Re-Conceptualizing Africa*. The construction of African Historical Identity. 2002. ISBN 90 04 12420 9

84. BERG, R. VAN DEN, *Nyoongar People of Australia*. Perspectives on Racism and Multiculturalism. 2002. ISBN 90 04 12478 0

85. DOGAN, M. (ed.), *Elite Configurations at the Apex of Power*. 2003. ISBN 90 04 12808 5

86. SENGERS, G., *Women and Demons*. Cult Healing in Islamic Egypt. 2003. ISBN 90 04 12771 2

87. WILSON, H.T. *The Vocation of Reason*. Studies in Critical Theory and Social Science in the Age of Max Weber. Edited and with a Foreword by T.M. Kemple. 2003. ISBN 90 04 13631 2

88. ZEGEYE, A. and R.L. HARRIS, *Media, Identity and the Public Sphere in Post-Apartheid South Africa*. 2003. ISBN 90 04 12633 3

89. INGLEHART, R. (ed.), *Human Values and Social Change*. Findings from the Values Surveys. 2003. ISBN 90 04 12810 7

90. BEN-RAFAEL, E. (ed.), *Sociology and Ideology*. 2003. ISBN 90 04 13104 3

91. AL-HAJ, M., *Immigration and Ethnic Formation in a Deeply Divided Society*. The Case of the 1990s Immigrants from the Former Soviet Union in Israel. 2004. ISBN 90 04 13625 8

92. AMINEH, M., *Central Eurasia in World Politics*. Conflict, Security, and Development. 2004. ISBN 90 04 12809 3

93. VINKEN, H., J. SOETERS & P. ESTER (eds.). *Comparing Cultures*. Dimensions of Culture in a Comparative Perspective. 2004. ISBN 90 04 13115 9

94. ASSIÉ-LUMUMBA, N.T., *Cyberspace, Distance Learning, and Higher Education in Developing Countries*. Old and Emergent Issues of Access, Pedagogy, and Knowledge Production. 2004. ISBN 90 04 13121 3

95. HARRIS, R.L. and M. Seid, *Globalization and Health*. 2004. ISBN 90 04 14145 6